The Interesting Narrative of the Life of Olaudah Equiano

Written by Himself

Related Titles in
THE BEDFORD SERIES IN HISTORY AND CULTURE
Advisory Editors: Natalie Zemon Davis, Princeton University
Ernest R. May, Harvard University

---

*Narrative of the Life of Frederick Douglass, An American Slave,
Written by Himself*
Edited with an Introduction by David W. Blight, *Amherst College*

William Lloyd Garrison and the Fight against Slavery: Selections from
The Liberator
Edited with an Introduction by William E. Cain, *Wellesley College*

The Confessions of Nat Turner (forthcoming)
Edited with an Introduction by Kenneth Greenberg, *Suffolk University*

The Autobiography of Benjamin Franklin
Edited with an Introduction by Louis P. Masur, *City College of the City
University of New York*

Mary Rowlandson's The Sovereignty and Goodness of God (forthcoming)
Edited with an Introduction by Neal Salisbury, *Smith College*

THE BEDFORD SERIES IN HISTORY AND CULTURE

The Interesting Narrative of the Life of Olaudah Equiano

Written by Himself

Edited with an Introduction by

Robert J. Allison

Suffolk University

BEDFORD BOOKS

Boston   New York

For Bedford Books

President and Publisher: Charles H. Christensen
General Manager and Associate Publisher: Joan E. Feinberg
History Editor: Niels Aaboe
Developmental Editor: Louise D. Townsend
Editorial Assistant: Richard Keaveny
Managing Editor: Elizabeth M. Schaaf
Production Editor: Ann Sweeney
Production Assistant: Alanya Harter
Copyeditor: Barbara G. Flanagan
Indexer: Anne Holmes
Text Design: Claire Seng-Niemoeller
Cover Design: Richard Emery Design, Inc.
Cover Art: Portrait of Olaudah Equiano, 1789.

Manufactured in the United States of America.

9 8 7

f   e   d

For information, write: Bedford Books, 75 Arlington Street, Boston, MA 02116 (617–426–7440)

ISBN: 0-312-11127-4 (paperback)
ISBN: 0-312-12243-8 (hardcover)

Acknowledgments

Pages 206, 208, 209, 210: Reprinted by courtesy of the Boston Athenaeum.
Page 207: Courtesy of the Smithsonian Institution, photo no. 68-092.
Page 211: Courtesy of the Boston Public Library, Print Department, the Holt Collection.
Pages 28, 114: Courtesy of Manuscripts, Archives, and Rare Books Division, Schomburg Center for Research in Black Culture. The New York Public Library: Astor, Lenox, and Tilden Foundations.

Foreword

The Bedford Series in History and Culture is designed so that readers can study the past as historians do.

The historian's first task is finding the evidence. Documents, letters, memoirs, interviews, pictures, movies, novels, or poems can provide facts and clues. Then the historian questions and compares the sources. There is more to do than in a courtroom, for hearsay evidence is welcome, and the historian is usually looking for answers beyond act and motive. Different views of an event may be as important as a single verdict. How a story is told may yield as much information as what it says.

Along the way the historian seeks help from other historians and perhaps from specialists in other disciplines. Finally, it is time to write, to decide on an interpretation and how to arrange the evidence for readers.

Each book in this series contains an important historical document or group of documents, each document a witness from the past and open to interpretation in different ways. The documents are combined with some element of historical narrative—an introduction or a biographical essay, for example—that provides students with an analysis of the primary source material and important background information about the world in which it was produced.

Each book in the series focuses on a specific topic within a specific historical period. Each provides a basis for lively thought and discussion about several aspects of the topic and the historian's role. Each is short enough (and inexpensive enough) to be a reasonable one-week assignment in a college course. Whether as classroom or personal reading, each book in the series provides firsthand experience of the challenge—and fun—of discovering, recreating, and interpreting the past.

Natalie Zemon Davis
Ernest R. May

Preface

This is the story of an ordinary man who lived an extraordinary life. Olaudah Equiano witnessed some great events: battles in the Seven Years' War, the religious revival in Europe and America, opening scenes of the American Revolution, an expedition to the Arctic, an eruption of Mount Vesuvius. He knew some of the eighteenth century's great figures: generals, evangelists, merchants, politicians. But he also knew men and women whose names are lost to history, and he wrote of less celebrated features of the human experience: the African slave trade, the work of slaves in the West Indies and America, and the currents of trade between Africa, America, Asia, and Europe. Equiano's *Narrative,* first published in 1789, re-creates these disparate experiences as well as his own struggle for a religious and cultural identity.

The text of this Bedford Books edition follows the first American printing, *The Interesting Narrative of the Life of Olaudah Equiano, or Gustavus Vassa, The African* (New York, 1791). The only significant changes (other than minor spelling and punctuation corrections) are the insertion of paragraph breaks and notes to the text that explain some of the ideas and events of the late eighteenth century to which Equiano refers. The chronology shows the reader how Equiano's story of capture in Africa and enslavement in America compares with the experiences of others and also places Equiano's *Narrative* in the international movement to end slavery. The illustrations show the visual evidence used in this early abolition campaign. The introduction brings out the book's central themes—slavery, religion, and commerce—and examines the *Narrative*'s historical context as well as its political and literary contexts.

This is more than a book about slavery, though slavery was an important part of Equiano's life and his world. It is the story of one man who encountered this brutal world and learned to survive in it, physically and spiritually. In telling the story of one who survived, Equiano tells the stories of countless others who did not.

ACKNOWLEDGMENTS

I am deeply grateful to Charles Christensen and Niels Aaboe for this opportunity to work with the story of Equiano's eventful life. All of the extraordinary people at Bedford Books have my thanks: Louise Townsend's keen mind and skillful editing aided me at every stage of this project. I cannot thank her enough. Ann Sweeney has done a superb job in seeing this project safely to this point; Barbara Flanagan improved every sentence of the introduction, and every page of the book. Thanks also go to Richard Keaveny, Mary Lou Wilshaw, and Katie Blatt. Fred Anderson, Seymour Drescher, David Leviatin, Louis P. Masur, Werner Sollors, and Rafia Zafar critiqued the introduction with great care. Many others offered suggestions and counsel: Bernard Bailyn, Robert Bellinger, Thomas Brown, Father John Culloty, Barbara DeWolfe, Luckson Ejofodomi, David Gewanter, Brian Glennon, Kenneth S. Greenberg, Robert Hall, Robert Hannigan, Kevin Hermes, Susan Hunt, Phyllis Hunter, Sharon Lenzie, Daniel Mandell, Donald Ostrowski, Mark Peterson, Reverend Charles Rice, Claire Schen, Benjamin Schmidt, Jan Thaddeus, Vince Tompkins, Lauri Umansky, Mario Valdes, and Ted Widmer deserve thanks greater than I can convey. Special thanks to Catharina Slautterback of the Boston Athenaeum, Karen Smith Shafts of the Boston Public Library, and Jennifer Code and Nancy Burkett of the American Antiquarian Society. Students in History 160 at Suffolk University and Expo S-12 and History and Literature 97 at Harvard University read drafts of the introduction and challenged my interpretation of Equiano's story. Phyllis, John Robert, and Philip prodded me in their own special ways.

This remains Equiano's book. The credit for it remains firmly in his hands. Hoping to flatter the British Parliament into ending the slave trade, he inscribed his book to them. I dedicate this edition of his life to all the descendants of Africa, in every part of the world.

Robert J. Allison

Contents

The Interesting Narrative of the Life of Olaudah Equiano

Written by Himself

PART ONE

Introduction:
Equiano's Worlds

Olaudah Equiano (o-lah-*oo*-day ek-wee-*ah*-no) was born into the Ibo tribe in the Nigerian village of Isseke in 1745. At the age of eleven he was kidnapped by slave traders; he would spend ten years as a slave in the West Indies, in America, and in the British navy before becoming a free man in 1766. In 1788 he wrote *The Interesting Narrative of the Life of Olaudah Equiano, or Gustavus Vassa, the African.* Written as a protest against slavery during a sustained public campaign against the slave trade in both England and America, his book is one of the first antislavery books by a former slave. Equiano experienced virtually every kind of slavery and every part of the slave experience: capture in Africa, the "middle passage" from Africa to the Americas, plantation labor in Virginia and the West Indies, and ultimately service on a slave-trading ship between North America and the Caribbean. He was one of the few to survive and to write about the experience.

Equiano's *Narrative,* however, is more than a protest against brutality or a record of survival. In his African boyhood, his ten years as a slave, and his two decades as a free man in Europe and America, he had seen most of the world: he had been shipwrecked in the Bahamas and icebound in the Arctic; he had felt earthquakes in the Caribbean and seen Vesuvius erupt in Italy; he had worshiped in his Ibo village and at Quaker meetinghouses, had discussed theology with Catholic priests and Turkish Muslims, and had been baptized into the Anglican church. A veteran of the British navy, having fought against France in the Seven Years' War, in 1765 he watched Americans celebrate the repeal of the Stamp Act and in 1776 watched a British warship chase down and destroy an American privateer. His book is a meditation on power and liberty by one who knew what each word meant.

He remembered much of what he observed, the exotic as well as the mundane. He remembered holding an Indian king's scalp in his hand during the battle of Louisbourg in 1758 and the feel and smell of roast alligator at a festival on the Mosquito Coast in 1776. When he danced with the Mosquito people in Nicaragua, when he watched the Greek slaves dance in Turkey, he remembered the dancers in his Ibo village. He witnessed some great events and many unique or colorful ones. But the real power of the *Narrative* lies in Equiano's perspective. During his travels and adventures in this strange world, he is an average man, as he says "neither a saint, a hero, nor a tyrant," but an ordinary person forced to lead an extraordinary life.

OLAUDAH EQUIANO AND THE EIGHTEENTH-CENTURY WORLD

Equiano's journeys began when he was eleven years old. He did not choose to be a traveler, but his course was determined by others. The market in his Ibo village drew people from all over southeastern Nigeria, coming to trade for the Ibos' cotton, corn, and yams. From the south, Aro traders brought European goods: guns, cloth, and hats. The Aros also traded slaves. One day when the adults were at work in the fields, three Aro traders snatched Equiano and his sister, put them in large sacks, and carried them away. He would never see his parents again and was soon separated from his sister as well.

Slavery was not new to Equiano, for his father owned slaves. But among the Ibo, as among other African people, men or women became slaves through warfare or as punishment for a crime, such as adultery. The slave traders who came through Isseke had to prove that their captives were legally taken, or they risked becoming slaves themselves. As European demand for slaves grew, though, traders like the Aros took more risks in gathering slaves, and once they had caught a slave for the European market they would quickly move the captive away from his or her home. Equiano and his sister were both taken out of their neighborhood and traded by their captors. Over the next two months, the two lost sight of each other. Equiano was traded from village to village, in one place working for a goldsmith, at another being a companion to a boy his own age.

Though Equiano never saw a white person until he reached the African coast, his village was tied to the Atlantic economy. The market women traded iron pots and European cloth for their baskets, perfumes, dyes, and crops. His village also raised corn and tobacco, which had been grown only in America before 1492. The seeds had arrived through trading in the sixteenth century, long enough before Equiano's time for those crops to be a natural part of his world.

Slavery and commerce were familiar in his Ibo world as well. But Equiano discovered on reaching the Atlantic that Europeans understood both differently. Slavery to the Europeans was an economic relationship, and a slave a piece of property. Equiano was one of fifty thousand Africans carried to the New World in 1756. The slave trade, which had begun before Columbus reached the New World (the Portuguese had brought the first African slaves to Europe in 1441), by the 1750s was well organized and brutally efficient. Of the more than eleven million African slaves brought to America between 1518 and 1850, more than six million were carried over after 1750. Most of the slaves were taken to the Americas to work the sugar plantations of Brazil and the Caribbean and the rice, to-bacco, and cotton plantations of mainland North America.[1] Others worked on small farms, as servants in cities, as skilled artisans, or as sailors.

From Africa, Equiano was taken first to Barbados, the richest of Britain's New World colonies. The sugar plantations produced much of Europe's wealth and absorbed most of the slaves carried off from Africa. But no one bought him, so he was sent to Virginia, staying briefly on a tobacco plantation owned by a man named Campbell. Years later he remembered a few details of his weeks in Virginia: the cook wore an iron muzzle, and a wall clock and a portrait of a Campbell ancestor both seemed to watch the young African who was put to work brushing flies away from the dozing planter.

Campbell rested, but young Equiano kept moving. He was purchased by Michael Henry Pascal, an officer in the British navy, in 1757. Equiano sailed with Pascal, leaving Virginia for new worlds and experiences. Had he stayed in the Americas, either on a Caribbean sugar plantation or on a Virginia tobacco plantation, his life would have been quite different. It probably would have ended much sooner, and he almost certainly would not have had the chance to write about it. He probably would not have learned to read or write. But on Pascal's ship bound for England, he met Richard Baker, a white Virginian just a few years older than he, who explained the English alphabet and some of the strange ways of white people to the young African. Equiano pursued knowledge on land and sea, using every opportunity to improve his skills in reading and writing.

Equiano sailed from Virginia just as England and France went to war. The Seven Years' War, or French and Indian War, began in a series of skirmishes among British colonists, Native Americans, and French traders along the Ohio River. From these frontier encounters the war spread to every part of the world, as England and France, and their allies in Europe, Asia, Africa, and the Americas, fought on every continent except Antarctica. Equiano served his master and the empire on land and sea: in Canada, on the Atlantic, and in the Mediterranean.

In these years on British warships, from age twelve to seventeen, Equiano began to develop a new sense of who he was. Straddling two worlds, Europe and Africa, he even had two names: Olaudah Equiano, given him by his parents, and Gustavus Vassa, given by his European master. Both names were somewhat prophetic. To the Ibo, *ola* is "ring," a symbol of good luck, *ude* a pleasing sound. Modern Nigerian novelist Chinua Achebe interprets the name Equiano as "if they agree we shall stay," signifying a person whose fate is controlled by others. The name Gustavus Vassa is also rich in unintended irony, recalling a Swedish nobleman who led his nation's revolt against Denmark in the 1520s. As King Gustav I, the Swedish Vasa reigned for most of the sixteenth century; his exploits were popularized in an eighteenth-century English play, *Gustavus Vasa, the Deliverer of His Country.* Equiano's two names, Ibo and Swedish (by way of the London stage), signify the varied paths he would travel and the life he would survive to write about.[2]

A 1760 incident points to Equiano's shifting identification of himself. During a furlough on the Isle of Wight, Equiano, now a swaggering fifteen-year-old veteran, was surprised one day by a black boy his own age, a farmhand, who rushed toward him in great excitement. Equiano did not know the boy, so he turned away. But the black boy would not let him go. Greeting Equiano as "one of his own countrymen" the boy embraced him "as if I had been his brother," Equiano later recalled. This black boy on the Isle of Wight, having lived among the English, felt a bond Equiano did not yet understand. But he would come to understand it. Like the name Gustavus Vassa, his identity as an African was forced upon him, but he would come to use both the English name and the African identity. His years of slavery in the West Indies and life as a free man in Europe and at sea had given him a dual identity and made him recognize that though he was culturally an Englishman, he had become a son of Africa.[3]

He was reminded of his ambiguous status when the war ended. Expecting freedom in return for having served his master and the British Empire, he was instead forced onto a ship bound for the West Indies. Once again he was sold as a slave, this time to a Philadelphia Quaker on the island of Montserrat. The Quaker merchant, Robert King, had a business shipping sugar and slaves from the West Indies to Georgia and South Carolina, trading there for rice and beef to feed the Caribbean workforce. King recognized Equiano's value to his business: he was a skilled sailor who could read, write, and calculate. Equiano's former owner even attested to his honesty. Equiano thus became part of the trade network holding together the British colonial system in America. The network benefited the planters, the empire, and ultimately even Equiano, who began, while working for the Quaker, to buy and sell goods on his own. Equiano saved his money, and on July 10, 1766, ten years after he was kidnapped in Nigeria, he bought his freedom.

Slavery not only had deprived Equiano of his freedom but had cut him off from the Ibo spiritual universe. In his years as a slave and then as a free man, he sought to reconnect himself to a religious world. As a free man he had more opportunities to explore a religious identity he had begun to develop as a child and then as a slave. During his first English winter in 1757–58, two Englishwomen, the Guerin sisters, had introduced him to Christianity. He found special comfort in the stories of the ancient Jews, whose customs, creation legends, and social structure reminded him of his Ibo world. He had found the similarities so comforting and compelling, and the Guerins so kind, that he had accepted their faith and been baptized in 1759.

During these years, the early to mid-1700s, Europe and America were undergoing a spiritual revival that became known as the Great Awakening. Evangelists such as George Whitefield, whom Equiano heard preach in Savannah in 1765, John Wesley, the founder of Methodism and a reader of Equiano's *Narrative,* and other Protestant evangelists spread the fire of their brand of Christianity through Britain and America. Merely practicing a religion was not enough: only through an intense experience of Christ could men and women be saved. The Baptists and Methodists preached and also practiced the idea that all souls are equal before God. Itinerant preachers reached out to the poor and the enslaved, who responded enthusiastically. By the 1780s, Baptists and Methodists went beyond preaching equality: they demanded that believers show faith by freeing their slaves, and the faithful of all races formed integrated congregations, sometimes with black pastors, sometimes with white.

Both Baptists and Methodists also pressured the political establishment to end slavery, often preaching abolition in places like Virginia's legislature.[4]

But though the new evangelical Christianity included a radical opposition to slavery, not all evangelicals were abolitionists. Some, like many eighteenth-century people, had their moral opposition to slavery compromised by their direct or indirect involvement with slavery. George Whitefield, for example, the most important eighteenth-century evangelist, cooperated with his friend General James Oglethorpe in founding the colony of Georgia. Oglethorpe wanted Georgia to be a New World refuge for the Old World's poor, a place where Europe's oppressed could regenerate themselves and restore their human dignity. Whitefield, an Anglican clergyman, opened an orphanage in Georgia and toured both North America and Britain raising money for it. But though Oglethorpe tried to bar slavery from the colony, the white colonists quickly saw that their neighbors in South Carolina used slave labor to grow rice and thought that they would restore their dignity more quickly with slaves. By the 1750s Georgia was a slave colony, and even Whitefield's Bethesda orphanage was worked by slaves.

Equiano visited Savannah often in the 1760s. He would have been shocked to learn that Georgia was begun as a philanthropic enterprise, for every visit both as a slave and as a free man, brought him trouble. Once he was nearly beaten to death, another time he was arrested for having a light on after nine P.M., and on another trip he was almost kidnapped and sold into slavery. So he was very surprised one Sunday morning when he passed a church packed with Georgians, white and black. A crowded church was a rare sight in the West Indies, and a curious Equiano was even more intrigued when he learned that the great George Whitefield was preaching inside. He pushed into the building to see Whitefield "sweating as ever I did on Montserrat beach" and exhorting the Georgians to lead Christian lives. The Georgians, according to another contemporary report, were "truly sensible of the many and great obligations this province has from its infant state lain under to that worthy gentleman." Equiano did not know it, but Whitefield was bidding farewell to Georgia: the evangelist was in town to close the orphanage he had opened with such high hopes thirty years earlier. Georgia had prospered, though not as its philanthropic benefactors had imagined it would.[5]

Whitefield's complicity in slavery shows how powerful, how lucrative, and how widespread slavery was in the eighteenth century. Whitefield's death in 1770 inspired a slave girl in Boston, Phillis Wheatley, to publish her first poem, a eulogy to the evangelist. Though taken by "the hand of death," Whitefield now graced the heavens, she wrote. Imagining Whitefield preaching from heaven, Wheatley portrayed the evangelist as telling Americans to bring their complaints to Christ, telling Africans, like herself and Equiano, that their "Impartial Saviour" would wash them in "the fountain of redeeming blood" and make them all "sons, and kings, and priests to God." Perhaps fulfilling Wheatley's prophecy, Equiano said farewell to Georgia in 1767 by preaching a sermon of his own. A black mother could find no white minister to bury her dead child. Equiano consented to "act the parson" and bid his own farewell to Savannah by burying a black child in its sandy soil.[6]

Though he played the parson, Equiano was still not sure he had been saved. He took his religion seriously, studying the Bible, going to church when he could, and trying to observe all of the commandments. But as a sailor he found it very difficult to stop swearing and to observe the Sabbath. Pray as he might, he still felt that he was not saved. Worse, he still felt himself to be a sinner. Proof of his own sinfulness came in 1774, when, living a relatively good life as a free man in England, he failed to save his friend John Annis from death in the West Indies. Annis, a slave from St. Kitts, had arrived in England in the early 1770s with his owner, a Scotsman named Kirkpatrick. Annis's status as a slave in England was ambiguous: in the 1772 case of a slave from Massachusetts named James Somerset, brought to England under circumstances similar to Annis's, Lord Chief Justice William Mansfield had ruled that since Parliament had never established slavery in England, the institution of slavery could not exist there. So once Somerset, or any slave, set foot in England, he became free and could not be forced to return to slavery in a British colony. The *Somerset* decision seemed to put the law on John Annis's side. Equiano hired a lawyer, who took his money but did nothing. Kirkpatrick spirited Annis off to the West Indies in 1774 and had him tortured to death.[7]

Equiano blamed himself, not the lawyer or the British legal system, for Annis's death. Despondent over his failure to prevent his friend's suffering, reminded of his own complicity in slavery, Equiano wished to die himself. His life in England seemed meaningless. He overcame the wish to die, but not the feeling of sinfulness. He thought of leaving England for Turkey and converting to Islam. Instead, he sailed for Spain, still wondering why he was so filled with sin. At Cadiz he had a sudden vision of Christ dying to save him, and the date of this experience, October 6, 1774, was as important to him as the date he became free.

EQUIANO AND THE
WORLD OF ANTISLAVERY

Freedom and salvation, parallel themes in Equiano's *Narrative,* are also twin themes in the story of the antislavery movement. Equiano tormented himself over his minor sins of swearing and missing the Sabbath. John Annis's death brought home to him the horrible consequences of larger sins, such as his own role in the slave trade. Between the 1450s, when the pope approved the Portuguese practice of enslaving African "pagans and unbelievers," and the 1750s, when the Aro traders kidnapped Equiano, the African slave trade had become one of the largest economic enterprises in the world's history. It enriched the European nations whose merchants owned the ships, it allowed some African people to grow powerful and to prey on others, and it brought labor to develop the Americas. In 1750 few Europeans questioned either their right to enslave Africans or the economic benefits of doing so. By the 1780s, the high point of the African slave trade, when more than eighty-eight thousand Africans would be brought to the New World every year, the Atlantic slave trade was a well-established mercantile system connecting Africa, Europe, and the Americas in a web of commerce.

Equiano knew how formidable and profitable the institution of slavery was. Even men and women who agreed that slavery was wrong were not prepared to give up such a lucrative business. George Whitefield preached the equality of all souls before God but still allowed his benevolent enterprises to use slaves. The Quakers in 1727 had explicitly called the slave trade and slavery contrary to Christian ethics, yet for years individual Quakers still owned and traded slaves. Anthony Benezet, a Philadelphia Quaker, wrote his antislavery books in the 1760s partly to convince other Quakers that they should not own slaves. Two years after the Quakers barred slave traders from their meetings, Philadelphia Quaker Robert King bought Equiano to work in his slave-trading business. Equiano himself continued to work as a slave trader after he became free and in 1776 helped Charles Irving buy slaves for a Central American plantation. Slavery was a dominant feature of the eighteenth century, and nearly impossible to escape, as Equiano, John Annis, and George Whitefield learned.[8]

By 1750 the slave trade had become better organized, more efficient in both capturing and delivering slaves, and more profitable to the European and American traders. The slave trade was central to Europe's economy in this century of tremendous change: England, Holland, and France had become the leading slave traders, and their trade in slaves and sugar helped them become the world's leading economic powers. Only a few moral zealots and the slaves themselves challenged the right of one people to enslave another. No one would have guessed in 1750 that the slave trade was entering its final century. No one would have predicted that in the 1780s a massive public campaign would challenge the slave trade, that men and women who were not slaves would interest themselves in men and women who were, or that in the 1790s the slaves of Haiti, France's richest sugar colony, would successfully revolt against slavery on that island.

Part of the spark for the antislavery movement came from evangelical Christianity and from the persistent Quaker agitation. Another spark came from the American Revolution (1776–1783), though, paradoxically, that political movement also strengthened the institution of slavery. In the 1760s, when England began taxing the American colonies to pay for the Seven Years' War, Americans protested. Equiano remembered being in Charleston in 1765 to see one of the great demonstrations against the Stamp Act. The American colonists searched for an ideological basis for resisting British authority. Rather than simply saying they did not like to pay taxes, Americans argued that British taxes were a small part of a larger scheme to oppress them and that this oppression, if not stopped, would result in their enslavement. Some American leaders, like Benjamin Franklin and James Otis, took this opposition to "slavery" to its logical conclusion, saying that slavery was wrong both for white Americans and for Africans or African Americans. But in 1776 there were slaves in every American colony, from New Hampshire to Georgia. Some leaders equivocated when they wrote of slavery and liberty; others simply ignored the contradiction. Thomas Jefferson wrote the Declaration of Independence declaring that "all men are created equal" and equally endowed with the rights to "life, liberty, and the pursuit of happiness." The fact that Jefferson and other revolutionaries owned slaves (Jefferson himself owned nearly two hundred) led British writer Samuel Johnson to ridicule American claims of oppression, asking, "How is it that we hear the loudest yelps for liberty among the drivers of Negroes?"[9]

The rhetoric of liberty, however hypocritical, made it impossible for Americans to insist on their own freedom while denying freedom to others. In 1773 slaves in Massachusetts petitioned the colonial assembly, a center for resistance to British authority, for their own freedom. Though the assembly took no action on slavery, the slaves had raised an issue that would not go away. Six years later John Adams drew up a new constitution for the state of Massachusetts, beginning it with a declaration that "all men are born free and equal." Quok Walker, a slave in Boston, read this and asked the state's highest court how he could be the property of Nathaniel

Jennison if he was born "free and equal." The court agreed with him, and in 1783 slavery was declared illegal in Massachusetts.[10]

Slaveholders as well as slaves recognized the power of these words. One South Carolinian argued against a bill of rights, saying bluntly that bills of rights usually begin by declaring that "men are by nature born free. Now, we should make that declaration with a very bad grace, when a large part of our property consists in men who are actually born slaves."[11] The American revolutionaries, having introduced the language of equality into their political vocabulary, would have to reckon with the full power of these words. In the 1780s Pennsylvania, Connecticut, and Rhode Island passed laws for the gradual emancipation of slaves and barred their citizens from participating in the slave trade. Baptists and Methodists pushed the issue further, barring slaveholders from membership and urging others to emancipate their slaves. In 1787 the American Congress barred slavery from the territory north of the Ohio River, and the new American Constitution allowed Congress to prohibit the slave trade after 1807. The American antislavery movement thus was propelled by diverse people: Quakers, Baptists, and Methodists; free blacks, especially in cities like Boston, New York, and Philadelphia; slaves who challenged white authority by violence, by running away, or by simply resisting; and some revolutionaries who saw the inconsistency in basing their own freedom on the slavery of others.

Equiano, as a sailor, helped to link the world of American antislavery with the simultaneous British movement. He sailed to Philadelphia in 1784, attended a Quaker wedding there, visited the school for blacks that Benezet had founded, and joined a delegation of blacks to thank the Quakers for their antislavery work. He visited New York in 1785, the year before an antislavery society was founded in that city. In England, Equiano linked the various parts of British antislavery, from the evangelical Christians to the black workers (many of them Americans freed by the British during the Revolution) and London's African community as well as the upper reaches of the mainly white antislavery movement. His strong religious faith and his assurance that God had a purpose for him made him take an active role both in spreading ideas and in shaping those ideas into a strong antislavery platform.

These circles of interest and sentiments of antislavery were in place by 1783 when a case of mass murder brought the horrors of slavery to a wider public. Equiano helped break the story of the massacre on the slave ship *Zong*, which had left São Tomé (off West Africa) in September 1781 with 440 slaves. Two months later, when the *Zong* reached the Caribbean, 60 slaves and 7 crew were dead. Disease had ravaged the human cargo, and many of the surviving slaves were dying. The captain, thinking of his Liverpool owners and their dwindling profits, knew he could not sell even the remaining healthy slaves.

The captain made a business decision. Insurance would not pay for sick slaves or slaves killed by illness, but it would pay for slaves who drowned. He ordered 54 Africans chained together and thrown overboard. The next day, he ordered 42 more drowned, and 36 on the third day. Having covered all evidence of illness, the captain sold the rest of the cargo and sailed for England. When he arrived in Liverpool, the *Zong*'s owners filed an insurance claim for 132 drowned slaves.

The claim might have gone through quietly, but Equiano learned the true story. Perhaps a crew member told him: even men on slave ships had some conscience. Equiano quickly alerted Granville Sharp, the British abolitionist who had brought the *Somerset* case twelve years earlier. Sharp was horrified, but he knew the limits of British justice. The *Zong*'s captain and owners would never be charged as murderers. At best, the owners could be stopped from collecting insurance on slaves their company had murdered. But even this did not happen. Lord Chief Justice Mansfield, who ten years earlier had declared James Somerset free once he set foot on British soil, ruled that the *Zong*'s owners were entitled to collect insurance on the 132 slaves their captain had murdered. British courts did not protect John Annis and did not punish the murderers of 132 men and women. As Equiano would write of earthly courts, he saw "no help in them, nor by the law."[12] The *Zong* massacre was a horrifying example of what happens when men and women are treated as property, and the British court's failure to do justice showed Equiano that laws made by men could not prevent the evils done by men.

Equiano and Sharp knew the limits of British justice, but they also knew the power of public opinion. In the wake of the *Zong* massacre, which showed the horrors of the slave trade, Britain's relatively small groups of abolitionists expanded, using the public newspapers and lecture platforms to organize opposition to both the slave trade and slavery. Two of the most notable abolitionists who emerged after the *Zong* massacre were James Ramsay, a former minister in the West Indies, and Thomas Clarkson, a college student at Cambridge. Ramsay's *Essay on the Treatment and Conversion of African Slaves in the Sugar Colonies* (1784) attacked the West Indian planters for their cruelty, and Clarkson's *Essay on the Slavery and Commerce of the Human Species* (1786) included a cross-section drawing of the slave ship *Brookes,* showing how Africans were loaded into the cargo bays. This illustration (p. 206) became one of the most important images of the abolition movement. Abolition had been one reform movement among many in England and America; the *Zong* massacre made antislavery a force of its own. The abolition movement grew, but slavery was still a lucrative business. Englishmen were still making money from slaves and sugar and were not willing to give up this income in return for a clear conscience. One slave dealer said that "answering [to God] was a thing of another world" and that *his* "policy" was to make money. London merchant James Tobin, who had spent the years 1775–1783 operating a plantation on the island of Nevis, wrote three pamphlets defending slavery. Tobin's *Cursory Remarks upon the Reverend Mr. Ramsay's Essay* (1785) responded to Ramsay's attack on slavery by accusing the minister of hypocrisy (saying Ramsay had mistreated his own slaves in the West Indies) and by charging that blacks who were not slaves would not work. He pointed to the blacks who had come to England after the American Revolution and asked if Ramsay had ever seen one of them "employed in a laborious task. . . . On the contrary . . . out of the whole of this number, those who are not in livery are in rags; and such as are not servants, are thieves or mendicants."[13]

Equiano had so far worked behind the scenes, bringing news and propaganda from one level of society to another, from one continent to another. The whites, better connected to power, would do the rest. But by being invisible, Equiano could not challenge the defenders of slavery, especially now that men like Tobin argued that blacks were fit only to be slaves. Equiano had to emerge in public to refute the claims of laziness and of dishonesty.

Prodded by Tobin's charges as well as by the inability of white abolitionists to face the racist arguments squarely, Equiano took up the pen. Calling Tobin "an invective fibber" in a letter to London's *Public Advertiser,* Equiano apologized for having to descend to Tobin's level. "I wish I could say truths, but you oblige me to use ill manners, you lie faster than Old Nick can hear them."[14] To challenge slavery, Equiano had to challenge racism. Well-intentioned Americans and English people might agree that the slave trade was wicked, but they were deeply troubled by the prospect of slaves becoming free and of black men and women entering English or American society as the equals of whites. Tobin had struck a sensitive nerve in his white readers. If slaves were free, what would they do?

Tobin had tried to turn the argument against slavery around by turning the problem of slavery into the problem of race, which always lurked beneath the surface. Equiano offered a solution to both problems. If men like Tobin, or even white abolitionists, could not accept black men and women as their equals, Equiano would "encourage open, free, and generous loves upon Nature's own wide and extensive plain, subservient only to moral rectitude, without distinction of the color of a skin." Marriages between blacks and whites would make racism impossible by obliterating racial distinctions. Drawing on the Bible he knew so well, Equiano reminded his English audience that Moses had encouraged the Israelites to marry outsiders, and God had punished Aaron and Miriam for "vexing their brother for marrying the Ethiopian." Marriages between whites and blacks would eliminate the color line and strengthen the British nation. "Away . . . with your narrow, impolitic notion" of legally barring "what will be a national honour, national strength, and productive of national virtue—Intermarriages!"[15]

For Equiano this was a natural solution. But even the British people with whom he worked most closely still reminded him that he was different. In 1786 a group of white abolitionists, including Clarkson and Sharp, formed the Committee for Relief of the Black Poor. This committee planned to send blacks living in England, many of whom had been born in the United States, to Sierra Leone on the west coast of Africa. These black men and women, most living in London, either had fought for the British during the American Revolution or had been slaves to American Loyalists and had fled with them to England.

Equiano objected to the whole enterprise. Black people were not the problem. The problem was the institution of slavery, which treated men and women like property, and persistent racism, which gave white people an excuse for enslaving blacks. If the black people were settled in Africa, which, he pointed out, was not their homeland, what would stop English slave traders from reenslaving them? Despite Equiano's objections, the idea of colonization appealed to many white abolitionists, both in England and the United States, who could not imagine that black men and women could be incorporated into English or American society. Virtually every white American leader who spoke against slavery before the Civil War advocated colonization of freed black people in Africa or somewhere beyond the borders of the United States.[16]

Despite Equiano's objections, he was appointed as the expedition's commissary. The only black official in this white-run charity organization, he was immediately caught in the conflict between the good intentions of white philanthropists, the needs of the four hundred black people who had agreed to go (white organizers had hoped to attract seven hundred emigrants), and the self-interest of white businessmen hired to supply the goods needed for the voyage. Equiano discovered that the white agent paid to deliver supplies had not done so. When Equiano reported the agent's corruption to the treasury, the agent charged Equiano with incompetence. Equiano saw that even some English philanthropists would "serve (or use) the blacks the same as they do in the West Indies." He organized a protest by the black emigrants and wrote to a fellow Ibo in London, Ottabah Cugoano, "I do not know how this undertaking will end; I wish I had never been involved in it." By the time he wrote this, he was no longer involved. The expedition's sponsors had fired him.[17]

Equiano left the Sierra Leone expedition under a cloud, though the lords of the treasury ultimately cleared him and paid him his back wages. He had learned an important lesson from this experience. Though white abolitionists like Clarkson and Sharp had the best intentions, blacks had to be more than symbols and tokens. In response, Equiano and other blacks living in England organized the Sons of Africa. These black men would speak out on issues important to the black community, such as slavery and the slave trade. Equiano's fellow Ibo and fellow Son of Africa Ottabah Cugoano wrote *Thoughts and Sentiments on the Evil of Slavery* in 1787, introducing an African voice into the growing debate.[18] Equiano went to the home of Thomas Hardy, a London shoemaker and political radical, to write his own story.

EQUIANO'S *NARRATIVE* AS AN ABOLITIONIST TOOL

Equiano was uniquely qualified to write an antislavery book, and he began to do so in the spring of 1788. He knew the whole system of slavery, from the kidnapping of slaves in Africa, to the brutal middle passage across the Atlantic, to the plantations of the West Indies and the American mainland, to the intercolonial slave trade. He had experienced every part of the slave system. But he had also lived as a free man for twenty years. His life was more than a testament against slavery: it was a record of one man's survival of both a brutal institution and a savage age.

In presenting the case against slavery, Equiano presented himself as a human being. He kept his book focused on his own life and made himself a sympathetic character, one with whom his readers could identify. Thus he could make his readers see that if slavery was wrong for him, it would also be wrong for them. He was not "a saint, a hero, [or] a tyrant," he wrote. He knew that he was not perfect, and he understood that no other person was. His book was intended to move different readers in different ways, but to bring all to the same conclusion: that Equiano was a decent person, that he did not deserve to be enslaved, and that therefore no African deserved to be enslaved. That this seems obvious now shows how successful Equiano and other abolitionists were; that we have not completely overcome the legacy of slavery and racism should bring home to us the enormous obstacles in Equiano's way.

Equiano's *Narrative* came at a critical moment in the British antislavery movement. Opposition to slavery in England had already come from different segments of British society. Granville Sharp, Thomas Clarkson, and their intellectual or religious allies were moved by moral revulsion against the brutality of the institution. Ottabah Cugoano, Equiano, and other black refugees had directly experienced it. Working people feared that their own status as free men and women was in jeopardy if the wider British public accepted slavery, and some industrialists in the emerging cities of Manchester and Birmingham had to compete for capital with the slave traders of Liverpool. Each group—religious reformers, intellectuals, blacks, working people, capitalists—pursued its own agenda, often working against one another. But in 1788 this diverse coalition banded together to form one of the greatest mass movements in British history. Activists collected tens of thousands of signatures on petitions urging Parliament to end the slave trade. Equiano presented his own petition to Queen Charlotte, wife of George III, on March 21, 1788.

Equiano's *Narrative* became one crucial link between these segments of the British public. He knew the great English abolitionists Sharp, Clarkson, and Ramsay, but he also knew sailors and dockworkers, black refugees from the West Indies and America, and leaders of London's emerging radical working class. He was recognized by virtually every segment of the antislavery and reform movements, and he could speak of his own experiences in a way to move men and women at every level of society. Among the subscribers to the first edition of his book were members of the English royal family and political radicals who in a few short years would be charged with treason, pacifists and admirals, Anglican bishops and dissenting ministers, Africans living in London, and women and men committed to reform.[19]

After Equiano sold nearly two thousand copies of the *Narrative* on a trip to Ireland in 1791, a white abolitionist said that Equiano was "more use to the Cause than half the People in the country." Always wary of his own vanity, Equiano responded, "I wish to God, I could be so."[20] In the *Narrative,* Equiano presented two strong arguments against slavery. Though the moral argument is on virtually every page, Equiano knew that Englishmen would not stop doing something that earned them money just because it was sinful. So he also made an economic case for ending the slave trade. He appealed to an English audience whose own economic world was changing. The *Narrative* sold especially well in the rising industrial centers of Manchester and Birmingham. England's industrial transformation was well under way by the 1780s, and Equiano argued that freedom for slaves in the West Indies and an end to the African slave trade would actually speed up the transition to an industrial economy. Africa, he argued, could be a lucrative market for European goods. If England would stop making Africans their slaves and instead would sell them textiles and tools, English manufacturers could enjoy tremendous profits far beyond what English slave traders and sugar planters enjoyed. Equiano thus appealed to both the British soul and the British purse.

Equiano understood the economic change taking place in England. He offered a way out for planters fearful of an insurrection but not certain that the former slaves could be incorporated into society. White people feared that the former slaves would retaliate and shared James Tobin's suspicion that the freed people would not work. Equiano himself was hardworking and diligent, and he told the slaveholders that by "treating your slaves as men, every cause of fear would be banished. They would be faithful, honest, intelligent, and vigorous," and all would enjoy "peace, prosperity, and happiness."[21] England and America could survive, but only by treating their slaves as men and women, only by living up to the Christian precepts and ideological positions staked out by Europeans and Americans.

It would not be enough, he knew, for masters to be nicer to their slaves. Nor would it be enough to abolish the slave trade. The problem was that slavery gave some men too much power, and men with power would abuse those without power. He had learned this lesson both as a slave and as a free man. Five of the *Narrative*'s twelve chapters chronicle his life after slavery, and some of the most brutal evidence against slavery is from the stories of men like John Annis and Joseph Clipson, who escaped from slavery only to be forced back into it. Though free, these men could at any time be tricked or overpowered by whites.

Equiano's *Narrative* was such a successful tool that slavery's defenders tried to challenge his authority: they claimed he was not an African at all but had been born in the West Indies. If he had been born in the West Indies, he could not have experienced the middle passage. Two anonymous notes were planted in the London papers in 1792, while Equiano was in Scotland selling the fourth edition of his *Narrative,* charging that Equiano was actually from the island of St. Croix.[22] This was an easy charge to refute: Equiano still had friends in England who remembered his arrival there as a slave thirty years earlier.

These critics saw what a powerful weapon Equiano's *Narrative* was. It appealed to people at many different levels of British society, particularly men and women of the working class who might have regarded abolition as an upper-class hobby. Equiano was distinctly ordinary; he made clear that what had happened to him could happen to anyone. Ordinary readers could identify with him, as they might not identify with the nameless bodies in Clarkson's drawing of a slave ship or with the nearly naked slave kneeling in Josiah Wedgwood's medallion entitled "Am I Not a Man and a Brother" (p. 207). Though the drawing and the medallion became popular antislavery symbols, Equiano was a real person. He spoke directly to many different men and women in his audience, confessing his own sins and urging them to face their own.

THE LITERARY CONTEXT OF EQUIANO'S *NARRATIVE*

Equiano's *Narrative* is the first great African American slave narrative. It draws on a number of literary traditions: the spiritual autobiography, the picaresque novel, the travel or adventure book, and the sentimental novel. Equiano did not set out to create a literary genre, nor did he try to fit his life story into a literary form. Instead, he wrote the story of his life as he remembered it, shaping it into a coherent and forceful argument against slavery.

Scholars who have studied slave narratives have noted common themes and motifs in these stories. The author tells of his or her birth and childhood, a struggle for literacy (since in most cases slaves were not allowed to learn to read), and ultimately an escape. Throughout the story the author relates details of slavery, giving examples of cruelty as well as moments of courage or of assistance from either other blacks or friendly whites. Equiano's *Narrative* fits this pattern, though it might be more correct to say that his *Narrative* set the pattern.

Writers of slave narratives also used various strategies to prove that the story they told was true. The writer had a political purpose: to convince readers that slavery was brutal and wrong. It was important, then, for readers to believe that the author had in fact experienced all of the horrors he or she wrote about. Equiano, like later writers of slave narratives, included in his text letters from men who knew him as well as his own petition to Queen Charlotte. He included real, public documents that gave credibility to his story and his portrait, showing readers his face. Other writers of slave narratives, notably Frederick Douglass (whose title, *Narrative of the Life of Frederick Douglass, an American Slave, Written by Himself,* even echoes Equiano's) used similar tactics.[23]

Equiano's amazing memory, his ability to recall details after twenty or thirty years, also verified his story. He recalled the names of ships, the names of captains and friends, as well as the exotic smell of alligator meat or the feel of an Indian king's scalp he held in his hand. His memory was aided by a journal (he mentions nearly blowing up the ship when he used the ship's gunpowder room to write). Keeping a journal was a common way for an intensely religious person to record his own struggles with sin and temptation. For Equiano, the journal also was a way to record voyages, to record transactions (in which he might be cheated), and to remember the incredible world he lived in. Because he wrote down so many details, it is possible to check his accuracy against eighteenth-century port records and newspapers. Every voyage between the West Indies and Savannah, Charleston, and Philadelphia checks out.[24]

Equiano used his journal to help his memory, but he also borrowed descriptions and some details from other books, such as Anthony Benezet's *Some Historical Account of Guinea* (1771) and Constantin John Phipps's *Journal of a Voyage towards the North Pole* (1774). Today this would be considered plagiarism, but eighteenth-century writers freely borrowed from other sources. Why, though, would an African writer rely on an American who had never been to Africa for his description of Africa? It is important to note that Equiano copied Benezet's general geographical survey of West Africa and Benezet's account of West African governments. An eleven-year-old boy would not know these facts, and Benezet did not know the details of Isseke that Equiano knew. Equiano remembered the *igbu ichi* ceremony, the facial scarring he would have undergone had he stayed in Isseke; he remembered the perfumes and dances, the cultural significance of snakes, the folktales and proverbs, local details unknown to Benezet or any writer outside of Ibo society. A boy would know these things and would remember them long after he became a man.[25]

The use of detail, literary scholar Henry Louis Gates Jr. observed, is a feature that African American slave narratives have in common with the picaresque novel. Like the slave narrative, the picaresque focuses on a central character, a *picaro*, who is taken from his ordinary circumstances and set in motion in a hostile world, his fate controlled by unknown forces. The picaresque novel has its central character experience a series of improbable adventures or misfortunes, sometimes comic, sometimes tragic. The author uses these random episodes to comment satirically on contemporary society. Cervantes's *Don Quixote* and Jonathan Swift's *Gulliver's Travels* are the best-known picaresque novels. The authors of these novels used rich details to give their improbable stories the ring of truth. As Gates has noted, like African American slave authors, the *picaros* are outsiders looking into the society; they are propelled by forces they cannot control through a society in which they have been thrown against their will. Echoed in Equiano's *Narrative,* the picaresque tradition lives on in such masterpieces of modern fiction as Toni Morrison's *Beloved* and Ralph Ellison's *Invisible Man.* Both of these twentieth-century novels feature the continuing journeys of black men and women through a hostile world.[26]

Though Equiano's *Narrative* is a true story with elements of the picaresque, it also has elements of the sentimental novel, a literary form emerging in the eighteenth century. Like Equiano, the authors of sentimental fiction wanted their readers to feel a bond with their characters. These writers, such as Laurence Sterne, tried to engage readers' sympathy. In Sterne's *A Sentimental Journey through France and Italy,* a satire on both contemporary society and literature, the protagonist wants to elicit the audience's compassion for the "millions of my fellow creatures born to no inheritance but slavery" on West Indian plantations. But Sterne understood what too many moralists did not. Before readers will feel sympathy, they must identify with the sufferer, and a reader is more likely to be moved by one person's sad story than by the collective sorrows of a mob. Instead of the suffering millions, Sterne focused on one single prisoner in a European jail, his body wasted and heart broken by his "hope deferr'd."[27]

Equiano knew this as well as Sterne did. While countless thousands of Africans had died on the slave ships and on American plantations, it took the deaths of 132 countable Africans on the *Zong* to arouse British opinion. In 1787 Equiano had helped his friend Ottabah Cugoano write his *Thoughts and Sentiments,* an antislavery essay that failed as both literature and propaganda. Though Cugoano had experienced the middle passage and life in slavery just as Equiano had, his book is a sermon against slavery, not the story of one man's struggle with the institution. Learning from Cugoano's experience, Equiano cut down on the sermons, presenting himself instead as an argument against slavery, creating himself as a character with whom ordinary readers would empathize.

As the story of an ordinary man's life, Equiano's *Narrative* fits into a long tradition of autobiography. The idea that a common man had an important story to tell was relatively new, but Equiano's *Narrative* actually belongs to a very old tradition of spiritual autobiographies, the life histories of ordinary men and women who struggled against extraordinary hardships to preserve their religious faith. These stories are still very much a part of our literature and still follow the same pattern: the author falls into a life of sin, comes to see both the sinfulness of his or her own life and the sinfulness of society, and devotes the rest of his or her life to conquering personal sin and changing the nature of society. St. Augustine's *Confessions* (c. A.D. 400) set the pattern for spiritual autobiographies, and books like *The Autobiography of Malcolm X* have kept the tradition alive in our own century. Equiano himself read one of the most popular collection of spiritual biographies, John Foxe's *Acts and Monuments,* also known as *Book of Martyrs* (1563). Foxe's martyrs struggle to overcome their own sin and to challenge the social order that condemns them for doing so. Equiano struggled for his own salvation against a world that rejected him.[28]

Perhaps the most popular English book in the eighteenth century was John Bunyan's *Pilgrim's Progress* (1678), a fictionalized spiritual biography. Bunyan's central character, Christian, moves steadily toward the Celestial City, though he is slowed by bad characters such as Mr. Worldly Wise, or rough places, such as the Slough of Despond. Bunyan's influence on other writers transcended his religious message. His plain style, his use of dialogue, his message, and the central metaphor of travel to a better world have kept his book in print for three centuries. Benjamin Franklin, whose *Autobiography* presents a different kind of pilgrim's progress, admired Bunyan's style. Franklin's progress was toward material success, his Celestial City a secular American society. Equiano's *Narrative* has a Christian theme similar to Bunyan's, but he shares with Franklin the steady advancement toward material success, measured most dramatically in his purchase of himself.

Equiano's Christian theme, his travel toward a Celestial City, is apparent. Less obvious, but just as fundamental to the *Narrative,* is the movement toward material success. As literary scholar Houston Baker has shown, Equiano's accumulation of capital (in 1764 he bought a glass for a half bit in St. Eustatia and sold it for one bit in Montserrat, then returned to St. Eustatia to buy two glasses, which he again sold in Montserrat for twice what he had paid) gave him some control over the economic system that enslaved him. Through trade, Equiano was able to free himself from this brutal system of commerce and exploitation.[29]

By mastering economics Equiano managed to free himself from slavery. By mastering language, he was able to tell his story. As a young boy, Equiano watched his friend Dick Baker and his master Captain Pascal read books. "I had a great curiosity to talk to the books as I thought they did, and so to learn how all things had a beginning. For that purpose I have often taken up a book, and have talked to it, and then put my ears to it, when alone, in hopes it would answer me."[30] Other eighteenth-century Anglo-African writers wrote of "talking books" in this same way, as the first step in their own mastery of the language. (The motif appears in the

1770 autobiography of Ukawsaw Gronniosaw, in Cugoano's *Thoughts and Sentiments,* and in the 1790 *Narrative of the Life of John Marrant.*)[31] Henry Louis Gates Jr. sees this figure of the talking book as the first tradition of the slave narrative.[32] Equiano's mastery of the language and of literary form does more than merely allow him to write a book (as important as writing his book was): it allows him to remain free. On a visit to Savannah some men tried to claim him as a runaway slave. Equiano told them "to be still and keep off, for I had seen those kind of tricks played upon other free blacks, and they must not think to serve me so." The men realized that "I talked too good English" for them to trick.[33]

EQUIANO'S LEGACY

In 1792 Equiano paused in his antislavery labors to marry Susan Cullen, an Englishwoman from a town near Cambridge. She had subscribed to the *Narrative*'s first edition, and perhaps they met through the antislavery movement. The first of their two daughters, Anna Maria, was born the following year, their second, Johanna, in 1795. Susan Cullen Vassa died a few months after Johanna's birth, and Equiano died in April 1797. The two young girls were left without parents, and Anna Maria survived her father by just a few months. She is buried near her mother's hometown, in Old Chesterton, Cambridge. Her grave is marked by a "humble stone" that tells visitors that beneath it lies "A child of colour haply [by chance] not thine own." The epitaph tells how other village children "bedew'd with tears the white wreaths on their breast" as they dropped flowers into the grave and that Anna Maria had gone to that place "Where some of every clime shall joy in God."[34]

Equiano and Susan's other daughter, Johanna, turned twenty-one in 1816, inherited £950 from her parents' estate, and with it disappeared from the historical record. She would not have remembered her mother, who died when she was an infant. If she had a memory of her father, it would have been a very faint one. Though she would lead a private life, her father's life, set down in his *Narrative,* would continue to be a public one.

Equiano lived to see his book become an international bestseller, with eight English editions as well as American, Dutch, Russian, and French editions by the time he died. In 1814, during a renewed debate over slavery, a new edition appeared in England. In 1829 Abigail Field Mott published a shortened, illustrated version of Equiano's story to be given as a prize to black pupils in New York's Free African School. Isaac Knapp, business partner of abolitionist William Lloyd Garrison, published the entire *Narrative* in 1837, reaching back to Equiano to restate the case against slavery.

In the early nineteenth century the book was still a political tool: England and the United States would not be persuaded to end their own African slave trades until 1807, ten years after Equiano's death. Most of France's West Indian slaves would win their freedom through violent revolution: Haiti exploded in 1792, and violence continued to rage until 1804, when Haiti became the second independent nation in the Western Hemisphere and the first to abolish slavery. The revolutions in Spanish America of the 1810s and 1820s all drew on the support of black people, and most made emancipation a goal of their revolutions. England would not emancipate its West Indian slaves until 1832 and then would impose on the freed people a system of apprenticeship, which would not be lifted until 1837. In the United States, as in Haiti, slavery ended only after a civil war, which in America cost 600,000 lives. It destroyed slavery, but not the racism or injustice that made slavery possible.

With slavery destroyed, Equiano's *Narrative* disappeared. As with many other political texts, it seemed to have lost its value. But in the twentieth century, when descendants of Africans in America, the Caribbean, Europe, and Africa itself continued to struggle against racism, Equiano's voice reemerged. Arna Bontemps, African American author and veteran of the Harlem Renaissance of the 1920s and 1930s, spoke of the "whispered pride" with which African Americans trying to reclaim their own history cited Equiano's *Narrative*. Equiano's book survives as a record of one man's lifelong struggles and reminds us of the lives of millions who did not live to tell their stories.[35]

In his lifetime, Equiano considered himself lucky. Providence had chosen him and had preserved him. He was keenly aware that others suffered while he prospered and that his luck had little to do with his own merit. Providence had chosen him, he believed, to tell the stories of others, the millions who did not survive. He hated to think of his sister's fate, having seen too many young African girls raped by their captors. He was powerless to help them, just as he could not prevent Joseph Clipson or John Annis from being sent back into slavery. But while he could not prevent rape or torture, he could remember and record it. He reminded his readers that slavery was a brutal institution, even for the men and women who survived it. At any moment their lives or liberty could be taken away, not by an omnipotent God, but by other humans. Episodes of kindness or generosity and moments of compassion were not enough to check the power of human greed and bad men who thrived in an evil system.

Ultimately, England would give up the slave trade and abolish slavery.

England and the other slaveholding nations would adopt precisely the kind of system of commerce that Equiano advocated. A century after he wrote his book, the system he proposed was at its peak, and the European nations formalized their trade with Africa by drawing artificial boundaries on a map of Africa and claiming people and territory as their own. The Europeans gave up enslaving Africans but did not give up exploiting them. Equiano may have been a better economist than he knew. Europe would benefit as much from colonizing Africa as it had from enslaving Africans. The slave trade changed African society in ways we are only now beginning to understand, and the colonial system that replaced it made it almost impossible for African societies to recover.

The wealth amassed from slavery helped pay for England's industrial transformation. The coal barge replaced the slave ship on the world's waterways, but the new commercial system Equiano advocated did not end the exploitation he condemned. Equiano visited the coalfields and the emerging industrial cities of Manchester and Birmingham as he toured Britain speaking out against slavery. In Newcastle and Shropshire, he was shown the inside of a coal mine, where men dug out the fuel that would power England's industrial revolution. Equiano, who knew the whole process of slavery better than any of his contemporaries, from kidnapping in Africa to sale in the West Indies and brutal work on American plantations, now was able to see the first step in the process of industrial production. By relying on the power of coal, Equiano believed, England could extricate itself from the slave system that made some men into beasts of burden, others their brutal drivers. Deep in the coal mine, Equiano and his party felt the earth shake as an avalanche of coal crashed down upon them. One man was buried alive. Equiano survived.

NOTES

[1] The eleven million figure is an estimate; some calculations are as low as nine million, some as high as twenty million. See Philip D. Curtin, *The Atlantic Slave Trade* (Madison: University of Wisconsin Press, 1969); Paul E. Lovejoy, "The Volume of the Atlantic Slave Trade: A Synthesis," *Journal of African History* 23 (1980); and Joseph E. Inikori, "Measuring the Atlantic Slave Trade: An Assessment of Curtin and Anstey," *Journal of African History* 17 (1976). See also Joseph E. Inikori and Stanley L. Engerman, eds., *The Atlantic Slave Trade* (Durham: Duke University Press, 1992).

[2] Catherine Obianuju Acholonu, *The Igbo Roots of Olaudah Equiano* (Owerri, Nigeria: Afa Publications, 1989), 42–43; Achebe quoted in Paul Edwards, *Equiano's Travels: His Autobiography* (London: Heinemann, 1967), 180 n; Henry Brooke, *Gustavus Vasa, the Deliverer of His Country: A Tragedy in Five Acts* (London, 1739). Inside the cover of the 1791 New York

edition of Equiano's *Narrative* at the American Antiquarian Society, an anonymous cataloger asked, "Was not this book written by Henry Brooke?"

[3] Equiano, *Narrative*, 78. On the kinds of bonds formed by sailors, see especially Peter Linebaugh and Marcus Rediker, "The Many Headed Hydra: Sailors, Slaves, and the Atlantic Working Class in the Eighteenth Century," *Journal of Historical Sociology* 3 (1990); on African identity, see Patrick Manning, *Slavery and African Life* (Cambridge: Cambridge University Press, 1990), 25–26, 86–88.

[4] Donald G. Mathews, "Religion and Slavery—the Case of the American South," in *Anti-Slavery, Religion, and Reform,* ed. Christine Bolt and Seymour Drescher (Hamden, Conn.: Archon Books, 1980), 210–18; Rhys Isaac, "Evangelical Revolt: The Nature of the Baptists' Challenge to the Traditional Order in Virginia, 1765 to 1775," *William and Mary Quarterly*, 3rd ser., 31 (1974); Albert J. Raboteau, "The Slave Church in the Era of the American Revolution," in *Slavery and Freedom in the Era of the American Revolution,* ed. Ira Berlin and Ronald Hoffman (Urbana: University of Illinois Press for the United States Capitol Historical Society, 1986).

[5] Equiano, *Narrative*, 16; Georgia *Gazette*, February 21, 1765. Equiano indicates that he heard Whitefield in Philadelphia. Paul Edwards points out that Equiano and Whitefield were never in Philadelphia at the same time. But Equiano was in Savannah when Whitefield preached his farewell sermon on February 17, 1765; Equiano and the *Prudence* arrived in Savannah on February 7, the ship was loaded and cleared customs on February 16, and it sailed on February 22. (Georgia *Gazette*, February 14 and 21, 1765.) For Whitefield and Georgia, see Jennings B. Saunders, "George Whitefield 225 Years after His First Visit: An Interpretation," *Georgia Historical Quarterly* 48 (1969).

[6] Phillis Wheatley, "On the Death of the Rev. Mr. George Whitefield, 1770," *Poems on Various Subjects* (London, 1773), 22–23; Equiano, *Narrative*, 136.

[7] On the frequently misrepresented *Somerset* case, see Folarin Shyllon, *Black People in Britain, 1555–1833* (London: Oxford University Press for the Institute of Race Relations, 1977), 23–27.

[8] On the Quakers and slavery, see especially Jean R. Soderlund, *Quakers and Slavery: A Divided Spirit* (Princeton: Princeton University Press, 1985). On the Methodists, see Donald J. Mathews, *Slavery and Methodism* (Princeton: Princeton University Press, 1965).

[9] Samuel Johnson, *Taxation No Tyranny* (1775), in *The Yale Edition of the Works of Samuel Johnson,* vol. 10, *Political Writings,* ed. Donald J. Greene (New Haven: Yale University Press, 1977), 454.

[10] The Quok Walker case, *Commonwealth v. Jennison* (1783), had as ambiguous an effect as the *Somerset* decision. Levi Lincoln, Walker's attorney and future U.S. attorney general, argued that slavery violated natural law and was illegal since it had not been established by the Massachusetts legislature. See Arthur Zilversmit, *The First Emancipation* (Chicago: University of Chicago Press, 1967).

[11] Charles Cotesworth Pinckney, *The Debates in the Several State Conventions on the Adoption of the Federal Constitution,* 4 vols., ed. Jonathan Elliot (Washington, 1836), 4: 316.

[12] Prince Hoare, *Memoirs of Granville Sharp, Esq.,* 2 vos. (London, 1828), 1:352–67; Peter Fryer, *Staying Power: The History of Black People in Britain* (London: Pluto Press, 1984), 127–30; Equiano, "Miscellaneous Verses," *Narrative*, 162–65.

[13] Equiano, *Narrative*, 94. James Tobin, *Cursory Remarks* (1785), quoted in Folarin Shyllon, *James Ramsay: The Unknown Abolitionist* (Edinburgh: Canongate, 1977), 61–62. On the post-Revolutionary black population of England, see Shyllon, *Black People in Britain,* ch. 8.

[14] Gustavus Vassa to J. T., Esq., *The Public Advertiser*, January 28, 1788. Reprinted in Shyllon, *Black People in Britain,* 250.

[15] Gustavus Vassa to J. T., Esq., in Shyllon, *Black People in Britain,* 251.

[16] On colonization, see Johnson U. J. Asiegbu, *Slavery and the Politics of Liberation,*

1787–1861 (London: African Publishing Corporation, 1969). For the American colonization movement, see P. J. Staudenraus, *The African Colonization Movement, 1816–1865* (New York: Columbia University Press, 1961), and George Fredrickson, *The Black Image in the White Mind: The Debate on Afro-American Character and Destiny, 1814–1917* (New York: Harper and Row, 1971).

[17] Gustavus Vassa to John Stewart [Ottabah Cugoano], March 24, 1787, reprinted in Shyllon, *Black People in Britain*, 246. When he wrote the *Narrative*, Equiano changed his tune on the Sierra Leone expedition: he praised the "benevolence of government" in supporting the "philanthropic individuals" whose plan "filled me with prayer and much rejoicing." Most likely he did not want to alienate the white philanthropists behind the Sierra Leone expedition. *Narrative*, 186.

[18] Gustavus Vassa to J. T., Esq., January 28, 1788, in Shyllon, *Black People in Britain*, 250; Paul Edwards, "Three West African Writers of the 1780s," in *The Slave's Narrative*, ed. Charles T. Davis and Henry Louis Gates Jr. (Oxford: Oxford University Press, 1985), 182–86.

[19] Equiano, *Narrative*, 191–92. See also James Walvin, "British Popular Sentiment for Abolition, 1787–1832," in *Anti-Slavery, Religion, and Reform*, ed. Bolt and Drescher, 149–53.

[20] Gustavus Vassa to Rev. G. Walker, February 27, 1792, ". . . written by himself: A Manuscript Letter of Olaudah Equiano," Paul Edwards, ed., *Notes and Queries* (June 1968).

[21] Equiano, *Narrative*, 100.

[22] The squibs are reprinted in Shyllon, *Black People in Britain*, 265 n.

[23] James Olney, " 'I Was Born': Slave Narratives, Their Status as Autobiography, and as Literature," in *The Slave's Narrative*, ed. Davis and Gates, 154–55.

[24] For example, though Equiano did not record the name of the ship that brought him from Barbados to Virginia, he recalled that it was a sloop. It arrived in Virginia, he thought, in the late summer or early fall of 1756. It went first into a large bay and then a long way up a river. Once it docked, he stayed on the plantation of a man named Campbell. Only two slave ships arrived in Virginia in 1756: one came directly from Africa and unloaded four hundred slaves in the port of Hampton. The other, a smaller ship called the *Kingston*, sailed up the York River before September 29. Far up the York River, in King and Queen County, a man named either Campbell or Kammel owned a plantation. Perhaps Equiano sailed on the *Kingston*, which only sold two or three slaves. Elizabeth Donnan, *Documents Illustrative of the History of the Slave Trade to America* (Washington, D.C.: Carnegie Institute, 1935), 4:225.

[25] S. E. Ogude, "Facts into Fiction: Equiano's *Narrative* Revisited," *Research in African Literatures*, 13, 1 (Spring 1982), does not trust Equiano's veracity because of this borrowing from Benezet and other sources. Catherine Acholonu, though, has traced Equiano's village of Essaka to the village of Isseke and has noted similarities between customs and even words Equiano used and those of contemporary Ibo society. Acholonu, *Igbo Roots*, 15.

[26] Henry Louis Gates Jr., "Binary Opposition in Chapter One of *Narrative of the Life of Frederick Douglass, an American Slave, Written by Himself*," in *Afro-American Literature: The Reconstruction of Instruction* ed. Dexter Fisher and Robert B. Stepto (New York: Modern Language Association, 1978), 214. On the picaresque in general and other emerging literary forms, see Michael McKeon, *Origins of the English Novel, 1600–1740* (Baltimore: Johns Hopkins University Press, 1987). See also Angelo Costanzo, *Surprizing Narrative: Olaudah Equiano and the Beginnings of Black Autobiography* (Westport, Conn.: Greenwood Press, 1987), 46–48.

[27] Laurence Sterne, *A Sentimental Journey through France and Italy by Mr. Yorick*, ed. Gardner Stout Jr. (Berkeley: University of California Press, 1967), 195–202.

[28] Costanzo, *Surprizing Narrative*, 125–26 n.

[29] Houston A. Baker Jr., *Blues, Ideology, and Afro-American Literature: A Vernacular Theory* (Chicago: University of Chicago Press, 1984), 34–38.

[30] Equiano, *Narrative,* 64.

[31] Costanzo, *Surprizing Narrative,* 72, 127 n.

[32] Henry Louis Gates Jr., "James Gronniosaw and the Trope of the Talking Book," *Southern Review* 22 (1986).

[33] Equiano, *Narrative,* 135.

[34] Richard A. Coates, "Anna Maria Equiano's Epitaph," *Notes and Queries* (July/August 1977).

[35] Arna Bontemps, *Great Slave Narratives* (Boston: Beacon Press, 1969), xiv.

PART TWO

The Document

Olaudah Equiano,

or

GUSTAVUS VASSA,

the African.

Publish'd March 1·1789 by G.Vassa

THE

INTERESTING NARRATIVE

OF

THE LIFE

OF

OLAUDAH EQUIANO,

OR

GUSTAVUS VASSA,

THE AFRICAN.

WRITTEN BY HIMSELF.

VOL. I.

---

*Behold, God is my salvation : I will trust and not
be afraid, for the Lord Jehovah is my strength
and my song ; he also is become my salvation.
And in that day shall ye say, Praise the Lord, call
upon his name, declare his doings among the people,*
Isaiah xii. 2, 4.

FIRST AMERICAN EDITION.

NEW-YORK:
Printed and Sold by W. DURELL, at his
Book-Store and Printing-Office, No. 19, Q. Street.
M,DCC,XCI.

TO THE LORDS SPIRITUAL AND TEMPORAL, AND THE COMMONS OF THE
PARLIAMENT OF GREAT BRITAIN

My Lords and Gentlemen,
Permit me, with the greatest deference and respect, to lay at your feet the
following genuine narrative; the chief design of which is to excite in your
august assemblies a sense of compassion for the miseries which the
Slave-Trade has entailed on my unfortunate countrymen. By the horrors
of that trade I was first torn away from all the tender connections that
were naturally dear to my heart; but these, through the mysterious ways
of Providence, I ought to regard as infinitely more than compensated by
the introduction I have thence obtained to the knowledge of the Christian
religion, and of a nation which, by its liberal sentiments, its humanity,
the glorious freedom of its government, and its proficiency in arts and
sciences, has exalted the dignity of human nature.
I am sensible I ought to entreat your pardon for addressing to you a
work wholly devoid of literary merit; but, as the production of an un-
lettered African, who is actuated by the hope of becoming an instrument
towards the relief of his suffering countrymen, I trust that *such a man,*
pleading in *such a cause,* will be acquitted of boldness and presumption.
May the God of Heaven inspire your hearts with peculiar benevolence
on that important day when the question of Abolition is to be discussed,
when thousands, in consequence of your determination, are to look for
Happiness or Misery!
I am, My Lords and Gentlemen,
Your most obedient,
And devoted humble servant,

OLAUDAH EQUIANO,
or
GUSTAVUS VASSA
No. 4, Taylor's Buildings, St. Martin's Lane, October 30, 1790.

Contents

The Interesting Narrative of the Life of Olaudah Equiano

CHAPTER 1

The author's account of his country, and their manners and customs— Administration of justice—Embrenche—Marriage ceremony, and public entertainments—Mode of living—Dress—Manufactures—Buildings— Commerce—Agriculture—War and religion—Superstition of the natives—Funeral ceremonies of the priests or magicians—Curious mode of discovering poison—Some hints concerning the origin of the author's countrymen, with the opinions of different writers on that subject.

I believe it is difficult for those who publish their own memoirs to escape the imputation of vanity; nor is this the only disadvantage under which they labor: it is also their misfortune that what is uncommon is rarely, if ever, believed, and what is obvious we are apt to turn from with disgust, and to charge the writer with impertinence. People generally think those memoirs only worthy to be read or remembered which abound in great or striking events, those, in short, which in a high degree excite either admiration or pity; all others they consign to contempt and oblivion. It is therefore, I confess, not a little hazardous in a private and obscure individual, and a stranger too, thus to solicit the indulgent attention of the public, especially when I own I offer here the history of neither a saint, a hero, nor a tyrant. I believe there are few events in my life which have not happened to many; it is true the incidents of it are numerous, and, did I consider myself an European, I might say my sufferings were great; but when I compare my lot with that of most of my countrymen, I regard myself as a *particular favorite of heaven,* and acknowledge the mercies of Providence in every occurrence of my life. If, then, the following narrative does not appear sufficiently interesting to engage general attention, let my motive be some excuse for its publication. I am not so foolishly vain as to expect from it either immortality or literary reputation. If it affords any satisfaction to my numerous friends, at whose request it has been written, or in the smallest degree promotes the interests of humanity, the ends for which it was undertaken will be fully attained, and every wish of my heart gratified. Let it therefore be remembered, that, in wishing to avoid censure, I do not aspire to praise.

That part of Africa, known by the name of Guinea, to which the trade for slaves is carried on, extends along the coast above 3400 miles, from Senegal to Angola, and includes a variety of kingdoms. Of these the most considerable is the kingdom of Benin,[1] both as to extent and wealth, the richness and cultivation of the soil, the power of its king, and the number and warlike disposition of the inhabitants. It is situated nearly under the line,[2] and extends along the coast about 170 miles, but runs back into the interior part of Africa to a distance hitherto, I believe, unexplored by any traveller, and seems only terminated at length by the empire of Abyssinia, near 1500 miles from its beginning. This kingdom is divided into many provinces or districts, in one of the most remote and fertile of which, I was born, in the year 1745, situated in a charming fruitful vale, named Essaka. The distance of this province from the capital of Benin and the sea coast must be very considerable, for I had never heard of white men or Europeans, nor of the sea; and our subjection to the king of Benin was little more than nominal, for every transaction of the government, as far as my slender observation extended, was conducted by the chief or elders of the place. The manners and government of a people who have little commerce with other countries are generally very simple, and the history of what passes in one family or village may serve as a specimen of the whole nation.

My father was one of those elders or chiefs I have spoken of, and was styled Embrenche, a term, as I remember, importing the highest distinction, and signifying in our language a *mark* of grandeur. This mark is conferred on the person entitled to it, by cutting the skin across at the top of the forehead, and drawing it down to the eyebrows; and while it is in this situation applying a warm hand, and rubbing it until it shrinks up into a thick *weal* across the lower part of the forehead.[3] Most of the judges and senators were thus marked; my father had long borne it; I had seen it conferred on one of my brothers, and I also was *destined* to receive it by my parents. Those Embrenche, or chief men, decided disputes and

---

[1] The kingdom of Benin, with its capital in the city of Benin, extended from the Niger delta to the city of Lagos.

[2] The equator.

[3] The Ibo phrase *igbu ichi* refers to this scarring of the face, and *mgburichi*, which Equiano renders as *Embrenche*, means "men who bear such scars." Both derive from *ichi*, "to crown." (Catherine Obianuju Acholonu, *The Igbo Roots of Olaudah Equiano: An Anthropological Research* [Owerri, Nigeria: Afa Publications, 1989], 10–12, 29–30.)

punished crimes, for which purpose they always assembled together. The proceedings were generally short, and in most cases the law of retaliation prevailed.

I remember a man was brought before my father, and the other judges, for kidnapping a boy; and, although he was the son of a chief or senator, he was condemned to make recompense by a man or woman slave. Adultery, however, was sometimes punished with slavery or death, a punishment which I believe is inflicted on it throughout most of the nations of Africa,[4] so sacred among them is the honor of the marriage bed, and so jealous are they of the fidelity of their wives. Of this I recollect an instance—a woman was convicted before the judges of adultery, and delivered over, as the custom was, to her husband, to be punished. Accordingly he determined to put her to death; but it being found, just before her execution, that she had an infant at her breast, and no woman being prevailed on to perform the part of a nurse, she was spared on account of the child. The men, however, do not preserve the same constancy to their wives which they expect from them; for they indulge in a plurality, though seldom in more than two.

Their mode of marriage is thus—both parties are usually betrothed when young by their parents (though I have known the males to betroth themselves). On this occasion a feast is prepared, and the bride and bridegroom stand up in the midst of all their friends, who are assembled for the purpose, while he declares she is henceforth to be looked upon as his wife, and that no other person is to pay any addresses to her. This is also immediately proclaimed in the vicinity, on which the bride retires from the assembly. Some time after, she is brought home to her husband, and then another feast is made, to which the relations of both parties are invited; her parents then deliver her to the bridegroom, accompanied with a number of blessings, and at the same time they tie round her waist a cotton string of the thickness of a goose-quill, which none but married women are permitted to wear; she is now considered as completely his wife; and at this time the dowry is given to the new married pair, which generally consists of portions of land, slaves, and cattle, household goods, and implements of husbandry. These are offered by the friends of both parties; besides which the parents of the bridegroom present gifts to those of the bride, whose property she is looked upon before marriage; but after it she is esteemed the sole property of her husband. The ceremony being

[4] See Benezet's "Account of Guinea," throughout. [Equiano's note.] Anthony Benezet (1713–1784), a Philadelphia Quaker, wrote *Some Historical Account of Guinea: Its situation, produce, and the general disposition of its inhabitants with an inquiry into the rise and progress of the Slave Trade its nature and lamentable effects* (1771) and other antislavery tracts.

now ended, the festival begins, which is celebrated with bonfires and loud acclamations of joy, accompanied with music and dancing.

We are almost a nation of dancers, musicians, and poets. Thus every great event, such as a triumphant return from battle or other cause of public rejoicing, is celebrated in public dances, which are accompanied with songs and music suited to the occasion. The assembly is separated into four divisions, which dance either apart or in succession, and each with a character peculiar to itself. The first division contains the married men, who in their dances frequently exhibit feats of arms and the representation of a battle. To these succeed the married women, who dance in the second division. The young men occupy the third, and the maidens the fourth. Each represents some interesting scene of real life, such as a great achievement, domestic employment, a pathetic story, or some rural sport; and as the subject is generally founded on some recent event, it is therefore ever new. This gives our dances a spirit and variety which I have scarcely seen elsewhere.[5] We have many musical instruments, particularly drums of different kinds, a piece of music which resembles a guitar, and another much like a stickado. These last are chiefly used by betrothed virgins, who play on them on all grand festivals.

As our manners are simple, our luxuries are few. The dress of both sexes is nearly the same. It generally consists of a long piece of calico, or muslin, wrapped loosely round the body, somewhat in the form of a highland plaid. This is usually dyed blue, which is our favorite color. It is extracted from a berry, and is brighter and richer than any I have seen in Europe. Besides this, our women of distinction wear golden ornaments, which they dispose with some profusion on their arms and legs. When our women are not employed with the men in tillage, their usual occupation is spinning and weaving cotton, which they afterwards dye, and make into garments. They also manufacture earthen vessels, of which we have many kinds. Among the rest, tobacco pipes, made after the same fashion, and used in the same manner, as those in Turkey.[6]

Our manner of living is entirely plain; for as yet the natives are unacquainted with those refinements in cookery which debauch the taste: bullocks, goats, and poultry supply the greatest part of their food. These constitute likewise the principal wealth of the country, and the chief articles of its commerce. The flesh is usually stewed in a pan; to make it

[5] When I was in Smyrna I have frequently seen the Greeks dance after this manner. [Equiano's note.]
[6] The bowl is earthen, curiously figured, to which a long reed is fixed as a tube. This tube is sometimes so long as to be borne by one, and frequently out of grandeur, two boys. [Equiano's note.]

savory we sometimes use pepper, and other spices, and we have salt made of wood ashes. Our vegetables are mostly plantains, eadas,[7] yams, beans, and Indian corn. The head of the family usually eats alone; his wives and slaves have also their separate tables. Before we taste food we always wash our hands; indeed, our cleanliness on all occasions is extreme, but on this it is an indispensable ceremony. After washing, libation is made, by pouring out a small portion of the drink on the floor, and tossing a small quantity of the food in a certain place, for the spirits of departed relations, which the natives suppose to preside over their conduct and guard them from evil. They are totally unacquainted with strong or spirituous liquors; and their principal beverage is palm wine. This is got from a tree of that name, by tapping it at the top and fastening a large gourd to it; and sometimes one tree will yield three or four gallons in a night. When just drawn it is of a most delicious sweetness; but in a few days it acquires a tartish and more spirituous flavor, though I never saw anyone intoxicated by it. The same tree also produces nuts and oil. Our principal luxury is in perfumes: one sort of these is an odoriferous wood of delicious fragrance, the other a kind of earth, a small portion of which thrown into the fire diffuses a most powerful odor.[8] We beat this wood into powder, and mix it with palm oil, with which both men and women perfume themselves.[9]

In our buildings we study convenience rather than ornament. Each master of a family has a large square piece of ground, surrounded with a moat or fence, or enclosed with a wall made of red earth tempered, which, when dry, is as hard as brick. Within this, are his houses to accommodate his family and slaves, which, if numerous, frequently present the appearance of a village. In the middle, stands the principal building, appropriated to the sole use of the master and consisting of two apartments; in one of which he sits in the day with his family, the other is left apart for the reception of his friends. He has besides these a distinct apartment in which he sleeps, together with his male children. On each side are the apartments of his wives, who have also their separate day and night houses. The habitations of the slaves and their families are distributed throughout the rest of the enclosure. These houses never exceed one story in height; they are always built of wood, or stakes driven into the ground, crossed with wattles, and neatly plastered within and without. The roof is thatched

---

[7] Probably eddo, or cocoa yam.

[8] When I was in Smyrna I saw the same kind of earth, and brought some of it with me to England; it resembles musk in strength, but is more delicious in scent, and is not unlike the smell of a rose. [Equiano's note.]

[9] Camwood, or *uhie,* was ground to a powder, mixed with oil, then spread on the skin; the *uhiguihi* is a fruit resembling a piece of wood that produces a fragrance when burned. (Acholonu, *Igbo Roots,* 21.)

with reeds. Our day houses are left open at the sides; but those in which we sleep are always covered, and plastered in the inside, with a composition mixed with cow-dung, to keep off the different insects which annoy us during the night. The walls and floors also of these are generally covered with mats. Our beds consist of a platform, raised three or four feet from the ground, on which are laid skins, and different parts of a spongy tree, called plantain. Our covering is calico or muslin, the same as our dress. The usual seats are a few logs of wood; but we have benches, which are generally perfumed to accommodate strangers: these compose the greater part of our household furniture. Houses so constructed and furnished require but little skill to erect them. Every man is a sufficient architect for the purpose. The whole neighborhood afford their unanimous assistance in building them, and in return receive and expect no other recompense than a feast.

As we live in a country where nature is prodigal of her favors, our wants are few and easily supplied; of course we have few manufactures. They consist for the most part of calicoes, earthen ware, ornaments, and instruments of war and husbandry.[10] But these make no part of our commerce, the principal articles of which, as I have observed, are provisions. In such a state, money is of little use; however, we have some small pieces of coin, if I may call them such. They are made something like an anchor, but I do not remember either their value or denomination. We have also markets, at which I have been frequently with my mother. These are sometimes visited by stout mahogany-colored men from the south-west of us: we call them *Oye-Eboe*, which term signifies red men living at a distance.[11] They generally bring us fire-arms, gun-powder, hats, beads, and dried fish. The last we esteemed a great rarity, as our waters were only brooks and springs. These articles they barter with us for odoriferous woods and earth, and our salt of wood ashes. They always carry slaves through our land; but the strictest account is exacted of their manner of procuring them before they are suffered to pass. Sometimes, indeed, we sold slaves to them, but they were only prisoners of war, or such among us as had been convicted of kidnapping, or adultery, and some other crimes, which we esteemed heinous. This practice of kidnapping induces me to think, that, notwithstanding all our strictness, their principal business among us was to trepan[12] our people. I remember too, they

---

[10] Farming.

[11] *Oyibo* is "light-colored person." Acholonu suggests that these may have been Aro people, a mahogany-colored people from south of Isseke. Those from Arochukwu were involved in the slave trade, exchanging their captives for guns, gunpowder, and other European goods. (Acholonu, *Igbo Roots*, 14.)

[12] To trick or trap.

carried great sacks along with them, which not long after, I had an opportunity of fatally seeing applied to that infamous purpose.

Our land is uncommonly rich and fruitful, and produces all kinds of vegetables in great abundance. We have plenty of Indian corn, and vast quantities of cotton and tobacco. Our pineapples grow without culture; they are about the size of the largest sugar-loaf, and finely flavored. We have also spices of different kinds, particularly pepper, and a variety of delicious fruits which I have never seen in Europe, together with gums of various kinds, and honey in abundance. All our industry is exerted to improve these blessings of nature. Agriculture is our chief employment; and everyone, even the children and women, are engaged in it. Thus we are all habituated to labor from our earliest years. Everyone contributes something to the common stock; and, as we are unacquainted with idleness, we have no beggars. The benefits of such a mode of living are obvious. The West India planters prefer the slaves of Benin or Eboe[13] to those of any other part of Guinea, for their hardiness, intelligence, integrity, and zeal. Those benefits are felt by us in the general healthiness of the people, and in their vigor and activity; I might have added, too, in their comeliness. Deformity is indeed unknown amongst us, I mean that of shape. Numbers of the natives of Eboe now in London might be brought in support of this assertion: for, in regard to complexion, ideas of beauty are wholly relative. I remember while in Africa to have seen three Negro children who were tawny, and another quite white, who were universally regarded by myself, and the natives in general, as far as related to their complexions, as deformed. Our women, too, were, in my eye at least, uncommonly graceful, alert, and modest to a degree of bashfulness; nor do I remember to have heard of an instance of incontinence[14] amongst them before marriage. They are also remarkably cheerful. Indeed, cheerfulness and affability are two of the leading characteristics of our nation.

Our tillage is exercised in a large plain or common, some hour's walk from our dwellings, and all the neighbors resort thither in a body. They use no beasts of husbandry; and their only instruments are hoes, axes, shovels, and beaks, or pointed iron, to dig with. Sometimes we are visited by locusts, which come in large clouds, so as to darken the air, and destroy our harvest. This, however, happens rarely, but when it does, a famine is produced by it. I remember an instance or two wherein this happened. This common is often the theatre of war; and therefore when our people go out to till their land, they not only go in a body, but generally take their arms with them for fear of a surprise; and when they apprehend an

[13] Ibo or Igbo.
[14] Lack of self-restraint, especially related to sexual appetites.

invasion, they guard the avenues to their dwellings, by driving sticks into the ground, which are so sharp at one end as to pierce the foot, and are generally dipt in poison. From what I can recollect of these battles, they appear to have been irruptions of one little state or district on the other, to obtain prisoners or booty. Perhaps they were incited to this by those traders who brought the European goods I mentioned, amongst us. Such a mode of obtaining slaves in Africa is common; and I believe more are procured this way, and by kidnapping, than any other.[15] When a trader wants slaves, he applies to a chief for them, and tempts him with his wares. It is not extraordinary, if on this occasion he yields to the temptation with as little firmness, and accepts the price of his fellow creature's liberty, with as little reluctance as the enlightened merchant. Accordingly he falls on his neighbors, and a desperate battle ensues. If he prevails and takes prisoners, he gratifies his avarice by selling them; but, if his party be vanquished, and he falls into the hands of the enemy, he is put to death; for, as he has been known to foment their quarrels, it is thought dangerous to let him survive, and no ransom can save him, though all other prisoners may be redeemed. We have fire-arms, bows and arrows, broad two-edged swords and javelins; we have shields also which cover a man from head to foot. All are taught the use of these weapons; even our women are warriors, and march boldly out to fight along with the men. Our whole district is a kind of militia: on a certain signal given, such as the firing of a gun at night, they all rise in arms and rush upon their enemy. It is perhaps something remarkable, that when our people march to the field a red flag or banner is borne before them.

I was once a witness to a battle in our common. We had been all at work in it one day as usual, when our people were suddenly attacked. I climbed a tree at some distance, from which I beheld the fight. There were many women as well as men on both sides; among others my mother was there, and armed with a broad sword. After fighting for a considerable time with great fury, and many had been killed, our people obtained the victory, and took their enemy's Chief a prisoner. He was carried off in great triumph, and, though he offered a large ransom for his life, he was put to death. A virgin of note among our enemies had been slain in the battle, and her arm was exposed in our marketplace, where our trophies were always exhibited. The spoils were divided according to the merit of the warriors. Those prisoners which were not sold or redeemed, we kept as slaves; but how different was their condition from that of the slaves in the West Indies! With us, they do no more work than other members of the community,

---

[15] See Benezet's "Account of Guinea," throughout. [Equiano's note.]

even their master; their food, clothing, and lodging were nearly the same as theirs (except that they were not permitted to eat with those who were free-born); and there was scarce any other difference between them, than a superior degree of importance which the head of a family possesses in our state, and that authority which, as such, he exercises over every part of his household. Some of these slaves have even slaves under them as their own property, and for their own use.

As to religion, the natives believe that there is one Creator of all things, and that he lives in the sun, and is girted round with a belt; that he may never eat or drink, but, according to some, he smokes a pipe, which is our own favorite luxury. They believe he governs events, especially our deaths or captivity; but, as for the doctrine of eternity, I do not remember to have ever heard of it; some, however, believe in the transmigration of souls in a certain degree. Those spirits which were not transmigrated, such as their dear friends or relations, they believe always attend them, and guard them from the bad spirits or their foes. For this reason they always, before eating, as I have observed, put some small portion of the meat, and pour some of their drink, on the ground for them; and they often make oblations of the blood of beasts or fowls at their graves. I was very fond of my mother, and almost constantly with her. When she went to make these oblations at her mother's tomb, which was a kind of small solitary thatched house, I sometimes attended her. There she made her libations, and spent most of the night in cries and lamentations. I have been often extremely terrified on these occasions. The loneliness of the place, the darkness of the night, and the ceremony of libation, naturally awful and gloomy, were heightened by my mother's lamentations; and these concurring with the doleful cries of birds, by which these places were frequented, gave an inexpressible terror to the scene.

We compute the year from the day on which the sun crosses the line, and on its setting that evening, there is a general shout throughout the land; at least, I can speak from my own knowledge, throughout our vicinity. The people at the same time make a great noise with rattles, not unlike the basket rattles used by children here, though much larger, and hold up their hands to heaven for a blessing. It is then the greatest offerings are made; and those children whom our wise men foretell will be fortunate are then presented to different people. I remember many used to come to see me, and I was carried about to others for that purpose. They have many offerings, particularly at full moons; generally two, at harvest, before the fruits are taken out of the ground; and when any young animals are killed, sometimes they offer up part of them as a sacrifice. These offerings, when made by one of the heads of a family, serve for the whole. I remember we often had them at my father's and my uncle's, and their families have been present. Some of our offerings are eaten with bitter herbs. We had a saying among us to anyone of a cross temper, "That if they were to be eaten, they should be eaten with bitter herbs."

We practised circumcision like the Jews, and made offerings and feasts on that occasion, in the same manner as they did. Like them also, our children were named from some event, some circumstance, or fancied foreboding, at the time of their birth. I was named *Olaudah*, which in our language signifies vicissitude, or fortunate; also, one favored, and having a loud voice and well spoken.[16] I remember we never polluted the name of the object of our adoration; on the contrary, it was always mentioned with the greatest reverence; and we were totally unacquainted with swearing, and all those terms of abuse and reproach which find their way so readily and copiously into the language of more civilized people. The only expressions of that kind I remember were, "May you rot, or may you swell, or may a beast take you."

I have before remarked that the natives of this part of Africa are extremely cleanly. This necessary habit of decency was with us a part of religion, and therefore we had many purifications and washings; indeed almost as many, and used on the same occasions, if my recollection does not fail me, as the Jews. Those that touched the dead at any time were obliged to wash and purify themselves before they could enter a dwelling-house. Every woman, too, at certain times was forbidden to come into a dwelling-house, or touch any person, or anything we eat. I was so fond of my mother I could not keep from her, or avoid touching her at some of those periods, in consequence of which I was obliged to be kept out with her, in a little house made for that purpose, till offering was made, and then we were purified.

Though we had no places of public worship, we had priests and magicians, or wise men. I do not remember whether they had different offices, or whether they were united in the same persons, but they were held in great reverence by the people. They calculated our time, and foretold events, as their name imported, for we called them *Ah-affoe-way-cah*, which signifies calculators or yearly men, our year being called *Ah-affoe*.[17] They wore their beards, and when they died, they were succeeded by their sons. Most of their implements and things of value were interred

---

[16] *Ola*, or ring, is a symbol of good fortune to the Ibo. *Ude* means "pleasing sound." (Acholonu, *Igbo Roots*, 42–43.)

[17] *Ofo-nwanchi* were traveling men who calculated the years. Often dwarfs, they were sometimes called *afo-nwa-ika*, or "funny monkeys," by children in the villages they visited. Local priests were *nze nzu*. (Acholonu, *Igbo Roots*, 18–19.)

along with them. Pipes and tobacco were also put into the grave with the corpse, which was always perfumed and ornamented, and animals were offered in sacrifice to them. None accompanied their funerals, but those of the same profession or tribe. They buried them after sunset, and always returned from the grave by a different way from that which they went.

These magicians were also our doctors or physicians. They practised bleeding by cupping, and were very successful in healing wounds and expelling poisons. They had likewise some extraordinary method of discovering jealousy, theft, poisoning, the success of which, no doubt, they derived from the unbounded influence over the credulity and superstition of the people. I do not remember what those methods were, except that as to poisoning; I recollect an instance or two, which I hope it will not be deemed impertinent here to insert, as it may serve as a kind of specimen of the rest, as is still used by the Negroes in the West Indies. A young woman had been poisoned, but it was not known by whom; the doctors ordered the corpse to be taken up by some persons, and carried to the grave. As soon as the bearers had raised it on their shoulders, they seemed seized with some[18] sudden impulse, and ran to and fro, unable to stop themselves. At last, after having passed through a number of thorns and prickly bushes unhurt, the corpse fell from them close to a house, and defaced it in the fall; and the owner being taken up, he immediately confessed the poisoning.[19]

The natives are extremely cautious about poison. When they buy any eatables, the seller kisses it all round before the buyer, to shew him it is not poisoned; and the same is done when any meat or drink is presented, particularly to a stranger. We have serpents of different kinds, some of which are esteemed ominous when they appear in our houses, and these we never molest. I remember two of those ominous snakes, each of which

[18] See also Lieutenant Matthew's Voyage, p. 123. [Equiano's note.] John Matthews, *A Voyage to the River Sierra Leone . . . with a Letter on the . . . African Slave Trade* (London, 1788).

[19] An instance of this kind happened at Montserrat, in the West Indies, in the year 1763. I then belonged to the *Charming Sally*, Capt. Doran. The chief mate, Mr. Mansfield, and some of the crew being one day on shore, were present at the burying of a poisoned Negro girl. Though they had often heard of the circumstance of the running in such cases, and had even seen it, they imagined it to be a trick of the corpse bearers. The mate therefore desired two of the sailors to take up the coffin, and carry it to the grave. The sailors, who were all of the same opinion, readily obeyed, but they had scarcely raised it to their shoulders before they began to run furiously about, quite unable to direct themselves, till at last, without intention, they came to the hut of him who had poisoned the girl. The coffin then immediately fell from their shoulders against the hut, and damaged part of the wall. The owner of the hut was taken into custody on this, and confessed the poisoning. I give this story as it was related by the mate and crew on their return to the ship. The credit which is due to it, I leave with the reader. [Equiano's note.]

was as thick as the calf of a man's leg, and in color resembling a dolphin in the water, crept at different times into my mother's night house, where I always lay with her, and coiled themselves into folds, and each time they crowed like a cock. I was desired by some of our wise men to touch these, that I might be interested in the good omens, which I did, for they were quite harmless, and would tamely suffer themselves to be handled; and then they were put into a large earthen pan, and set on one side of the highway. Some of our snakes, however, were poisonous; one of them crossed the road one day as I was standing on it, and passed between my feet without offering to touch me, to the great surprise of many who saw it; and these incidents were accounted by the wise men, and likewise by my mother and the rest of the people, as remarkable omens in my favor.

Such is the imperfect sketch my memory has furnished me with, of the manners and customs of a people among whom I first drew my breath. And here I cannot forbear suggesting what has long struck me very forcibly, namely, the strong analogy which even by this sketch, imperfect as it is, appears to prevail in the manners and customs of my countrymen and those of the Jews, before they reached the land of promise, and particularly the patriarchs while they were yet in that pastoral state which is described in Genesis—an analogy, which alone would induce me to think that the one people had sprung from the other. Indeed, this is the opinion of Dr. Gill, who, in his commentary on Genesis, very ably deduces the pedigree of the Africans from Afer and Afra, the descendents of Abraham by Keturah his wife and concubine (for both these titles are applied to her). It is also conformable to the sentiments of Dr. John Clarke, formerly Dean of Sarum, in his truth of the Christian religion; both these authors concur in ascribing to us this original.[20] The reasonings of those gentlemen are still further confirmed by the scripture chronology; and if any further corroboration were required, this resemblance in so many respects, is a strong evidence in support of the opinion. Like the Israelites in their primitive state, our government was conducted by our chiefs or judges, our wise men and elders; and the head of a family with us enjoyed a similar authority over his household, with that which is ascribed to Abraham and the other patriarchs. The law of retaliation obtained almost universally with us as with them: and even their religion appeared to have shed upon us a ray of its glory, though broken and spent in its passage, or eclipsed by the cloud with which time, tradition, and ignorance might have enveloped it; for we had our circumcision (a rule, I believe, peculiar to that people),

---

[20] Dr. John Gill (1697–1771), a Baptist divine, published his multivolume *Exposition of the Holy Scriptures* in 1766. John Clarke's *Truth of the Christian Religion, in Six Books* (1711) is a translation of Hugo Grotius (1583–1645), *De veritatus religionis christianae* (1627).

we had also our sacrifices and burnt-offerings, our washings and purifications, and on the same occasions as they did.

As to the difference of color between the Eboan Africans and the modern Jews, I shall not presume to account for it. It is a subject which has engaged the pens of men of both genius and learning, and is far above my strength. The most able and Reverend Mr. T. Clarkson, however, in his much admired *Essay on the Slavery and Commerce of the Human Species,* [21] has ascertained the cause in a manner that at once solves every objection on that account, and, on my mind at least, has produced the fullest conviction. I shall therefore refer to that performance for the theory, [22] contenting myself with extracting a fact as related by Dr. Mitchel. [23] "The Spaniards, who have inhabited America, under the torrid zone, for any time, are become as dark colored as our native Indians of Virginia; of which *I myself have been a witness.*" There is also another instance [24] of a Portuguese settlement at Mitomba, a river in Sierra Leone, where the inhabitants are bred from a mixture of the first Portuguese discoverers with the natives, and are now become in their complexion, and in the woolly quality of their hair, *perfect Negroes,* retaining however a smattering of the Portuguese language. [25]

These instances, and a great many more which might be adduced, while they show how the complexions of the same persons vary in different climates, it is hoped may tend also to remove the prejudice that some conceive against the natives of Africa on account of their color. Surely the minds of the Spaniards did not change with their complexions! Are there not causes enough to which the apparent inferiority of an African may be ascribed, without limiting the goodness of God, and supposing he forebore to stamp understanding on certainly his own image, because "carved in ebony." Might it not naturally be ascribed to their situation? When they come among Europeans, they are ignorant of their language, religion, manners, and customs. Are any pains taken to teach them these? Are they treated as men? Does not slavery itself depress the mind, and extinguish

[21] Thomas Clarkson, *Essay on the Slavery and Commerce of the Human Species, Particularly the African* (London, 1786). Clarkson (1760–1846) wrote this essay for an academic competition at Cambridge in 1785. He won the contest and became a lifelong abolitionist. His documentation of the horrors of the slave trade became a foundation for antislavery activity. His brother John, a Royal Navy officer, helped to found the Sierra Leone colony.

[22] Pages 178 to 216. [Equiano's note.]

[23] Philos. Trans. No. 476, Sec. 4, cited by Mr. Clarkson, p. 205. [Equiano's note.] John Mitchell, "An Essay upon the Causes of the Different Colours of People in Different Climates," *Philosophical Transactions of the Royal Society* 43 (1746).

[24] Same page. [Equiano's note.]

[25] The Portuguese established a trading post at Mitombe, Sierra Leone, in the 1460s.

all its fire and every noble sentiment? But, above all, what advantages do not a refined people possess, over those who are rude and uncultivated? Let the polished and haughty European recollect that his ancestors were once, like the Africans, uncivilized, and even barbarous. Did Nature make *them* inferior to their sons? and should *they too* have been made slaves? Every rational mind answers, No. Let such reflections as these melt the pride of their superiority into sympathy for the wants and miseries of their sable brethren, and compel them to acknowledge that understanding is not confined to feature or color. If, when they look round the world, they feel exultation, let it be tempered with benevolence to others, and gratitude to God, "who hath made of one blood all nations of men for to dwell on all the face of the earth";[26] "and whose wisdom is not our wisdom, neither are our ways his ways."

[26] Acts 17:26. [Equiano's note.]

CHAPTER 2

The author's birth and parentage—His being kidnapped with his sister— Their separation—Surprise at meeting again—Are finally separated— Account of the different places and incidents the author met with till his arrival on the coast—The effect the sight of a slave-ship had on him—He sails for the West Indies—Horrors of a slave-ship—Arrives at Barbadoes, where the cargo is sold and dispersed.

I hope the reader will not think I have trespassed on his patience in introducing myself to him with some account of the manners and customs of my country. They had been implanted in me with great care, and made an impression on my mind, which time could not erase, and which all the adversity and variety of fortune I have since experienced, served only to rivet and record: for, whether the love of one's country be real or imaginary, or a lesson of reason, or an instinct of nature, I still look back with pleasure on the first scenes of my life, though that pleasure has been for the most part mingled with sorrow.

I have already acquainted the reader with the time and place of my birth. My father, besides many slaves, had a numerous family, of which seven lived to grow up, including myself and sister, who was the only daughter. As I was the youngest of the sons, I became, of course, the greatest favorite with my mother, and was always with her; and she used to take particular pains to form my mind.[1] I was trained up from my earliest years in the art of war: my daily exercise was shooting and throwing javelins, and my mother adorned me with emblems, after the manner of our greatest warriors. In this way I grew up till I had turned the age of eleven, when an end was put to my happiness in the following manner: Generally, when the grown people in the neighborhood were gone far in the fields to labor, the children assembled together in some of the neighboring premises to play; and commonly some of us used to get up a tree to look out for any assailant, or kidnapper, that might come upon us—for they sometimes took those opportunities of our parents' absence, to attack and carry off as many as they could seize. One day as I was watching at the top of a tree in our yard, I saw one of those people come into the yard of our next neighbor but one, to kidnap, there being many stout young people in it. Immediately on this I gave the alarm of the rogue, and he was surrounded by the stoutest of them, who entangled him with cords, so that he could not escape, till some of the grown people came and secured him. But, alas! ere long it was my fate to be thus attacked, and to be carried off, when none of the grown people were nigh.

One day, when all our people were gone out to their works as usual, and only I and my dear sister were left to mind the house, two men and a woman got over our walls, and in a moment seized us both, and, without giving us time to cry out, or make resistance, they stopped our mouths, and ran off with us into the nearest wood. Here they tied our hands, and continued to carry us as far as they could, till night came on, when we reached a small house, where the robbers halted for refreshment, and spent the night. We were then unbound, but were unable to take any food; and, being quite overpowered by fatigue and grief, our only relief was some sleep, which allayed our misfortune for a short time. The next morning we left the house, and continued travelling all the day. For a long time we had kept the woods, but at last we came into a road which I believed I knew. I had now some hopes of being delivered; for we had advanced but a little way before I discovered some people at a distance, on which I began to cry out for their assistance; but my cries had no other effect than to make them tie me faster and stop my mouth, and then they put me into a large sack. They also stopped my sister's mouth, and tied her hands; and in this manner we proceeded till we were out of sight of these people. When we went to rest the following night, they offered us

---

[1] Acholonu identifies Equiano's father as Ichie Ekwealuo, born about 1700, and his mother as Nwansoro, from the village of Uli. (Acholonu, *Igbo Roots*, 42–43.)

some victuals, but we refused it; and the only comfort we had was in being in one another's arms all that night, and bathing each other with our tears. But alas! we were soon deprived of even the small comfort of weeping together.

The next day proved a day of greater sorrow than I had yet experienced; for my sister and I were then separated, while we lay clasped in each other's arms. It was in vain that we besought them not to part us; she was torn from me, and immediately carried away, while I was left in a state of distraction not to be described. I cried and grieved continually; and for several days did not eat anything but what they forced into my mouth. At length, after many days' travelling, during which I had often changed masters, I got into the hands of a chieftain, in a very pleasant country. This man had two wives and some children, and they all used me extremely well, and did all they could do to comfort me; particularly the first wife, who was something like my mother. Although I was a great many days' journey from my father's house, yet these people spoke exactly the same language with us. This first master of mine, as I may call him, was a smith, and my principal employment was working his bellows, which were the same kind as I had seen in my vicinity. They were in some respects not unlike the stoves here in gentlemen's kitchens, and were covered over with leather; and in the middle of that leather a stick was fixed, and a person stood up, and worked it in the same manner as is done to pump water out of a cask with a hand pump. I believe it was gold he worked, for it was of a lovely bright yellow color, and was worn by the women on their wrists and ankles.

I was there I suppose about a month, and they at last used to trust me some little distance from the house. This liberty I used in embracing every opportunity to inquire the way to my own home; and I also sometimes, for the same purpose, went with the maidens, in the cool of the evenings, to bring pitchers of water from the springs for the use of the house. I had also remarked where the sun rose in the morning, and set in the evening, as I had travelled along; and I had observed that my father's house was towards the rising of the sun. I therefore determined to seize the first opportunity of making my escape, and to shape my course for that quarter; for I was quite oppressed and weighed down by grief after my mother and friends; and my love of liberty, ever great, was strengthened by the mortifying circumstance of not daring to eat with the free-born children, although I was mostly their companion.

While I was projecting my escape, one day an unlucky event happened, which quite disconcerted my plan, and put an end to my hopes. I used to be sometimes employed in assisting an elderly slave to cook and take care of the poultry; and one morning, while I was feeding some chickens, I happened to toss a small pebble at one of them, which hit it on the middle, and directly killed it. The old slave, having soon after missed the chicken, inquired after it; and on my relating the accident (for I told her the truth, for my mother would never suffer me to tell a lie), she flew into a violent passion, and threatened that I should suffer for it; and, my master being out, she immediately went and told her mistress what I had done. This alarmed me very much, and I expected an instant flogging, which to me was uncommonly dreadful, for I had seldom been beaten at home. I therefore resolved to fly; and accordingly I ran into a thicket that was hard by, and hid myself in the bushes. Soon afterwards my mistress and the slave returned, and, not seeing me, they searched all the house, but not finding me, and I not making answer when they called to me, they thought I had run away, and the whole neighborhood was raised in the pursuit of me.

In that part of the country, as in ours, the houses and villages were skirted with woods, or shrubberies, and the bushes were so thick that a man could readily conceal himself in them, so as to elude the strictest search. The neighbors continued the whole day looking for me, and several times many of them came within a few yards of the place where I lay hid. I expected every moment, when I heard a rustling among the trees, to be found out, and punished by my master; but they never discovered me, though they were often so near that I even heard their conjectures as they were looking about for me; and I now learned from them that any attempts to return home would be hopeless. Most of them supposed I had fled towards home; but the distance was so great, and the way so intricate, that they thought I could never reach it, and that I should be lost in the woods. When I heard this I was seized with a violent panic, and abandoned myself to despair. Night, too, began to approach, and aggravated all my fears. I had before entertained hopes of getting home, and had determined when it should be dark to make the attempt; but I was now convinced it was fruitless, and began to consider that, if possibly I could escape all other animals, I could not those of the human kind; and that, not knowing the way, I must perish in the woods. Thus was I like the hunted deer—

——Every leaf and every whisp'ring breath,
Convey'd a foe, and every foe a death.

I heard frequent rustlings among the leaves, and being pretty sure they were snakes, I expected every instant to be stung by them. This increased my anguish, and the horror of my situation became now quite insupportable. I at length quitted the thicket, very faint and hungry, for I had not eaten or drank anything all the day, and crept to my master's kitchen, from whence I set out at first, which was an open shed, and laid myself down in the ashes with an anxious wish for death, to relieve me from all my pains. I was scarcely awake in the morning, when the old woman slave, who was the first up, came to light the fire, and saw me in the fireplace. She was very much surprised to see me, and could scarcely believe her own eyes. She now promised to intercede for me, and went for her master, who soon after came, and, having slightly reprimanded me, ordered me to be taken care of, and not ill treated.

Soon after this, my master's only daughter, and child by his first wife, sickened and died, which affected him so much that for sometime he was almost frantic, and really would have killed himself, had he not been watched and prevented. However, in a short time afterwards he recovered, and I was again sold. I was now carried to the left of the sun's rising, through many dreary wastes and dismal woods, amidst the hideous roarings of wild beasts. The people I was sold to used to carry me very often, when I was tired, either on their shoulders or on their backs. I saw many convenient well-built sheds along the road, at proper distances, to accommodate the merchants and travellers, who lay in those buildings along with their wives, who often accompany them; and they always go well armed.

From the time I left my own nation, I always found somebody that understood me till I came to the sea coast. The languages of different nations did not totally differ, nor were they so copious as those of the Europeans, particularly the English. They were therefore easily learned; and, while I was journeying thus through Africa, I acquired two or three different tongues. In this manner I had been travelling for a considerable time, when, one evening, to my great surprise, whom should I see brought to the house where I was but my dear sister! As soon as she saw me, she gave a loud shriek, and ran into my arms—I was quite overpowered; neither of us could speak, but, for a considerable time, clung to each other in mutual embraces, unable to do anything but weep. Our meeting affected all who saw us; and, indeed, I must acknowledge, in honor of those sable destroyers of human rights, that I never met with any ill treatment, or saw any offered to their slaves, except tying them, when necessary, to keep them from running away.

When these people knew we were brother and sister, they indulged us to be together; and the man, to whom I supposed we belonged, lay with us, he in the middle, while she and I held one another by the hands across his breast all night; and thus for a while we forgot our misfortunes, in the joy of being together; but even this small comfort was soon to have an end;

for scarcely had the fatal morning appeared when she was again torn from me forever! I was now more miserable, if possible, than before. The small relief which her presence gave me from pain, was gone, and the wretchedness of my situation was redoubled by my anxiety after her fate, and my apprehensions lest her sufferings should be greater than mine, when I could not be with her to alleviate them. Yes, thou dear partner of all my childish sports! thou sharer of my joys and sorrows! happy should I have ever esteemed myself to encounter every misery for you and to procure your freedom by the sacrifice of my own. Though you were early forced from my arms, your image has been always riveted in my heart, from which neither time nor fortune have been able to remove it; so that, while the thoughts of your sufferings have damped my prosperity, they have mingled with adversity and increased its bitterness. To that Heaven which protects the weak from the strong, I commit the care of your innocence and virtues, if they have not already received their full reward, and if your youth and delicacy have not long since fallen victims to the violence of the African trader, the pestilential stench of a Guinea ship, the seasoning in the European colonies, or the lash and lust of a brutal and unrelenting overseer.

I did not long remain after my sister. I was again sold, and carried through a number of places, till after travelling a considerable time, I came to a town called Tinmah, in the most beautiful country I had yet seen in Africa.[2] It was extremely rich, and there were many rivulets which flowed through it, and supplied a large pond in the centre of the town, where the people washed. Here I saw for the first time cocoanuts, which I thought superior to any nuts I had ever tasted before; and the trees, which were loaded, were also interspersed among the houses, which had commodious shades adjoining, and were in the same manner as ours the insides being neatly plastered and whitewashed. Here I also saw and tasted for the first time, sugar-cane. Their money consisted of little white shells, the size of the finger nail. I was sold here for one hundred and seventy-two of them, by a merchant who lived and brought me there.

I had been about two or three days at his house, when a wealthy widow, a neighbor of his, came there one evening, and brought with her an only son, a young gentleman about my own age and size. Here they saw me; and, having taken a fancy to me, I was bought of the merchant, and went home with them. Her house and premises were situated close to one of those rivulets I have mentioned, and were the finest I ever saw in Africa: they were very extensive, and she had a number of slaves to attend her.

[2] Possibly Utuma, Utu Etim, or Tinan, villages on the border between Ibo and Ibibio. (Acholonu, *Igbo Roots*, 7–9.)

The next day I was washed and perfumed, and when meal time came, I was led into the presence of my mistress, and ate and drank before her with her son. This filled me with astonishment; and I could scarce help expressing my surprise that the young gentleman should suffer me, who was bound, to eat with him who was free; and not only so, but that he would not at any time either eat or drink till I had taken first, because I was the eldest, which was agreeable to our custom. Indeed, every thing here, and all their treatment of me, made me forget that I was a slave. The language of these people resembled ours so nearly, that we understood each other perfectly. They had also the very same customs as we. There were likewise slaves daily to attend us, while my young master and I, with other boys, sported with our darts and bows and arrows, as I had been used to do at home. In this resemblance to my former happy state, I passed about two months; and I now began to think I was to be adopted into the family, and was beginning to be reconciled to my situation, and to forget by degrees my misfortunes, when all at once the delusion vanished; for, without the least previous knowledge, one morning early, while my dear master and companion was still asleep, I was awakened out of my reverie to fresh sorrow, and hurried away even amongst the uncircumcised.

Thus, at the very moment I dreamed of the greatest happiness, I found myself most miserable; and it seemed as if fortune wished to give me this taste of joy only to render the reverse more poignant. The change I now experienced was as painful as it was sudden and unexpected. It was a change indeed, from a state of bliss to a scene which is inexpressible by me, as it discovered to me an element I had never before beheld, and till then had no idea of, and wherein such instances of hardship and cruelty continually occurred, as I can never reflect on but with horror.

All the nations and people I had hitherto passed through, resembled our own in their manners, customs, and language; but I came at length to a country, the inhabitants of which differed from us in all those particulars. I was very much struck with this difference, especially when I came among a people who did not circumcise, and ate without washing their hands. They cooked also in iron pots, and had European cutlasses and cross bows, which were unknown to us, and fought with their fists among themselves. Their women were not so modest as ours, for they ate, and drank, and slept with their men. But above all, I was amazed to see no sacrifices or offerings among them. In some of those places the people ornamented themselves with scars, and likewise filed their teeth very sharp. They wanted sometimes to ornament me in the same manner, but I would not suffer them; hoping that I might some time be among a people who did not thus disfigure themselves, as I thought they did. At last I came to the banks of a large river which was covered with canoes, in which the people appeared to live with their household utensils, and provisions of all kinds. I was beyond measure astonished at this, as I had never before seen any water larger than a pond or a rivulet; and my surprise was mingled with no small fear when I was put into one of these canoes, and we began to paddle and move along the river. We continued going on thus till night, and when we came to land, and made fires on the banks, each family by themselves; some dragged their canoes on shore, others stayed and cooked in theirs, and laid in them all night. Those on the land had mats, of which they made tents, some in the shape of little houses; in these we slept; and after the morning meal, we embarked again and proceeded as before. I was often very much astonished to see some of the women, as well as the men, jump into the water, dive to the bottom, come up again, and swim about.

Thus I continued to travel, sometimes by land, sometimes by water, through different countries and various nations, till, at the end of six or seven months after I had been kidnapped, I arrived at the sea coast. It would be tedious and uninteresting to relate all the incidents which befell me during this journey, and which I have not yet forgotten; of the various hands I passed through, and the manners and customs of all the different people among whom I lived—I shall therefore only observe, that in all the places where I was, the soil was exceedingly rich; the pumpkins, eadas, plantains, yams, &c. &c., were in great abundance, and of incredible size. There were also vast quantities of different gums, though not used for any purpose, and everywhere a great deal of tobacco. The cotton even grew quite wild, and there was plenty of red-wood. I saw no mechanics whatever in all the way, except such as I have mentioned. The chief employment in all these countries was agriculture, and both the males and females, as with us, were brought up to it, and trained in the arts of war.

The first object which saluted my eyes when I arrived on the coast, was the sea, and a slave ship, which was then riding at anchor, and waiting for its cargo. These filled me with astonishment, which was soon converted into terror, when I was carried on board. I was immediately handled, and tossed up to see if I were sound, by some of the crew; and I was now persuaded that I had gotten into a world of bad spirits, and that they were going to kill me. Their complexions, too, differing so much from ours, their long hair, and the language they spoke (which was very different from any I had ever heard), united to confirm me in this belief. Indeed, such were the horrors of my views and fears at the moment, that, if ten thousand worlds had been my own, I would have freely parted with them all to have exchanged my condition with that of the meanest slave in my own country. When I looked round the ship too, and saw a large furnance of copper boiling, and a multitude of black people of every description chained together, every one of their countenances expressing dejection and sorrow, I no longer doubted of my fate; and, quite overpowered with horror and anguish, I fell motionless on the deck and fainted. When I recovered a little, I found some black people about me, who I believed were some of those who had brought me on board, and had been receiving their pay; they talked to me in order to cheer me, but all in vain. I asked them if we were not to be eaten by those white men with horrible looks, red faces, and long hair. They told me I was not, and one of the crew brought me a small portion of spirituous liquor in a wine glass; but being afraid of him, I would not take it out of his hand. One of the blacks therefore took it from him and gave it to me, and I took a little down my palate, which, instead of reviving me, as they thought it would, threw me into the greatest consternation at the strange feeling it produced, having never tasted any such liquor before. Soon after this, the blacks who brought me on board went off, and left me abandoned to despair.

I now saw myself deprived of all chance of returning to my native country, or even the least glimpse of hope of gaining the shore, which I now considered as friendly; and I even wished for my former slavery in preference to my present situation, which was filled with horrors of every kind, still heightened by my ignorance of what I was to undergo. I was not long suffered to indulge my grief; I was soon put down under the decks, and there I received such a salutation in my nostrils as I had never experienced in my life: so that, with the loathsomeness of the stench, and crying together, I became so sick and low that I was not able to eat, nor had I the least desire to taste anything. I now wished for the last friend, death, to relieve me; but soon, to my grief, two of the white men offered me eatables; and, on my refusing to eat, one of them held me fast by the hands, and laid me across, I think, the windlass, and tied my feet, while the other flogged me severely. I had never experienced anything of this kind before, and, although not being used to the water, I naturally feared that element the first time I saw it, yet, nevertheless, could I have got over the nettings, I would have jumped over the side, but I could not; and besides, the crew used to watch us very closely who were not chained down to the decks, lest we should leap into the water; and I have seen some of these poor African prisoners most severely cut, for attempting to do so, and hourly whipped for not eating. This indeed was often the case with myself.

In a little time after, amongst the poor chained men, I found some of my own nation, which in a small degree gave ease to my mind. I inquired of these what was to be done with us? They gave me to understand, we were to be carried to these white people's country to work for them. I then was a little revived, and thought, if it were no worse than working, my situation was not so desperate; but still I feared I should be put to death, the white people looked and acted, as I thought, in so savage a manner; for I had never seen among any people such instances of brutal cruelty; and this not only shown towards us blacks, but also to some of the whites themselves. One white man in particular I saw, when we were permitted to be on deck, flogged so unmercifully with a large rope near the foremast, that he died in consequence of it; and they tossed him over the side as they would have done a brute. This made me fear these people the more; and I expected nothing less than to be treated in the same manner. I could not help expressing my fears and apprehensions to some of my countrymen; I asked them if these people had no country, but lived in this hollow place (the ship)? They told me they did not, but came from a distant one. "Then," said I, "how comes it in all our country we never heard of them?" They told me because they lived so very far off. I then asked where were their women? had they any like themselves? I was told they had. "And why," said I, "do we not see them?" They answered, because they were left behind. I asked how the vessel could go? They told me they could not tell; but that there was cloth put upon the masts by the help of the ropes I saw, and then the vessel went on; and the white men had some spell or magic they put in the water when they liked, in order to stop the vessel. I was exceedingly amazed at this account, and really thought they were spirits. I therefore wished much to be from amongst them, for I expected they would sacrifice me; but my wishes were vain—for we were so quartered that it was impossible for any of us to make our escape.

While we stayed on the coast I was mostly on deck; and one day, to my great astonishment, I saw one of these vessels coming in with the sails up. As soon as the whites saw it, they gave a great shout, at which we were amazed; and the more so, as the vessel appeared larger by approaching nearer. At last, she came to an anchor in my sight, and when the anchor was let go, I and my countrymen who saw it, were lost in astonishment to observe the vessel stop—and were now convinced it was done by magic. Soon after this the other ship got her boats out, and they came on board of us, and the people of both ships seemed very glad to see each other. Several of the strangers also shook hands with us black people, and made motions with their hands, signifying I suppose, we were to go to their country, but we did not understand them.

At last, when the ship we were in, had got in all her cargo, they made ready with many fearful noises, and we were all put under deck, so that we could not see how they managed the vessel. But this disappointment was the least of my sorrow. The stench of the hold while we were on the coast was so intolerably loathsome, that it was dangerous to remain there for any time, and some of us had been permitted to stay on the deck for the fresh air; but now that the whole ship's cargo were confined together, it became absolutely pestilential. The closeness of the place, and the heat of the climate, added to the number in the ship, which was so crowded that each had scarcely room to turn himself, almost suffocated us. This produced copious perspirations, so that the air soon became unfit for respiration, from a variety of loathsome smells, and brought on a sickness among the slaves, of which many died—thus falling victims to the improvident avarice, as I may call it, of their purchasers. This wretched situation was again aggravated by the galling of the chains, now became insupportable, and the filth of the necessary tubs,[3] into which the children often fell, and were almost suffocated. The shrieks of the women, and the groans of the dying, rendered the whole a scene of horror almost inconceivable. Happily perhaps, for myself, I was soon reduced so low here that it was thought necessary to keep me almost always on deck; and from my extreme youth I was not put in fetters. In this situation I expected every hour to share the fate of my companions, some of whom were almost daily brought upon deck at the point of death, which I began to hope would soon put an end to my miseries. Often did I think many of the inhabitants of the deep much more happy than myself. I envied them the freedom they enjoyed, and as often wished I could change my condition for theirs. Every circumstance I met with, served only to render my state more painful, and heightened my apprehensions, and my opinion of the cruelty of the whites.

One day they had taken a number of fishes; and when they had killed and satisfied themselves with as many as they thought fit, to our astonishment who were on deck, rather than give any of them to us to eat, as we expected, they tossed the remaining fish into the sea again, although we begged and prayed for some as well as we could, but in vain; and some of my countrymen, being pressed by hunger, took an opportunity, when they thought no one saw them, of trying to get a little privately; but they were discovered, and the attempt procured them some very severe floggings.

One day, when we had a smooth sea and moderate wind, two of my wearied countrymen who were chained together (I was near them at the time), preferring death to such a life of misery, somehow made through

---

[3] Latrines.

the nettings and jumped into the sea; immediately, another quite dejected fellow, who, on account of his illness, was suffered to be out of irons, also followed their example; and I believe many more would very soon have done the same, if they had not been prevented by the ship's crew, who were instantly alarmed. Those of us that were the most active, were in a moment put down under the deck; and there was such a noise and confusion amongst the people of the ship as I never heard before, to stop her, and get the boat out to go after the slaves. However, two of the wretches were drowned, but they got the other, and afterwards flogged him unmercifully, for thus attempting to prefer death to slavery. In this manner we continued to undergo more hardships than I can now relate, hardships which are inseparable from this accursed trade. Many a time we were near suffocation from the want of fresh air, which we were often without for whole days together. This, and the stench of the necessary tubs, carried off many.

During our passage, I first saw flying fishes, which surprised me very much; they used frequently to fly across the ship, and many of them fell on the deck. I also now first saw the use of the quadrant; I had often with astonishment seen the mariners make observations with it, and I could not think what it meant. They at last took notice of my surprise; and one of them, willing to increase it, as well as to gratify my curiosity, made me one day look through it. The clouds appeared to me to be land, which disappeared as they passed along. This heightened my wonder; and I was now more persuaded than ever, that I was in another world, and that every thing about me was magic.

At last we came in sight of the island of Barbadoes, at which the whites on board gave a great shout, and made many signs of joy to us. We did not know what to think of this; but as the vessel drew nearer, we plainly saw the harbor, and other ships of different kinds and sizes, and we soon anchored amongst them, off Bridgetown. Many merchants and planters now came on board, though it was in the evening. They put us in separate parcels, and examined us attentively. They also made us jump, and pointed to the land, signifying we were to go there. We thought by this, we should be eaten by these ugly men, as they appeared to us; and, when soon after we were all put down under the deck again, there was much dread and trembling among us, and nothing but bitter cries to be heard all the night from these apprehensions, insomuch, that at last the white people got some old slaves from the land to pacify us. They told us we were not to be eaten, but to work, and were soon to go on land, where we should see many of our country people. This report eased us much. And sure enough, soon after we were landed, there came to us Africans of all languages.

We were conducted immediately to the merchant's yard, where we were all pent up together, like so many sheep in a fold, without regard to sex or age. As every object was new to me, everything I saw filled me with surprise. What struck me first, was, that the houses were built with bricks and stories, and in every other respect different from those I had seen in Africa; but I was still more astonished on seeing people on horseback. I did not know what this could mean; and, indeed, I thought these people were full of nothing but magical arts. While I was in this astonishment, one of my fellow prisoners spoke to a countryman of his, about the horses, who said they were the same kind they had in their country. I understood them, though they were from a distant part of Africa; and I thought it odd I had not seen any horses there; but afterwards, when I came to converse with different Africans, I found they had many horses amongst them, and much larger than those I then saw.

We were not many days in the merchant's custody, before we were sold after their usual manner, which is this: On a signal given (as the beat of a drum), the buyers rush at once into the yard where the slaves are confined, and make choice of that parcel they like best. The noise and clamor with which this is attended, and the eagerness visible in the countenances of the buyers, serve not a little to increase the apprehension of terrified Africans, who may well be supposed to consider them as the ministers of that destruction to which they think themselves devoted. In this manner, without scruple, are relations and friends separated, most of them never to see each other again.

I remember, in the vessel in which I was brought over, in the men's apartment, there were several brothers, who, in the sale, were sold in different lots; and it was very moving on this occasion, to see and hear their cries at parting. O, ye nominal Christians! might not an African ask you—Learned you this from your God, who says unto you, Do unto all men as you would men should do unto you? Is it not enough that we are torn from our country and friends, to toil for your luxury and lust of gain? Must every tender feeling be likewise sacrificed to your avarice? Are the dearest friends and relations, now rendered more dear by their separation from their kindred, still to be parted from each other, and thus prevented from cheering the gloom of slavery, with the small comfort of being together, and mingling their sufferings and sorrows? Why are parents to lose their children, brothers their sisters, or husbands their wives? Surely, this is a new refinement in cruelty, which, while it has no advantage to atone for it, thus aggravates distress, and adds fresh horrors even to the wretchedness of slavery.

CHAPTER 3

The author is carried to Virginia—His distress—Surprise at seeing a picture and a watch—Is bought by Captain Pascal, and sets out for England—His terror during the voyage—Arrives in England—His wonder at a fall of snow—Is sent to Guernsey, and in some time goes on board a ship of war with his master—Some account of the expedition against Louisburg under the command of Admiral Boscawen, in 1758.

I now totally lost the small remains of comfort I had enjoyed in conversing with my countrymen; the women too, who used to wash and take care of me were all gone different ways, and I never saw one of them afterwards.

I stayed in this island for a few days, I believe it could not be above a fortnight, when I, and some few more slaves that were not saleable amongst the rest, from very much fretting, were shipped off in a sloop for North America. On the passage we were better treated than when we were coming from Africa, and we had plenty of rice and fat pork. We were landed up a river a good way from the sea, about Virginia county, where we saw few or none of our native Africans, and not one soul who could talk to me. I was a few weeks weeding grass and gathering stones in a plantation; and at last all my companions were distributed different ways, and only myself was left. I was now exceedingly miserable, and thought myself worse off than any of the rest of my companions, for they could talk to each other, but I had no person to speak to that I could understand. In this state, I was constantly grieving and pining, and wishing for death rather than anything else.

While I was in this plantation, the gentleman, to whom I suppose the estate belonged, being unwell, I was one day sent for to his dwelling-house to fan him; when I came into the room where he was I was very much affrighted at some things I saw, and the more so as I had seen a black woman slave as I came through the house, who was cooking the dinner, and the poor creature was cruelly loaded with various kinds of iron machines; she had one particularly on her head, which locked her mouth so fast that she could scarcely speak; and could not eat nor drink. I was much astonished and shocked at this contrivance, which I afterwards learned was called the iron muzzle. Soon after I had a fan put in my hand, to fan the gentleman while he slept; and so I did indeed with great fear. While he was fast asleep I indulged myself a great deal in looking about the room, which to me appeared very fine and curious.

The first object that engaged my attention was a watch which hung on the chimney, and was going. I was quite surprised at the noise it made, and was afraid it would tell the gentleman anything I might do amiss; and when I immediately after observed a picture hanging in the room, which appeared constantly to look at me, I was still more affrighted, having never seen such things as these before. At one time I thought it was something relative to magic; and not seeing it move, I thought it might be some way the whites had to keep their great men when they died, and offer them libations as we used to do our friendly spirits. In this state of anxiety I remained till my master awoke, when I was dismissed out of the room, to my no small satisfaction and relief; for I thought that these people were all made up of wonders.

In this place I was called Jacob; but on board the *African Snow*, I was called Michael. I had been some time in this miserable, forlorn, and much dejected state, without having anyone to talk to, which made my life a burden, when the kind and unknown hand of the Creator (who in every deed leads the blind in a way they know not) now began to appear, to my comfort; for one day the captain of a merchant ship, called the *Industrious Bee*, came on some business to my master's house. This gentleman, whose name was Michael Henry Pascal, was a lieutenant in the Royal Navy, but now commanded this trading ship, which was somewhere in the confines of the county many miles off. While he was at my master's house, it happened that he saw me, and liked me so well that he made a purchase of me. I think I have often heard him say he gave thirty or forty pounds sterling for me; but I do not remember which. However, he meant me for a present to some of his friends in England: and as I was sent accordingly from the house of my then master (one Mr. Campbell) to the place where the ship lay; I was conducted on horseback by an elderly black man (a mode of travelling which appeared very odd to me). When I arrived I was carried on board a fine large ship, loaded with tobacco, &c., and just ready to sail for England.

I now thought my condition much mended; I had sails to lie on, and plenty of good victuals to eat; and everybody on board used me very kindly, quite contrary to what I had seen of any white people before; I therefore began to think that they were not all of the same disposition. A few days after I was on board we sailed for England. I was still at a loss to conjecture my destiny. By this time, however, I could smatter a little imperfect English; and I wanted to know as well as I could where we were going. Some of the people of the ship used to tell me they were going to carry me back to my own country, and this made me very happy. I was quite rejoiced at the idea of going back, and thought if I could get home what wonders I should have to tell. But I was reserved for another fate, and was soon undeceived when we came within sight of the English coast.

While I was on board this ship, my captain and master named me *Gustavus Vassa.*[1] I at that time began to understand him a little, and refused to be called so, and told him as well as I could that I would be called Jacob; but he said I should not, and still called me Gustavus: and when I refused to answer to my new name, which I at first did, it gained me many a cuff; so at length I submitted, and by which I have been known ever since.

The ship had a very long passage; and on that account we had very short allowance of provisions. Towards the last, we had only one pound and a half of bread per week, and about the same quantity of meat, and one quart of water a day. We spoke with only one vessel the whole time we were at sea, and but once we caught a few fishes. In our extremities the captain and people told me in jest they would kill and eat me; but I thought them in earnest, and was depressed beyond measure, expecting every moment to be my last. While I was in this situation, one evening they caught, with a good deal of trouble, a large shark, and got it on board. This gladdened my poor heart exceedingly, as I thought it would serve the people to eat instead of their eating me; but very soon, to my astonishment, they cut off a small part of the tail, and tossed the rest over the side. This renewed my consternation; and I did not know what to think of these white people, though I very much feared they would kill and eat me.

There was on board the ship a young lad who had never been at sea before, about four or five years older than myself: his name was Richard Baker. He was a native of America, had received an excellent education, and was of a most amiable temper. Soon after I went on board, he showed me a great deal of partiality and attention, and in return I grew extremely fond of him. We at length became inseparable; and, for the space of two years, he was of very great use to me, and was my constant companion and instructor. Although this dear youth had many slaves of his own, yet he and I have gone through many sufferings together on shipboard; and we have many nights lain in each other's bosoms when we were in great distress. Thus such a friendship was cemented between us as we cherished till his death, which, to my very great sorrow, happened in the year 1759, when he was up the Archipelago, on board his Majesty's ship the *Preston:* an event which I have never ceased to regret, as I lost at once a kind interpreter, an agreeable companion, and a faithful friend; who, at the age of fifteen, discovered a mind superior to prejudice; and who was not

[1] Gustavus Ericksson Vasa, a Swedish nobleman, led a successful revolt against Danish rule in the 1520s; as Gustavus I he ruled Sweden from 1523 to 1560. At the time of Equiano's capture Henry Brooke's *Gustavus Vasa, the Deliverer of His Country* was a popular English play.

ashamed to notice, to associate with, and to be the friend and instructor of one who was ignorant, a stranger, of a different complexion, and a slave! My master had lodged in his mother's house in America; he respected him very much, and made him always eat with him in the cabin. He used often to tell him jocularly that he would kill and eat me. Sometimes he would say to me—the black people were not good to eat, and would ask me if we did not eat people in my country. I said, No; then he said he would kill Dick (as he always called him) first, and afterwards me. Though this hearing relieved my mind a little as to myself, I was alarmed for Dick, and whenever he was called I used to be very much afraid he was to be killed; and I would peep and watch to see if they were going to kill him; nor was I free from this consternation till we made the land.

One night we lost a man overboard; and the cries and noise were so great and confused, in stopping the ship, that I, who did not know what was the matter, began, as usual, to be very much afraid, and to think they were going to make an offering with me, and perform some magic; which I still believed they dealt in. As the waves were very high, I thought the Ruler of the seas was angry, and I expected to be offered up to appease him. This filled my mind with agony, and I could not any more, that night, close my eyes again to rest. However, when daylight appeared, I was a little eased in my mind; but still, every time I was called, I used to think it was to be killed. Some time after this, we saw some very large fish, which I afterwards found were called grampusses. They looked to me exceedingly terrible, and made their appearance just at dusk, and were so near as to blow the water on the ship's deck. I believed them to be the rulers of the sea; and as the white people did not make any offerings at any time, I thought they were angry with them; and, at last, what confirmed my belief was, the wind just then died away, and a calm ensued, and in consequence of it the ship stopped going. I supposed that the fish had performed this, and I hid myself in the fore part of the ship, through fear of being offered up to appease them, every minute peeping and quaking; but my good friend Dick came shortly towards me, and I took an opportunity to ask him, as well as I could, what these fish were. Not being able to talk much English, I could but just make him understand my question; and not at all, when I asked him if any offerings were to be made to them; however, he told me these fish would swallow anybody which sufficiently alarmed me. Here he was called away by the captain, who was leaning over the quarter-deck railing, and looking at the fish; and most of the people were busied in getting a barrel of pitch[2] to light for them to play

²Black tarlike substance used to seal the hull of a ship.

with. The captain now called me to him, having learned some of my apprehensions from Dick; and having diverted himself and others for some time with my fears, which appeared ludicrous enough in my crying and trembling, he dismissed me. The barrel of pitch was now lighted and put over the side into the water. By this time it was just dark, and the fish went after it; and, to my great joy, I saw them no more.

However, all my alarms began to subside when we got sight of land; and at last the ship arrived at Falmouth, after a passage of thirteen weeks. Every heart on board seemed gladdened on our reaching the shore, and none more than mine. The captain immediately went on shore, and sent on board some fresh provisions, which we wanted very much. We made good use of them, and our famine was soon turned into feasting, almost without ending. It was about the beginning of the spring 1757, when I arrived in England, and I was near twelve years of age at that time. I was very much struck with the buildings and the pavement of the streets in Falmouth; and, indeed, every object I saw, filled me with new surprise.

One morning, when I got upon deck, I saw it covered all over with the snow that fell over night. As I had never seen anything of the kind before, I thought it was salt: so I immediately ran down to the mate, and desired him, as well as I could, to come and see how somebody in the night had thrown salt all over the deck. He, knowing what it was, desired me to bring some of it down to him. Accordingly I took up a handful of it, which I found very cold indeed; and when I brought it to him he desired me to taste it. I did so, and I was surprised beyond measure. I then asked him what it was; he told me it was snow, but I could not in anywise understand him. He asked me, if we had no such thing in my country; I told him, No. I then asked him the use of it, and who made it; he told me a great man in the heavens, called God. But here again I was to all intents and purposes at a loss to understand him; and the more so, when a little after I saw the air filled with it, in a heavy shower, which fell down on the same day.

After this I went to church; and having never been at such a place before, I was again amazed at seeing and hearing the service. I asked all I could about it, and they gave me to understand it was worshipping God, who made us and all things. I was still at a great loss, and soon got into an endless field of inquiries, as well as I was able to speak and ask about things. However, my little friend Dick used to be my best interpreter; for I could make free with him, and he always instructed me with pleasure. And from what I could understand by him of this God, and in seeing these white people did not sell one another as we did, I was much pleased; and in this I thought they were much happier than we Africans. I was astonished at the wisdom of the white people in all things I saw; but was amazed at their not sacrificing, or making any offerings, and eating with unwashed hands, and touching the dead. I likewise could not help remarking the particular slenderness of their women, which I did not at first like; and I thought they were not so modest and shame-faced as the African women.

I had often seen my master and Dick employed in reading; and I had a great curiosity to talk to the books as I thought they did, and so to learn how all things had a beginning. For that purpose I have often taken up a book, and have talked to it, and then put my ears to it, when alone, in hopes it would answer me; and I have been very much concerned when I found it remained silent.

My master lodged at the house of a gentleman in Falmouth, who had a fine little daughter about six or seven years of age, and she grew prodigiously fond of me, insomuch that we used to eat together, and had servants to wait on us. I was so much caressed by this family that it often reminded me of the treatment I had received from my little noble African master. After I had been here a few days, I was sent on board of the ship; but the child cried so much after me that nothing could pacify her till I was sent for again. It is ludicrous enough, that I began to fear I should be betrothed to this young lady; and when my master asked me if I would stay there with her behind him, as he was going away with the ship, which had taken in the tobacco again, I cried immediately, and said I would not leave him. At last, by stealth, one night I was sent on board the ship again; and in a little time we sailed for Guernsey, where she was in part owned by a merchant, one Nicholas Doberry.

As I was now amongst a people who had not their faces scarred, like some of the African nation where I had been, I was very glad I did not let them ornament me in that manner when I was with them. When we arrived at Guernsey, my master placed me to board and lodge with one of his mates, who had a wife and family there; and some months afterwards he went to England, and left me in care of this mate, together with my friend Dick. This mate had a little daughter, aged about five or six years, with whom I used to be much delighted. I had often observed that when her mother washed her face it looked very rosy, but when she washed mine it did not look so. I therefore tried oftentimes myself if I could not by washing make my face of the same color as my little play-mate, Mary, but it was all in vain; and I now began to be mortified at the difference in our complexions. This woman behaved to me with great kindness and attention, and taught me everything in the same manner as she did her own child, and, indeed, in every respect, treated me as such. I remained here till the summer of the year 1757, when my master, being appointed first lieutenant of his Majesty's ship the *Roebuck*, sent for Dick and me, and his old mate. On this we all left Guernsey, and set out for England in a sloop, bound for London.

As we were coming up towards the Nore,[3] where the *Roebuck* lay, a man-of-war's boat came along side to press[4] our people, on which each man run to hide himself. I was very much frightened at this, though I did not know what it meant, or what to think or do. However I went and hid myself also under a hencoop. Immediately afterwards, the press-gang came on board with their swords drawn, and searched all about, pulled the people out by force, and put them into the boat. At last I was found out also; the man that found me held me up by the heels while they all made their sport of me, I roaring and crying out all the time most lustily; but at last the mate, who was my conductor, seeing this, came to my assistance, and did all he could to pacify me; but all to very little purpose, till I had seen the boat go off. Soon afterwards we came to the Nore, where the *Roebuck* lay; and, to our great joy, my master came on board to us, and brought us to the ship.

When I went on board this large ship, I was amazed indeed to see the quantity of men and the guns. However, my surprise began to diminish as my knowledge increased; and I ceased to feel those apprehensions and alarms which had taken such strong possession of me when I first came among the Europeans, and for some time after. I began now to pass to an opposite extreme; I was so far from being afraid of anything new which I saw, that after I had been some time in this ship, I even began to long for an engagement. My griefs, too, which in young minds are not perpetual, were now wearing away; and I soon enjoyed myself pretty well, and felt tolerably easy in my present situation. There was a number of boys on board, which still made it more agreeable; for we were always together, and a great part of our time was spent in play.

I remained in this ship a considerable time, during which we made several cruises, and visited a variety of places; among others we were twice in Holland, and brought over several persons of distinction from it, whose names I do not now remember. On the passage, one day, for the diversion of those gentlemen, all the boys were called on the quarter-deck, and were paired proportionably, and then made to fight; after which the gentlemen gave the combatants from five to nine shillings each. This was the first time I ever fought with a white boy; and I never knew what it was to have a bloody nose before. This made me fight most desperately, I suppose considerably more than an hour; and at last, both of us being

---

[3] Island near the mouth of the Thames.
[4] To force into service. To obtain sailors for the British navy, press-gangs would travel through the countryside and the seaport towns impressing men into service.

weary, we were parted. I had a great deal of this kind of sport afterwards, in which the captain and the ship's company used very much to encourage me.

Sometime afterwards, the ship went to Leith in Scotland, and from thence to the Orkneys, where I was surprised in seeing scarcely any night; and from thence we sailed with a great fleet, full of soldiers, for England. All this time we had never come to an engagement, though we were frequently cruising off the coast of France; during which we chased many vessels, and took in all seventeen prizes. I had been learning many of the maneuvres of the ship during our cruise; and I was several times made to fire the guns. One evening, off Havre de Grace, just as it was growing dark, we were standing off shore, and met with a fine large French built frigate. We got all things immediately ready for fighting; and I now expected I should be gratified in seeing an engagement, which I had so long wished for in vain. But the very moment the word of command was given to fire, we heard those on board the other ship cry, "Haul down the jib"; and in that instant she hoisted English colors. There was instantly with us an amazing cry of—"Avast!" or stop firing; and I think one or two guns had been let off, but happily they did no mischief. We had hailed them several times, but they not hearing, we received no answer, which was the cause of our firing. The boat was then sent on board of her, and she proved to be the *Ambuscade*, man-of-war, to my no small disappointment.

We returned to Portsmouth, without having been in any action, just at the trial of Admiral Byng[5] (whom I saw several times during it); and my master having left the ship, and gone to London for promotion, Dick and I were put on board the *Savage*, sloop-of-war, and we went in her to assist in bringing off the *St. George*, man-of-war, that had run ashore somewhere on the coast. After staying a few weeks on board the *Savage*, Dick and I were sent on shore at Deal, where we remained some short time, till my master sent for us to London, the place I had long desired exceedingly to see. We therefore both with great pleasure got into a wagon, and came to London, where we were received by a Mr. Guerin, a relation of my master. This gentleman had two sisters, very amiable ladies, who took much notice and great care of me.

Though I had desired so much to see London, when I arrived in it I was

---

[5] Admiral John Byng (1704–1757) had been sent to relieve Fort St. Philip on Minorca in 1756. He was unable to do so, and the island surrendered to the French. An embarrassed English government, unprepared for the war it had begun, tried Byng for cowardice and negligence. His court-martial at Portsmouth (December 28, 1756–January 27, 1757) ended with his conviction, and he faced a firing squad on March 14, 1757.

unfortunately unable to gratify my curiosity; for I had at this time the chilblains[6] to such a degree that I could not stand for several months, and I was obliged to be sent to St. George's hospital. There I grew so ill that the doctors wanted to cut my leg off, at different times, apprehending a mortification; but I always said I would rather die than suffer it, and happily (I thank God) I recovered without the operation. After being there several weeks, and just as I had recovered, the smallpox broke out on me, so that I was again confined; and I thought myself now particularly unfortunate. However, I soon recovered again; and by this time, my master having been promoted to be first lieutenant of the *Preston,* man-of-war, of fifty guns, then new at Deptford, Dick and I were sent on board her, and soon after, we went to Holland to bring over the late Duke of Cumberland to England.

While I was in the ship an incident happened, which, though trifling, I beg leave to relate, as I could not help taking particular notice of it, and considered it then as a judgment of God. One morning a young man was looking up to the foretop, and in a wicked tone, common on shipboard, d———d his eyes about something. Just at the moment some small particles of dirt fell into his left eye, and by the evening it was very much inflamed. The next day it grew worse, and within six or seven days he lost it.

From this ship my master was appointed a lieutenant on board the *Royal George.* When he was going he wished me to stay on board the *Preston,* to learn the French horn; but the ship being ordered for Turkey, I could not think of leaving my master, to whom I was very warmly attached; and I told him if he left me behind, it would break my heart. This prevailed on him to take me with him; but he left Dick on board the *Preston,* whom I embraced at parting for the last time. The *Royal George* was the largest ship I had ever seen, so that when I came on board of her I was surprised at the number of people, men, women, and children, of every denomination; and the largeness of the guns, many of them also of brass, which I had never seen before. Here were also shops or stalls of every kind of goods, and people crying their different commodities about the ship as in a town.

To me it appeared a little world, into which I was again cast without a friend, for I had no longer my dear companion Dick. We did not stay long here. My master was not many weeks on board before he got an appointment to the sixth lieutenant of the *Namur,* which was then at Spithead,

---

[6] Painful inflammation and swelling of hands and feet caused by exposure to cold.

fitting up for Vice-admiral Boscawen, who was going with a large fleet on an expedition against Louisburg.[7]

The crew of the *Royal George* were turned over to her, and the flag of that gallant admiral was hoisted on board, the blue at the maintop gallant mast head. There was a very great fleet of men-of-war of every description assembled together for this expedition, and I was in hopes soon to have an opportunity of being gratified with a sea-fight. All things being now in readiness, this mighty fleet (for there was also Admiral Cornish's fleet in company, destined for the East Indies) at last weighed anchor, and sailed. The two fleets continued in company for several days, and then parted; Admiral Cornish, in the *Lenox,* having first saluted our Admiral in the *Namur,* which he returned. We then steered for America; but, by contrary winds, we were driven to Tenerife, where I was struck with its noted peak. Its prodigious height, and its form, resembling a sugar loaf, filled me with wonder. We remained in sight of this island some days, and then proceeded for America, which we soon made, and got into a very commodious harbor called St. George, in Halifax, where we had fish in great plenty, and all other fresh provisions. We were here joined by different men-of-war and transport ships with soldiers; after which, our fleet being increased to a prodigious number of ships of all kinds, we sailed for Cape Breton in Nova Scotia. We had the good and gallant General Wolfe on board our ship, whose affability made him highly esteemed and beloved by all the men.[8] He often honored me, as well as other boys, with marks of his notice, and saved me once a flogging for fighting with a young gentleman.

We arrived at Cape Breton in the summer of 1758; and here the soldiers were to be landed, in order to make an attack upon Louisburg. My master had some part in superintending the landing; and here I was in a small measure gratified in seeing an encounter between our men and the enemy. The French were posted on the shore to receive us, and disputed our landing for a long time; but at last they were driven from their trenches, and a complete landing was effected. Our troops pursued them as far as the town of Louisburg. In this action many were killed on both sides.

One thing remarkable I saw this day. A lieutenant of the *Princess*

[7] Edward Boscawen (1711–1761). Louisbourg, at the tip of the Cape Breton peninsula, sits at the entrance to the St. Lawrence River. This strategic point could control entry into the interior of Canada and to the Great Lakes, as well as into the Ohio River Valley and, through Lake Champlain, into New York and New England.

[8] General James Wolfe (1727–1759), England's greatest hero of the war. His successful assault on Quebec in 1759 destroyed French power in North America, though it also cost Wolfe his life.

Amelia, who, as well as my master, superintended the landing, was giving the word of command, and while his mouth was open, a musket ball went through it, and passed out at his cheek. I had that day, in my hand, the scalp of an Indian king, who was killed in the engagement; the scalp had been taken off by an Highlander. I saw the king's ornaments too, which were very curious, and made of feathers.

Our land forces laid siege to the town of Louisburg, while the French men-of-war were blocked up in the harbor by the fleet, the batteries at the same time playing upon them from the land. This they did with such effect, that one day I saw some of the ships set on fire by the shells from the batteries, and I believe two or three of them were quite burnt. At another time, about fifty boats belonging to the English men-of-war, commanded by Captain George Belfour, of the *Etna,* fire ship, and Mr. Laforey, another junior Captain, attacked and boarded the only two remaining French men-of-war in the harbor. They also set fire to a seventy-gun ship, but a sixty-four, called the *Bienfaisant,* they brought off. During my stay here, I had often an opportunity of being near Captain Belfour, who was pleased to notice me, and liked me so much that he often asked my master to let him have me, but he would not part with me; and no consideration could have induced me to leave him.

At last, Louisburg was taken,[9] and the English men-of-war came into the harbor before it, to my very great joy; for I had now more liberty of indulging myself, and I went often on shore. When the ships were in the harbor, we had the most beautiful procession on the water I ever saw. All the Admirals and Captains of the men-of-war, full dressed, and in their barges, well ornamented with pendants, came alongside of the *Namur.* The Vice-admiral then went on shore in his barge, followed by the other officers in order of seniority, to take possession, as I suppose, of the town and fort. Some time after this, the French governor and his lady, and other persons of note, came on board our ship to dine. On this occasion our ships were dressed with colors of all kinds, from the top-gallant mast head to the deck; and this, with the firing of guns, formed a most grand and magnificent spectacle.

As soon as everything here was settled, Admiral Boscawen sailed with part of the fleet for England, leaving some ships behind with Rear-admirals Sir Charles Hardy and Durell. It was now winter; and one evening, during our passage home, about dusk, when we were in the channel, or near soundings, and were beginning to look for land, we descried[10] seven sail of large men-of-war, which stood off shore. Several people on board of our

[9] Louisbourg surrendered July 2, 1758.
[10] Caught sight of.

ship said, as the two fleets were (in forty minutes from the first sight) within hail of each other, that they were English men-of-war; and some of our people even began to name some of the ships. By this time both fleets began to mingle, and our Admiral ordered his flag to be hoisted. At that instant, the other fleet, which were French, hoisted their ensigns, and gave us a broadside as they passed by. Nothing could create greater surprise and confusion among us than this. The wind was high, the sea rough, and we had our lower and middle deck guns housed in, so that not a single gun on board was ready to be fired at any of the French ships. However, the *Royal William* and the *Somerset,* being our sternmost ships, became a little prepared, and each gave the French ships a broadside as they passed by.

I afterwards heard this was a French squadron, commanded by Monsieur Corflans; and certainly, had the Frenchmen known our condition, and had a mind to fight us, they might have done us great mischief. But we were not long before we were prepared for an engagement. Immediately many things were tossed overboard, the ships were made ready for fighting as soon as possible, and about ten at night we had bent a new main-sail, the old one being split. Being now in readiness for fighting, we wore ship, and stood after the French fleet, who were one or two ships in number more than we. However we gave them chase, and continued pursuing them all night; and at day-light we saw six of them, all large ships of the line, and an English East Indiaman, a prize they had taken. We chased them all day till between three and four o'clock in the evening, when we came up with, and passed within a musket shot of one seventy-four-gun ship, and the Indiaman also, who now hoisted her colors, but immediately hauled them down again. On this we made a signal for the other ships to take possession of her; and, supposing the man-of-war would likewise strike, we cheered, but she did not; though if we had fired into her, from being so near we must have taken her. To my utter surprise, the *Somerset,* who was the next ship astern of the *Namur,* made way likewise; and, thinking they were sure of this French ship, they cheered in the same manner, but still continued to follow us.

The French Commodore was about a gun-shot ahead of all, running from us with all speed; and about four o'clock he carried his foretopmast overboard. This caused another loud cheer with us; and a little after the topmast came close by us; but, to our great surprise, instead of coming up with her, we found she went as fast as ever, if not faster. The sea grew now much smoother; and the wind lulling, the seventy-four-gun ship we had passed, came again by us in the very same direction, and so near that we heard her people talk as she went by, yet not a shot was fired on either side; and about five or six o'clock, just as it grew dark, she joined her Commodore. We chased all night; but the next day we were out of sight, so that we saw no more of them; and we only had the old Indiaman (called *Carnarvon,* I think) for our trouble.

After this we stood in for the channel, and soon made the land; and, about the close of the year 1758–9, we got safe to St. Helen's. Here the *Namur* ran aground, and also another large ship astern of us; but, by starting our water, and tossing many things overboard to lighten her, we got the ships off without any damage. We stayed for a short time at Spithead, and then went into Portsmouth harbor to refit. From whence the Admiral went to London; and my master and I soon followed, with a press-gang, as we wanted some hands to complete our complement.

CHAPTER 4

The author is baptized—Narrowly escapes drowning—Goes on an expedition to the Mediterranean—Incidents he met with there—Is witness to an engagement between some English and French ships—A particular account of the celebrated engagement between Admiral Boscawen and Monsieur Le Clue, off Cape Logas, in August 1759—Dreadful explosion of a French ship—The author sails for England—His master appointed to the command of a fire ship—Meets a Negro boy, from whom he experiences much benevolence—Prepares for an expedition against Belle Isle—A remarkable story of a disaster which befell his ship—Arrives at Belle Isle—Operations of the landing and siege—The author's danger and distress, with his manner of extricating himself—Surrender of Belle Isle—Transactions afterwards on the coast of France—Remarkable instance of kidnapping— The author returns to England—Hears a talk of peace, and expects his freedom—His ship sails for Deptford to be paid off, and when he arrives there he is suddenly seized by his master and carried forcibly on board a West India ship and sold.

It was now between two and three years since I first came to England, a great part of which I had spent at sea; so that I became inured to that service, and began to consider myself as happily situated, for my master treated me always extremely well; and my attachment and gratitude to him were very great. From the various scenes I had beheld on shipboard, I soon grew a stranger to terror of every kind, and was, in that respect at least, almost an Englishman. I have often reflected with surprise that I never felt half the alarm at any of the numerous dangers I have been in, that I was filled with at the first sight of the Europeans, and at every act of theirs, even the most trifling, when I first came among them, and for some time afterwards. That fear, however, which was the effect of my ignorance, wore away as I began to know them. I could now speak English tolerably well, and I perfectly understood everything that was said. I not only felt myself quite easy with these new countrymen, but relished their society and manners. I no longer looked upon them as spirits, but as men superior to us; and therefore I had the stronger desire to resemble them, to imbibe their spirit, and imitate their manners. I therefore embraced every occasion of improvement, and every new thing that I observed I treasured up in my memory. I had long wished to be able to read and write; and for this purpose I took every opportunity to gain instruction, but had made as yet very little progress. However, when I went to London with my master, I had soon an opportunity of improving myself, which I gladly embraced. Shortly after my arrival, he sent me to wait upon the Miss Guerins, who had treated me with much kindness when I was there before; and they sent me to school.

While I was attending these ladies, their servants told me I could not go to Heaven unless I was baptized. This made me very uneasy, for I had now some faint idea of a future state: accordingly I communicated my anxiety to the eldest Miss Guerin, with whom I was become a favorite, and pressed her to have me baptized; when to my great joy, she told me I should. She had formerly asked my master to let me be baptized, but he had refused. However she now insisted on it; and he being under some obligation to her brother, complied with her request. So I was baptized in St. Margaret's church, Westminster, in February 1759, by my present name. The clergyman at the same time, gave me a book, called *A Guide to the Indians,* written by the Bishop of Sodor and Man.[1] On this occasion, Miss Guerin did me the honor to stand as god-mother, and afterwards gave me a treat.

I used to attend these ladies about the town, in which service I was extremely happy; as I had thus many opportunities of seeing London, which I desired of all things. I was sometimes, however, with my master at his rendezvous house, which was at the foot of Westminster bridge. Here I used to enjoy myself in playing about the bridge stairs, and often in the waterman's wherries,[2] with other boys. On one of these occasions there was another boy with me in a wherry, and we went out into the current of the river; while we were there, two more stout boys came to us

---

[1] Thomas Wilson (1697–1755), bishop of Sodor and Man, wrote *The Knowledge and Practice of Christianity Made Easy for the Meanest Mental Capacities; or, an Essay towards an Instruction for the Indians* (London, 1740) in the form of a dialogue between an Indian and a Christian.

[2] Long, light rowboats.

in another wherry, and abusing us for taking the boat, desired me to get into the other wherry-boat. Accordingly, I went to get out of the wherry I was in, but just as I had got one of my feet into the other boat, the boys shoved it off, so that I fell into the Thames; and, not being able to swim, I should unavoidably have been drowned, but for the assistance of some watermen who providentially came to my relief.

The *Namur* being again got ready for sea, my master, with his gang, was ordered on board; and, to my no small grief, I was obliged to leave my school-master, whom I liked very much, and always attended while I stayed in London, to repair on board with my master. Nor did I leave my kind patronesses, the Miss Guerins, without uneasiness and regret. They often used to teach me to read, and took great pains to instruct me in the principles of religion and the knowledge of God. I therefore parted from those amiable ladies with reluctance, after receiving from them many friendly cautions how to conduct myself, and some valuable presents.

When I came to Spithead, I found we were destined for the Mediterranean, with a large fleet, which was now ready to put to sea. We only waited for the arrival of the Admiral, who soon came on board. And about the beginning of the spring of 1759, having weighed anchor, and got under way, sailed for the Mediterranean; and in eleven days, from the Land's End, we got to Gibraltar. While we were here I used to be often on shore, and got various fruits in great plenty, and very cheap.

I had frequently told several people, in my excursions on shore, the story of my being kidnapped with my sister, and of our being separated, as I have related before; and I had as often expressed my anxiety for her fate, and my sorrow at having never met her again. One day, when I was on shore, and mentioning these circumstances to some persons, one of them told me he knew where my sister was, and, if I would accompany him, he would bring me to her. Improbable as this story was, I believed it immediately, and agreed to go with him, while my heart leaped for joy; and, indeed, he conducted me to a black young woman, who was so like my sister, that at first sight, I really thought it was her; but I was quickly undeceived. And, on talking to her, I found her to be of another nation.

While we lay here the *Preston* came in from the Levant.[3] As soon as she arrived, my master told me I should now see my old companion, Dick, who was gone in her when she sailed for Turkey. I was much rejoiced at this news, and expected every minute to embrace him; and when the captain came on board of our ship, which he did immediately after, I ran to inquire after my friend; but, with inexpressible sorrow, I learned from the boat's

[3] Eastern Mediterranean region.

crew that the dear youth was dead! and that they had brought his chest, and all his other things, to my master. These he afterwards gave to me, and I regarded them as a memorial of my friend, whom I loved, and grieved for, as a brother.

While we were at Gibraltar, I saw a soldier hanging by the heels, at one of the moles.[4] I thought this a strange sight, as I had seen a man hanged in London by his neck. At another time I saw the master of a frigate towed to shore on a grating, by several of the men-of-war's boats, and discharged the fleet, which I understood was a mark of disgrace for cowardice. On board the same ship there was also a sailor hung up at the yardarm.

After laying at Gibraltar for some time, we sailed up the Mediterranean, a considerable way above the Gulf of Lyons; where we were one night overtaken with a terrible gale of wind, much greater than any I had ever yet experienced. The sea ran so high, that, though all the guns were well housed, there was great reason to fear their getting loose, the ship rolled so much; and if they had, it must have proved our destruction. After we had cruised here for a short time, we came to Barcelona, a Spanish sea-port, remarkable for its silk manufactures. Here the ships were all to be watered; and my master, who spoke different languages, and used often to interpret for the Admiral, superintended the watering of ours. For that purpose, he and the other officers of the ship, who were on the same service, had tents pitched in the bay; and the Spanish soldiers were stationed along the shore, I suppose to see that no depredations were committed by our men.

I used constantly to attend my master; and I was charmed with this place. All the time we stayed it was like a fair with the natives, who brought us fruits of all kinds, and sold them to us much cheaper than I got them in England. They used also to bring wine down to us in hog and sheep skins, which diverted me very much. The Spanish officers here treated our officers with great politeness and attention; and some of them, in particular, used to come often to my master's tent to visit him; where they would sometimes divert themselves by mounting me on the horses or mules, so that I could not fall, and setting them off at full gallop; my imperfect skill in horsemanship all the while affording them no small entertainment.

After the ships were watered, we returned to our old station of cruising off Toulon, for the purpose of intercepting a fleet of French men-of-war that lay there. One Sunday, in our cruise, we came off a place where there

---

[4] He had drowned himself in endeavoring to desert. [Equiano's note.] A mole is a pier.

were two small French frigates laying in shore; and our Admiral, thinking to take or destroy them, sent two ships in after them—the *Culloden* and the *Conqueror*. They soon came up to the Frenchmen, and I saw a smart fight here, both by sea and land; for the frigates were covered by batteries,[5] and they played upon our ships most furiously, which they as furiously returned; and for a long time a constant firing was kept up on all sides at an amazing rate. At last, one frigate sunk; but the people escaped, though not without much difficulty. And soon after, some of the people left the other frigate also, which was a mere wreck. However, our ships did not venture to bring her away, they were so much annoyed from the batteries, which raked them both in going and coming. Their topmasts were shot away, and they were otherwise so much shattered, that the Admiral was obliged to send in many boats to tow them back to the fleet. I afterwards sailed with a man who fought in one of the French batteries during the engagement, and he told me our ships had done considerable mischief that day, on shore and in the batteries.

After this we sailed for Gibraltar, and arrived there about August 1759. Here we remained with all our sails unbent, while the fleet was watering and doing other necessary things. While we were in this situation, one day the Admiral, with most of the principal officers and many people of all stations, being on shore, about seven o'clock in the evening we were alarmed by signals from the frigates stationed for that purpose; and in an instant there was a general cry that the French fleet was out, and just passing through the straits. The Admiral immediately came on board with some other officers; and it is impossible to describe the noise, hurry, and confusion throughout the whole fleet, in bending their sails and slipping their cables; many people and ship's boats were left on shore in the bustle. We had two captains on board of our ship who came away in the hurry and left their ships to follow. We showed lights from the gun-wales to the main topmast head; and all our lieutenants were employed amongst the fleet to tell the ships not to wait for their captains, but to put the sails to the yards, slip their cables, and follow us; and in this confusion of making ready for fighting, we set out for sea in the dark after the French fleet. Here I could have exclaimed with Ajax,

> O Jove! O father! if it be thy will
> That we must perish, we thy will obey,
> But let us perish by the light of day.[6]

---

[5] Guns in fortified positions on land.

[6] This is a misquotation of Alexander Pope's translation of Homer's *Iliad* (17. 728–32): "O King! O Father! hear my humble prayer . . . / If Greece must perish, we thy will obey, / But let us perish in the face of day." Ajax was a Greek warrior in the Trojan War.

They had got the start of us so far that we were not able to come up with them during the night; but at day light we saw seven sail of the line of battle some miles ahead. We immediately chased them till about four o'clock in the evening, when our ships came up with them; and, though we were about fifteen large ships, our gallant Admiral only fought them with his own division, which consisted of seven; so that we were just ship for ship. We passed by the whole of the enemy's fleet in order to come at their commander, Monsieur Le Clue, who was in the *Ocean,* an eighty-four gun ship. As we passed they all fired on us, and at one time three of them fired together, continuing to do so for some time. Notwithstanding which our Admiral would not suffer a gun to be fired at any of them, to my astonishment; but made us lie on our bellies on the deck until we came quite close to the *Ocean,* who was ahead of them all; when we had orders to pour the whole three tiers into her at once.

The engagement now commenced with great fury on both sides. The *Ocean* immediately returned our fire, and we continued engaged with each other for some time; during which I was frequently stunned with the thundering of the great guns, whose dreadful contents hurried many of my companions into awful eternity. At last the French line was entirely broken, and we obtained the victory, which was immediately proclaimed with loud huzzas and acclamations. We took three prizes, *La Modeste,* of sixty-four guns, and *Le Temeraire* and *Centaur,* of seventy-four guns each. The rest of the French ships took to flight with all the sail they could crowd. Our ship being very much damaged, and quite disabled from pursuing the enemy, the Admiral immediately quitted her and went in the broken and only boat we had left on board the *Newark,* with which, and some other ships, he went after the French. The *Ocean,* and another large French ship, called the *Redoubtable,* endeavoring to escape, ran ashore at Cape Logas, on the coast of Portugal, and the French Admiral and some of the crew got ashore; but we, finding it impossible to get the ships off, set fire to them both. About midnight I saw the *Ocean* blow up, with a most dreadful explosion. I never beheld a more awful scene. In less than a minute, the midnight for a certain space seemed turned into day by the blaze, which was attended with a noise louder and more terrible than thunder, that seemed to rend every element around us.

My station during the engagement was on the middle deck, where I was quartered with another boy, to bring powder to the aftermost gun; and here I was a witness of the dreadful fate of many of my companions, who, in the twinkling of an eye, were dashed in pieces, and launched into eternity. Happily I escaped unhurt, though the shot and splinters flew thick about me during the whole fight. Towards the latter part of it, my master was wounded, and I saw him carried down to the surgeon; but though I was much alarmed for him, and wished to assist him, I dared not leave my post. At this station, my gun-mate (a partner in bringing powder for the same gun) and I ran a very great risk, for more than half an hour, of blowing up the ship. For, when we had taken the cartridges out of the boxes, the bottoms of many of them proving rotten, the powder ran all about the deck, near the match tub; we scarcely had water enough at the last to throw on it. We were also, from our employment, very much exposed to the enemy's shots; for we had to go through nearly the whole length of the ship to bring the powder. I expected, therefore, every minute to be my last, especially when I saw our men fall so thick about me; but, wishing to guard as much against the dangers as possible, at first I thought it would be safest not to go for the powder till the Frenchmen had fired their broadside; and then, while they were charging, I could go and come with my powder. But immediately afterwards I thought this caution was fruitless; and, cheering myself with the reflection that there was a time allotted for me to die as well as to be born, I instantly cast off all fear or thought whatever of death, and went through the whole of my duty with alacrity; pleasing myself with the hope, if I survived the battle, of relating it and the dangers I had escaped to the Miss Guerins, and others, when I should return to London.

Our ship suffered very much in this engagement; for, besides the number of our killed and wounded, she was almost torn to pieces, and our rigging so much shattered, that our mizen-mast, main-yard, &c., hung over the side of the ship; so that we were obliged to get many carpenters, and others from some of the ships of the fleet, to assist in setting us in some tolerable order. And, notwithstanding which, it took us some time before we were completely refitted; after which we left Admiral Broderick to command, and we, with the prizes, steered for England. On the passage, and as soon as my master was something recovered of his wounds, the Admiral appointed him Captain of the *Etna*, fire ship, on which he and I left the *Namur*, and went on board of her at sea. I liked this little ship very much. I now became the captain's steward, in which situation I was very happy; for I was extremely well treated by all on board, and I had leisure to improve myself in reading and writing. The latter I had learned a little of before I left the *Namur*, as there was a school on board. When we arrived at Spithead, the *Etna* went into Portsmouth harbor to refit, which being done, we returned to Spithead and joined a large fleet that was thought to be intended against the Havannah; but about that time the king died.[7] Whether that prevented the expedition, I know not, but it caused our ship to be stationed at Cowes, in the isle of Wight, till the beginning of the year sixty-one. Here I spent my time very pleasantly; I was much on shore, all about this delightful island, and found the inhabitants very civil.

While I was here, I met with a trifling incident, which surprised me agreeably. I was one day in a field belonging to a gentleman who had a black boy about my own size; this boy having observed me from his master's house, was transported at the sight of one of his own country-men, and ran to meet me with the utmost haste. I not knowing what he was about, turned a little out of his way at first, but to no purpose: he soon came close to me, and caught hold of me in his arms, as if I had been his brother, though we had never seen each other before. After we had talked together for some time he took me to his master's house, where I was treated very kindly. This benevolent boy and I were very happy in frequently seeing each other, till about the month of March 1761, when our ship had orders to fit out again for another expedition. When we got ready, we joined a very large fleet at Spithead, commanded by Commodore Keppel, which was destined against Belle Isle;[8] and, with a number of transport ships, with troops on board, to make a descent on the place, we sailed once more in quest of fame. I longed to engage in new adventures, and see fresh wonders.

I had a mind on which every thing uncommon made its full impression and every event which I considered as marvellous. Every extraordinary escape, or signal deliverance, either of myself or others, I looked upon to be effected by the interposition of Providence. We had not been above ten days at sea, before an incident of this kind happened; which, whatever credit it may obtain from the reader, made no small impression on my mind.

We had on board a gunner, whose name was John Mondle, a man of very indifferent morals. This man's cabin was between the decks, exactly over where I lay, abreast of the quarter-deck ladder. One night, the 5th of April, being terrified with a dream, he awoke in so great a fright that he could not rest in his bed any longer, nor even remain in his cabin; and he went upon deck about four o'clock in the morning, extremely agitated. He immediately told those on the deck of the agonies of his mind, and the dream which occasioned it; in which he said he had seen many things very awful, and had been warned by St. Peter to repent, who told him time was

[7] King George II died on October 25, 1760, and was succeeded by his grandson George III. Britain captured Havana, Cuba, from Spain in 1762.
[8] Belle Isle (Belle-Île) is in the Bay of Biscay, off the French coast.

short. This he said had greatly alarmed him, and he was determined to alter his life. People generally mock the fears of others, when they are themselves in safety, and some of his shipmates who heard him only laughed at him. However, he made a vow that he never would drink strong liquors again; and he immediately got a light, and gave away his sea-stores of liquor. After which, his agitation still continuing, he began to read the Scriptures, hoping to find some relief; and soon afterwards he laid himself down again on his bed, and endeavored to compose himself to sleep, but to no purpose; his mind still continuing in a state of agony. By this time it was exactly half after seven in the morning. I was then under the half-deck at the great cabin door; and, all at once I heard the people in the waist cry out, most fearfully—"The Lord have mercy upon us! We are all lost! The Lord have mercy upon us!" Mr. Mondle hearing the cries, immediately ran out of his cabin; and we were instantly struck by the *Lynne,* a forty-gun ship, Captain Clark, which nearly run us down. This ship had just put about, and was by the wind, but had not got full headway, or we must all have perished, for the wind was brisk. However, before Mr. Mondle had got four steps from his cabin door, she struck our ship with her cutwater, right in the middle of his bed and cabin, and ran it up to the combings of the quarter-deck hatchway, and above three feet below water, and in a minute there was not a bit of wood to be seen where Mr. Mondle's cabin stood; and he was so near being killed, that some of the splinters tore his face. As Mr. Mondle must inevitably have perished from this accident, had he not been alarmed in the very extraordinary way I have related, I could not help regarding this as an awful interposition of Providence for his preservation.

The two ships for some time swung alongside of each other; for ours, being a fire ship, our grappling-irons caught the *Lynne* every way, and the yards and rigging went at an astonishing rate. Our ship was in such a shocking condition that we all thought she would instantly go down, and everyone run for their lives, and got as well as they could on board the *Lynne;* but our lieutenant, being the aggressor, he never quitted the ship. However, when we found she did not sink immediately, the captain came on board again, and encouraged our people to return to try to save her. Many, on this, came back, but some would not venture. Some of the ships in the fleet seeing our situation, immediately sent their boats to our assistance; but it took us the whole day to save the ship, with all their help. And, by using every possible means, particularly strapping her together with many hawsers,[9] and putting a great quantity of tallow[10] below water,

---

[9] Large ropes used for towing or mooring a ship.
[10] Animal fat, in this case probably used to plug the holes in the ship's hull.

where she was damaged, she was kept together. But it was well we did not meet with any gales of wind, or we must have gone to pieces; for we were in such a crazy condition, that we had ships to attend us till we arrived at Belle Isle, the place of our destination; and then we had all things taken out of the ship, and she was properly repaired. This escape of Mr. Mondle, which he, as well as myself, always considered as a singular act of Providence, I believe had a great influence on his life and conduct ever afterwards.

Now that I am on this subject, I beg leave to relate another instance or two which strongly raised my belief of the particular interposition of Heaven, and which might not otherwise have found a place here, from their insignificance. I belonged for a few days in the year 1758, to the *Jason*, of fifty-four guns, at Plymouth; and one night, when I was on board, a woman, with a child at her breast, fell from the upper-deck down into the hold, near the keel. Everyone thought that the mother and child must be both dashed to pieces; but, to our great surprise, neither of them was hurt. I myself one day fell headlong from the upper deck of the *Etna*, down the after-hold, when the ballast was out; and all who saw me fall cried out I was killed, but I received not the least injury. And in the same ship a man fell from the mast-head on the deck, without being hurt. In these, and in many more instances, I thought I could plainly trace the hand of God, without whose permission a sparrow cannot fall. I began to raise my fear from man to him alone, and to call daily on his holy name with fear and reverence. And I trust he heard my supplications, and graciously condescended to answer me according to his holy word, and to implant the seeds of piety in me, even one of the meanest of his creatures.

When we had refitted our ship, and all things were in readiness for attacking the place, the troops on board the transports were ordered to disembark; and my master, as a junior captain, had a share in the command of the landing. This was on the 12th of April. The French were drawn up on the shore, and had made every disposition to oppose the landing of our men, only a small part of them this day being able to effect it; most of them, after fighting with great bravery, were cut off; and General Crawford, with a number of others, were taken prisoners. In this day's engagement we had also our lieutenant killed.

On the 21st of April we renewed our efforts to land the men, while all the men-of-war were stationed along the shore to cover it, and fired at the French batteries and breast-works from early in the morning till about four o'clock in the evening, when our soldiers effected a safe landing. They immediately attacked the French; and, after a sharp encounter, forced them from the batteries. Before the enemy retreated, they blew up several of them, lest they should fall into our hands. Our men now proceeded to besiege the citadel, and my master was ordered on board to superintend the landing of all the materials necessary for carrying on the siege; in which service I mostly attended him.

While I was there I went about to different parts of the island; and one day, particularly, my curiosity almost cost me my life. I wanted very much to see the mode of charging the mortars, and letting off the shells, and for that purpose I went to an English battery that was but a very few yards from the walls of the citadel. There, indeed, I had an opportunity of completely gratifying myself in seeing the whole operation, and that not without running a very great risk, both from the English shells that burst while I was there, but likewise from those of the French. One of the largest of their shells bursted within nine or ten yards of me. There was a single rock close by, about the size of a butt; and I got instant shelter under it in time to avoid the fury of the shell. Where it burst, the earth was torn in such a manner that two or three butts might easily have gone into the hole it made, and it threw great quantities of stones and dirt to a considerable distance. Three shots were also fired at me and another boy, who was along with me, one of them in particular seemed

Wing'd with red lightning and impetuous rage;[11]

for, with a most dreadful sound it hissed close by me, and struck a rock at a little distance, which it shattered to pieces. When I saw what perilous circumstances I was in, I attempted to return the nearest way I could find, and thereby I got between the English and the French sentinels. An English sergeant, who commanded the out-posts, seeing me, and surprised how I came there (which was by stealth along the seashore), reprimanded me very severely for it, and instantly took the sentinel off his post into custody, for his negligence in suffering me to pass the lines.

While I was in this situation, I observed at a little distance a French horse, belonging to some islanders, which I thought I would now mount, for the greater expedition of getting off. Accordingly I took some cord, which I had about me, and making a kind of bridle of it, I put it round the horse's head, and the tame beast very quietly suffered me to tie him thus, and mount him. As soon as I was on the horse's back, I began to kick and beat him, and try every means to make him go quick, but all to very little purpose: I could not drive him out of a slow pace. While I was creeping along, still within reach of the enemy's shot, I met with a servant well

[11] John Milton, *Paradise Lost*, 1.175.

mounted on an English horse; I immediately stopped, and crying, told him my case, and begged of him to help me, and this he effectually did. For, having a fine large whip, he began to lash my horse with it so severely that he set off full speed with me towards the sea, while I was quite unable to hold or manage him. In this manner I went along till I came to a craggy precipice. I now could not stop my horse, and my mind was filled with apprehensions of my deplorable fate, should he go down the precipice, which he appeared fully disposed to do. I therefore thought I had better throw myself off him at once, which I did immediately, with a great deal of dexterity, and fortunately escaped unhurt. As soon as I found myself at liberty I made the best of my way for the ship, determined I would not be so foolhardy again in a hurry.

We continued to besiege the citadel till June, when it surrendered. During the siege, I have counted above sixty shells and carcases in the air at once. When this place was taken I went through the citadel, and in the bomb-proofs under it, which were cut in the solid rock; and I thought it a surprising place, both for strength and building: notwithstanding which our shots and shells had made amazing devastation, and ruinous heaps all around it.

After the taking of this island, our ships with some others commanded by Commodore Stanhope, in the *Swiftsure,* went to Basse road, where we blocked up a French fleet.[12] Our ships were there from June till February following; and in that time I saw a great many scenes of war, and stratagems on both sides to destroy each other's fleet. Sometimes we would attack the French with some ships of the line, at other times with boats, and frequently we made prizes. Once or twice the French attacked us by throwing shells with their bomb-vessels; and one day, as a French vessel was throwing shells at our ships, she broke from her springs, behind the isle of I-de-Re.[13] The tide being complicated, she came within a gun-shot of the *Nassau;* but the *Nassau* could not bring a gun to bear upon her, and thereby the Frenchman got off. We were twice attacked by their fire-floats, which they chained together, and then let them float down with the tide; but each time we sent boats with grapplings, and towed them safe out of the fleet.

We had different commanders while we were at this place, Commodores Stanhope, Dennis, Lord Howe, &c. From hence, before the Spanish war began, our ship and the *Wasp* sloop were sent to St. Sebastian, in Spain, by Commodore Stanhope; and Commodore Dennis after-

[12] Off La Rochelle and Rochefort, France.
[13] Île-de-Ré, in the Bay of Biscay.

wards sent our ship as a cartel, to Bayonne in France,[14] after which,[15] we went in February, in 1762, to Belle Isle, and there stayed till the summer, when we left it, and returned to Portsmouth.

After our ship was fitted out again for service, in September she went to Guernsey, where I was very glad to see my old hostess, who was now a widow, and my former little charming companion, her daughter. I spent some time here very happily with them, till October, when we had orders to repair to Portsmouth. We parted from each other with a great deal of affection; and I promised to return soon, and see them again, not knowing what all powerful fate had determined for me. Our ship having arrived at Portsmouth, we went into the harbor, and remained there till the latter end of November, when we heard great talk about a peace; and, to our very great joy, in the beginning of December we had orders to go up to London with our ship, to be paid off. We received this news with loud huzzas, and every other demonstration of gladness; and nothing but mirth was to be seen throughout every part of the ship. I too was not without my share of the general joy on this occasion.

I thought now of nothing but being freed, and working for myself, and thereby getting money to enable me to get a good education; for I always had a great desire to be able at least to read and write; and while I was on ship-board, I had endeavored to improve myself in both. While I was in the *Etna,* particularly, the captain's clerk taught me to write, and gave me a smattering of arithmetic, as far as the rule of three. There was also one Daniel Queen, about forty years of age, a man very well educated, who messed with me on board this ship, and he likewise dressed and attended the captain. Fortunately this man soon became very much attached to me, and took very great pains to instruct me in many things. He taught me to shave and dress hair a little, and also to read in the Bible, explaining many passages to me, which I did not comprehend. I was wonderfully surprised to see the laws and rules of my own country written almost exactly here; a

[14] Amongst others whom we brought from Bayonne were two gentlemen who had been in the West Indies, where they sold slaves; and they confessed they had made at one time a false bill of sale, and sold two Portuguese white men among a lot of slaves. [Equiano's note.]

[15] Some people have it, that sometimes shortly before persons die, their ward has been seen; that is, some spirit exactly in their likeness, though they are themselves at other places at the same time. One day while we were at Bayonne, Mr. Mondle saw one of our men, as he thought, in the gun-room; and a little after, coming on the quarter-deck, he spoke of some circumstances of this man to some of the officers. They told him that the man was then out of the ship, in one of the boats with the lieutenant; but Mr. Mondle would not believe it, and we searched the ship, when he found the man was actually out of her; and when the boat returned some time afterwards, we found the man had been drowned at the very time Mr. Mondle thought he saw him. [Equiano's note.]

circumstance which I believe tended to impress our manners and customs more deeply on my memory. I used to tell him of this resemblance, and many a time we have sat up the whole night together at this employment. In short, he was like a father to me, and some even used to call me after his name; they also styled me the black Christian. Indeed, I almost loved him with the affection of a son. Many things I have denied myself that he might have them; and when I used to play at marbles, or any other game, and won a few half-pence, or got any little money, which I sometimes did, for shaving anyone, I used to buy him a little sugar or tobacco, as far as my stock of money would go. He used to say, that he and I never should part; and that when our ship was paid off, as I was as free as himself, or any other man on board, he would instruct me in his business, by which I might gain a good livelihood.

This gave me new life and spirits; and my heart burned within me, while I thought the time long till I obtained my freedom. For though my master had not promised it to me, yet, besides the assurances I had received, that he had no right to detain me, he always treated me with the greatest kindness, and reposed in me an unbounded confidence; he even paid attention to my morals, and would never suffer me to deceive him, or tell lies, of which he used to tell me the consequences; and that if I did so, God would not love me. So that, from all this tenderness, I had never once supposed, in all my dreams of freedom, that he would think of detaining me any longer than I wished.

In pursuance of our orders, we sailed from Portsmouth for the Thames, and arrived at Deptford the 10th of December, where we cast anchor just as it was high water. The ship was up about half an hour, when my master ordered the barge to be manned; and all in an instant, without having before given me the least reason to suspect anything of the matter, he forced me into the barge, saying, I was going to leave him, but he would take care I should not. I was so struck with the unexpectedness of this proceeding, that for some time I did not make a reply, only I made an offer to go for my books and chest of clothes, but he swore I should not move out of his sight, and if I did, he would cut my throat, at the same time taking his hanger. I began, however, to collect myself, and plucking up courage, I told him I was free, and he could not by law serve me so. But this only enraged him the more: and he continued to swear, and said he would soon let me know whether he would or not, and at that instant sprung himself into the barge from the ship, to the astonishment and sorrow of all on board.

The tide, rather unluckily for me, had just turned downward, so that we quickly fell down the river along with it, till we came among some outward-bound West Indiamen; for he was resolved to put me on board the first vessel he could get to receive me. The boat's crew, who pulled against their will, became quite faint, different times, and would have gone ashore, but he would not let them. Some of them strove then to cheer me, and told me he could not sell me, and that they would stand by me, which revived me a little, and I still entertained hopes; for, as they pulled along, he asked some vessels to receive me, but they would not. But, just as we had got a little below Gravesend, we came alongside of a ship which was going away the next tide for the West Indies. Her name was the *Charming Sally,* Captain James Doran, and my master went on board, and agreed with him for me; and in a little time I was sent for into the cabin.

When I came there, Captain Doran asked me if I knew him. I answered that I did not. "Then," said he, "you are now my slave." I told him my master could not sell me to him, nor to anyone else. "Why," said he, "did not your master buy you?" I confessed he did. "But I have served him," said I, "many years, and he has taken all my wages and prize-money, for I had only got one six pence during the war; besides this I have been baptizcd, and by the laws of the land no man has a right to sell me." And I added that I had heard a lawyer and others at different times tcll my master so. They both then said that those people who told me so, were not my friends; but I replied, "It was very extraordinary that other people did not know the law as well as they."

Upon this Captain Doran said I talked too much English; and if I did not behave myself well, and be quiet, he had a method on board to make me. I was too well convinced of his power over me to doubt what he said; and my former sufferings in the slave-ship presenting themselves to my mind, the recollection of them made me shudder. However, before I retired I told them that, as I could not get any right among men here, I hoped I should hereafter in Heaven; and I immediately left the cabin, filled with resentment and sorrow. The only coat I had with me my master took away with him, and said, "If your prize money had been £10,000, I had a right to it all, and would have taken it."

I had about nine guineas, which, during my long sea-faring life, I had scraped together from trifling perquisites and little ventures; and I hid it at that instant, lest my master should take that from me likewise, still hoping that by some means or other I should make my escape to the shore; and indeed some of my old shipmates told me not to despair, for they would get me back again; and that, as soon as they could get their pay, they would immediately come to Portsmouth to me, where the ship was going. But, alas! all my hopes were baffled, and the hour of my deliverance was yet far off. My master, having soon concluded his bargain with the captain, came out of the cabin, and he and his people got into the boat and put off. I followed them with aching eyes as long as I could, and when they were out of sight I threw myself on the deck, with a heart ready to burst with sorrow and anguish.

CHAPTER 5

The author's reflections on his situation—Is deceived by a promise of being delivered—His despair at sailing for the West Indies—Arrives at Montserrat, where he is sold to Mr. King—Various interesting instances of oppression, cruelty, and extortion, which the author saw practised upon the slaves in the West Indies, during his captivity from the years 1763 to 1766—Address on it to the planters.

Thus, at the moment I expected all my toils to end, was I plunged, as I supposed, in a new slavery; in comparison of which, all my service hitherto had been perfect freedom; and whose horrors, always present to my mind, now rushed on it with tenfold aggravation. I wept very bitterly for some time: and began to think I must have done something to displease the Lord, that he thus punished me so severely. This filled me with painful reflections on my past conduct; I recollected that on the morning of our arrival at Deptford, I had rashly sworn that as soon as we reached London I would spend the day in rambling and sport. My conscience smote me for this unguarded expression: I felt that the Lord was able to disappoint me in all things, and immediately considered my present situation as a judgment of Heaven, on account of my presumption in swearing: I therefore, with contrition of heart, acknowledged my transgression to God, and poured out my soul before him with unfeigned repentance, and with earnest supplications I besought him not to abandon me in my distress, nor cast me from his mercy forever. In a little time, my grief, spent with its own violence, began to subside, and after the first confusion of my thoughts was over, I reflected with more calmness on my present condition. I considered that trials and disappointments are sometimes for our good, and I thought God might perhaps have permitted this, in order to teach me wisdom and resignation; for he had hitherto shadowed me with the wings of his mercy, and by his invisible but powerful hand brought me the way I knew not. These reflections gave me a little comfort, and I rose at last from the deck with dejection and sorrow in my countenance, yet mixed with some faint hope that the *Lord would appear* for my deliverance.

Soon afterwards, as my new master was going on shore, he called me to him, and told me to behave myself well, and do the business of the ship the same as any of the rest of the boys, and that I should fare the better for it; but I made him no answer. I was then asked if I could swim, and I said, No. However, I was made to go under the deck, and was well watched. The next tide the ship got under way, and soon after arrived at the Mother Bank, Portsmouth, where she waited a few days for some of the West India convoy. While I was here I tried every means I could devise, amongst the people of the ship, to get me a boat from the shore, as there was none suffered to come alongside of the ship; and their own, whenever it was used, was hoisted in again immediately. A sailor on board took a guinea from me on pretence of getting me a boat, and promised me, time after time, that it was hourly to come off. When he had the watch upon deck, I watched also, and looked long enough, but all in vain; I could never see either the boat or my guinea again. And what I thought was still the worst of all, the fellow gave information, as I afterwards found, all the while to the mates, of my intention to go off, if I could in any way do it; but, rogue-like, he never told them he had got a guinea from me to procure my escape. However, after we had sailed, and his trick was made known to the ship's crew, I had some satisfaction in seeing him detested and despised by them all, for his behavior to me.

I was still in hopes that my old shipmates would not forget their promise to come for me at Portsmouth. And, indeed, at last, but not till the day before we sailed, some of them did come there, and sent me off some oranges, and other tokens of their regard. They also sent me word they would come off to me themselves the next day or the day after; and a lady also, who lived in Gosport, wrote to me that she would come and take me out of the ship at the same time. This lady had been once very intimate with my former master. I used to sell and take care of a great deal of property for her, in different ships; and in return she always showed great friendship for me, and used to tell my master that she would take me away to live with her: but, unfortunately for me, a disagreement soon afterwards took place between them; and she was succeeded in my master's good graces by another lady, who appeared sole mistress of the *Etna,* and mostly lodged on board. I was not so great a favorite with this lady as with the former; she had conceived a pique against me on some occasion when she was on board, and she did not fail to instigate my master to treat me in the manner he did.[1]

---

[1] Thus was I sacrificed to the envy and resentment of this woman for knowing that the lady whom she had succeeded in my master's good graces, designed to take me into her service; which, had I once got on shore, she would not have been able to prevent. She felt her pride alarmed at the superiority of her rival, in being attended by a black servant. It was not less to prevent this, than to be revenged on me, that she caused the captain to treat me thus cruelly. [Equiano's note.]

However, the next morning, the 30th of December, the wind being brisk and easterly, the *Eolus* frigate, which was to escort the convoy, made a signal for sailing. All the ships then got up their anchors; and, before any of my friends had an opportunity to come off to my relief, to my inexpressible anguish, our ship had got under way. What tumultuous emotions agitated my soul when the convoy got under sail, and I a prisoner on board, now without hope! I kept my swimming eyes upon the land in a state of unutterable grief; not knowing what to do, and despairing how to help myself. While my mind was in this situation, the fleet sailed on, and in one day's time I lost sight of the wished-for land. In the first expression of my grief I reproached my fate, and wished I had never been born. I was ready to curse the tide that bore us, the gale that wafted my prison, and even the ship that conducted us; and I called on death to relieve me from the horrors I felt and dreaded, that I might be in that place

> Where slaves are free, and men oppress no more.
> Fool that I was, inur'd so long to pain,
> To trust to hope, or dream of joy again.
> . . . .
> Now dragg'd once more beyond the western main,
> To groan beneath some dastard planter's chain;
> Where my poor countrymen in bondage wait
> The long enfranchisement of a ling'ring fate.
> Hard ling'ring fate! while, ere the dawn of day,
> Rous'd by the lash they go their cheerless way;
> And as their souls with shame and anguish burn,
> Salute with groans unwelcome morn's return;
> And, chiding ev'ry hour the slow pac'd sun,
> Pursue their toils till all his race is run.
> No eye to mark their suff'rings with a tear,
> No friend to comfort, and no hope to cheer;
> Then, like the dull unpity'd brutes, repair
> To stalls as wretched, and as coarse a fare;
> Thank heaven one day of misery was o'er,
> Then sink to sleep, and wish to wake no more.[2]

The turbulence of my emotions, however, naturally gave way to calmer thoughts, and I soon perceived what fate had decreed no mortal on earth

---

[2] "The Dying Negro" [by Thomas Day], a poem originally published in 1773. Perhaps it may not be deemed impertinent here to add, that this elegant and pathetic little poem was occasioned, as appears by the advertisement prefixed to it, by the following incident. "A black, who, a few days before had run away from his master, and got himself christened, with intent to marry a white woman, his fellow-servant, being taken and sent on board a ship in the Thames, took an opportunity of shooting himself through the head." [Equiano's note.]

could prevent. The convoy sailed on without any accident, with a pleasant gale and smooth sea, for six weeks, till February, when one morning the *Eolus* ran down a brig, one of the convoy, and she instantly went down, and was engulfed in the dark recesses of the ocean. The convoy was immediately thrown into great confusion till it was day-light; and the *Eolus* was illumined with lights, to prevent any further mischief. On the 13th of February, 1763, from the mast-head, we descried our destined island, Montserrat; and soon after I beheld those

> Regions of sorrow, doleful shades, where peace
> And rest can rarely dwell. Hope never comes
> That comes to all, but torture without end
> Still urges.[3]

At the sight of this land of bondage, a fresh horror ran through all my frame, and chilled me to the heart. My former slavery now rose in dreadful review to my mind, and displayed nothing but misery, stripes, and chains; and, in the first paroxysm of my grief, I called upon God's thunder, and his avenging power, to direct the stroke of death to me, rather than permit me to become a slave, and be sold from lord to lord.

In this state of my mind our ship came to anchor, and soon after discharged her cargo. I now knew what it was to work hard; I was made to help unload and load the ship. And, to comfort me in my distress in that time, two of the sailors robbed me of all my money, and ran away from the ship. I had been so long used to a European climate, that at first I felt the scorching West India sun very painful, while the dashing surf would toss the boat and the people in it, frequently above high water mark. Sometimes our limbs were broken with this, or even attended with instant death, and I was day by day mangled and torn.

About the middle of May, when the ship was got ready to sail for England, I all the time believing that fate's blackest clouds were gathering over my head, and expecting their bursting would mix me with the dead, Captain Doran sent for me ashore one morning, and I was told by the messenger that my fate was then determined. With trembling steps and fluttering heart, I came to the captain, and found with him one Mr. Robert King, a Quaker, and the first merchant in the place. The captain then told me my former master had sent me there to be sold; but that he had desired him to get me the best master he could, as he told him I was a very deserving boy, which Captain Doran said he found to be true; and if he were to stay in the West Indies, he would be glad to keep me himself; but he could not venture to take me to London, for he was very sure that when

[3] Milton, *Paradise Lost,* 1.65–68.

I came there I would leave him. I at that instant burst out a crying, and begged much of him to take me to England with him, but all to no purpose. He told me he had got me the very best master in the whole island, with whom I should be as happy as if I were in England, and for that reason he chose to let him have me, though he could sell me to his own brother-in-law for a great deal more money than what he got from this gentleman. Mr. King, my new master, then made a reply, and said the reason he had bought me was on account of my good character; and as he had not the least doubt of my good behavior, I should be very well off with him. He also told me he did not live in the West Indies, but at Philadelphia, where he was going soon; and, as I understood something of the rules of arithmetic, when we got there he would put me to school, and fit me for a clerk.

This conversation relieved my mind a little, and I left those gentlemen considerably more at ease in myself than when I came to them; and I was very thankful to Captain Doran, and even to my old master, for the character they had given me: a character which I afterwards found of infinite service to me. I went on board again, and took leave of all my ship-mates, and the next day the ship sailed. When she weighed anchor, I went to the waterside and looked at her with a very wishful and aching heart, and followed her with my eyes until she was totally out of sight. I was so bowed down with grief, that I could not hold up my head for many months; and if my new master had not been kind to me, I believe I should have died under it at last. And, indeed, I soon found that he fully deserved the good character which Captain Doran gave me of him, for he possessed a most amiable disposition and temper, and was very charitable and humane. If any of his slaves behaved amiss he did not beat or use them ill, but parted with them. This made them afraid of disobliging him; and as he treated his slaves better than any other man on the island, so he was better and more faithfully served by them in return. By this kind treatment I did at last endeavor to compose myself; and with fortitude, though moneyless, determined to face whatever fate had decreed for me. Mr. King soon asked me what I could do; and at the same time said he did not mean to treat me as a common slave. I told him I knew something of seamanship, and could shave and dress hair pretty well; and I could refine wines, which I had learned on shipboard, where I had often done it; and that I could write, and understood arithmetic tolerably well, as far as the Rule of Three. He then asked me if I knew anything of gauging;[4] and, on my answering that I did not, he said one of his clerks should teach me to gauge.

---

[4] Measuring.

Mr. King dealt in all manner of merchandise, and kept from one to six clerks. He loaded many vessels in a year; particularly to Philadelphia, where he was born; and was connected with a great mercantile house in that city. He had, besides, many vessels and droggers,[5] of different sizes, which used to go about the island; and others, to collect rum, sugar, and other goods. I understood pulling and managing those boats very well; and this hard work, which was the first that he set me to, in the sugar seasons used to be my constant employment. I have rowed the boat, and slaved at the oars, from one hour to sixteen in the twenty-four, during which I had fifteen pence sterling per day to live on, though sometimes only ten pence.

However, this was considerably more than was allowed to other slaves that used to work often with me, and belonged to other gentlemen on the island. Those poor souls had never more than nine pence per day, and seldom more than six pence, from their masters or owners, though they earned them three or four pistareens.[6] For it is a common practice in the West Indies for men to purchase slaves, though they have not plantations themselves, in order to let them out to planters and merchants at so much a piece by the day, and they give what allowance they choose out of this product of their daily work to their slaves for subsistence; this allowance is often very scanty. My master often gave the owners of the slaves two and a half of these pieces per day, and found the poor fellows in victuals himself, because he thought their owners did not feed them well enough according to the work they did.

The slaves used to like this very well; and, as they knew my master to be a man of feeling, they were always glad to work for him, in preference to any other gentleman; some of whom, after they had been paid for these poor people's labors, would not give them their allowance out of it. Many times have I even seen these unfortunate wretches beaten for asking for their pay; and often severely flogged by their owners if they did not bring them their daily or weekly money exactly to the time; though the poor creatures were obliged to wait on the gentlemen they had worked for, sometimes more than half the day before they could get their pay; and this generally on Sundays, when they wanted the time for themselves. In particular, I knew a countryman of mine who once did not bring the weekly money directly that it was earned; and, though he brought it the same day to his master, yet he was staked to the ground for his pretended negligence, and was just going to receive a hundred lashes, but for a gentleman who begged him off with fifty.

This poor man was very industrious; and by his frugality, had saved so

[5] [droggers]. Slow, clumsy boats.
[6] These pistareens are of the value of a shilling. [Equiano's note.]

much money by working on ship-board, that he had got a white man to buy him a boat, unknown to his master. Some time after he had this little estate, the governor wanted a boat to bring his sugar from different parts of the island; and, knowing this to be a Negro man's boat, he seized upon it for himself, and would not pay the owner a farthing. The man, on this, went to his master, and complained to him of this act of the governor; but the only satisfaction he received was to be damned very heartily by his master, who asked him how dared any of his Negroes to have a boat. If the justly merited ruin of the governor's fortune could be any gratification to the poor man he had thus robbed, he was not without consolation. Extortion and rapine are poor providers; and some time after this the governor died in the King's Bench[7] in England, as I was told, in great poverty. The last war favored this poor Negro man, and he found some means to escape from his Christian master. He came to England, where I saw him afterwards several times. Such treatment as this often drives these miserable wretches to despair, and they run away from their masters at the hazard of their lives. Many of them, in this place, unable to get their pay when they have earned it, and fearing to be flogged, as usual, if they return home without it, run away where they can for shelter, and a reward is often offered to bring them in dead or alive. My master used sometimes, in these cases, to agree with their owners, and to settle with them himself; and thereby he saved many of them a flogging.

Once, for a few days, I was let out to fit a vessel, and I had no victuals allowed me by either party; at last I told my master of this treatment, and he took me away from it. In many of the estates, on the different islands where I used to be sent for rum or sugar, they would not deliver it to me, or any other Negro; he was therefore obliged to send a white man along with me to those places; and then he used to pay him from six to ten pistareens a day. From being thus employed, during the time I served Mr. King, in going about the different estates on the island, I had all the opportunity I could wish for, to see the dreadful usage of the poor men; usage that reconciled me to my situation, and made me bless God for the hands into which I had fallen.

I had the good fortune to please my master in every department in which he employed me; and there was scarcely any part of his business, or household affairs, in which I was not occasionally engaged. I often supplied the place of a clerk, in receiving and delivering cargoes to the ships, in tending stores, and delivering goods. And besides this, I used to shave and dress my master when convenient, and take care of his horse; and when it

[7] A London prison.

was necessary, which was very often, I worked likewise on board of different vessels of his. By these means I became very useful to my master, and saved him, as he used to acknowledge, above a hundred pounds a year. Nor did he scruple to say I was of more advantage to him than any of his clerks; though their usual wages in the West Indies are from sixty to a hundred pounds current a year.

I have sometimes heard it asserted that a Negro cannot earn his master the first cost; but nothing can be further from the truth. I suppose nine-tenths of the mechanics throughout the West Indies are Negro slaves; and I well know the coopers[8] among them earn two dollars a day, the carpenters the same, and oftentimes more; as also the masons, smiths, and fishermen, &c. and I have known many slaves whose masters would not take a thousand pounds current for them. But surely this assertion refutes itself; for, if it be true, why do the planters and merchants pay such a price for slaves? And, above all, why do those who make this assertion exclaim the most loudly against the abolition of the slave trade? So much are men blinded, and to such inconsistent arguments are they driven by mistaken interest! I grant, indeed, that slaves are sometimes, by half-feeding, half-clothing, over-working, and stripes, reduced so low, that they are turned out as unfit for service, and left to perish in the woods, or expire on a dung-hill.

My master was several times offered by different gentlemen one hundred guineas for me, but he always told them he would not sell me, to my great joy. And I used to double my diligence and care, for fear of getting into the hands of those men who did not allow a valuable slave the common support of life. Many of them even used to find fault with my master for feeding his slaves so well as he did, although I often went hungry, and an Englishman might think my fare very indifferent; but he used to tell them he always would do it, because the slaves thereby looked better and did more work.

While I was thus employed by my master, I was often a witness to cruelties of every kind, which were exercised on my unhappy fellow slaves. I used frequently to have different cargoes of new Negroes in my care for sale; and it was almost a constant practice with our clerks, and other whites, to commit violent depredations on the chastity of the female slaves; and these I was, though with reluctance, obliged to submit to at all times, being unable to help them. When we have had some of these slaves on board my master's vessels, to carry them to other islands, or to America, I have known our mates to commit these acts most shamefully,

---

[8] Barrel makers.

to the disgrace, not of Christians only, but of men. I have even known them to gratify their brutal passion with females not ten years old; and these abominations, some of them practised to such scandalous excess, that one of our captains discharged the mate and others on that account. And yet in Montserrat I have seen a Negro man staked to the ground, and cut most shockingly, and then his ears cut off bit by bit, because he had been connected with a white woman who was a common prostitute; as if it were no crime in the whites to rob an innocent African girl of her virtue, but most heinous in a black man only to gratify a passion of nature, where the temptation was offered by one of a different color, though the most abandoned woman of her species.

One Mr. D—— told me that he had sold 41,000 Negroes, and that he once cut off a Negro man's leg for running away. I asked him if the man had died in the operation, how he, as a Christian, could answer for the horrid act before God? and he told me, answering was a thing of another world, what he thought and did were policy. I told him that the Christian doctrine taught us to do unto others as we would that others should do unto us. He then said that his scheme had the desired effect—it cured that man and some others of running away.

Another Negro man was half hanged, and then burnt, for attempting to poison a cruel overseer. Thus by repeated cruelties, are the wretched first urged to despair, and then murdered, because they still retain so much of human nature about them as to wish to put an end to their misery, and retaliate on their tyrants! These overseers are indeed for the most part persons of the worst character of any denomination of men in the West Indies. Unfortunately, many humane gentlemen, by not residing on their estates, are obliged to leave the management of them in the hands of these human butchers, who cut and mangle the slaves in a shocking manner on the most trifling occasions, and altogether treat them in every respect like brutes. They pay no regard to the situation of pregnant women, nor the least attention to the lodging of the field Negroes. Their huts, which ought to be well covered, and the place dry where they take their little repose, are often open sheds, built in damp places; so that when the poor creatures return tired from the toils of the field, they contract many disorders, from being exposed to the damp air in this uncomfortable state, while they are heated, and their pores are open. This neglect certainly conspires with many others to cause a decrease in the births as well as in the lives of the grown Negroes.

I can quote many instances of gentlemen who reside on their estates in the West Indies, and then the scene is quite changed; the Negroes are treated with lenity and proper care, by which their lives are prolonged, and their masters profited. To the honor of humanity, I knew several gentlemen who managed their estates in this manner, and they found that benevolence was their true interest. And, among many I could mention in several of the islands, I knew one in Monserrat[9] whose slaves looked remarkably well, and never needed any fresh supplies of Negroes; and there are many other estates, especially in Barbadoes, which, from such judicious treatment, need no fresh stock of Negroes at any time. I have the honor of knowing a most worthy and humane gentleman, who is a native of Barbadoes, and has estates there.[10] This gentleman has written a treatise on the usage of his own slaves. He allows them two hours of refreshment at mid-day, and many other indulgencies and comforts, particularly in their lodging; and, besides this, he raises more provisions on his estate than they can destroy; so that by these attentions he saves the lives of his Negroes, and keeps them healthy, and as happy as the condition of slavery can admit. I myself, as shall appear in the sequel, managed an estate, where, by those attentions, the Negroes were uncommonly cheerful and healthy, and did more work by half than by the common mode of treatment they usually do. For want, therefore, of such care and attention to the poor Negroes, and otherwise oppressed as they are, it is no wonder that the decrease should require 20,000 new Negroes annually to fill up the vacant places of the dead.

Even in Barbadoes, notwithstanding those humane exceptions which I have mentioned, and others I am acquainted with, which justly make it quoted as a place where slaves meet with the best treatment, and need fewest recruits of any in the West Indies, yet this island requires 1,000 Negroes annually to keep up the original stock, which is only 80,000. So that the whole term of a Negro's life may be said to be there but sixteen years![11] And yet the climate here in every respect is the same as that from which they are taken, except in being more wholesome. Do the British colonies decrease in this manner? And yet what prodigious difference is there between an English and West India climate?

While I was in Montserrat I knew a Negro man, named Emanuel Sankey, who endeavored to escape from his miserable bondage, by concealing himself on board of a London ship: but fate did not favor the poor oppressed man; for, being discovered when the vessel was under sail, he was delivered up again to his master. This *Christian master* immediately pinned the wretch down to the ground at each wrist and ankle, and then took some sticks of sealing wax, and lighted them, and dropped it all over

[9] Mr. Dubury, and many others, Montserrat. [Equiano's note.]
[10] Sir Phillip Gibbes, Baronet, Barbadoes. [Equiano's note.]
[11] Benezet's "Account of Guinea," p. 16. [Equiano's note.]

his back. There was another master who was noted for cruelty; and I believe he had not a slave but what had been cut, and had pieces fairly taken out of the flesh. And after they had been punished thus, he used to make them get into a long wooden box or case he had for that purpose, in which he shut them up during pleasure. It was just about the height and breadth of a man; and the poor wretches had no room, when in the case, to move.

It was very common in several of the islands, particularly in St. Kitts, for the slaves to be branded with the initial letters of their master's name; and a load of heavy iron hooks hung about their necks. Indeed on the most trifling occasions they were loaded with chains; and often instruments of torture were added. The iron muzzle, thumb-screws, &c., are so well known as not to need a description, and were sometimes applied for the slightest faults. I have seen a Negro beaten till some of his bones were broken, for only letting a pot boil over. Is it surprising that usage like this should drive the poor creatures to despair, and make them seek a refuge in death from those evils which render their lives intolerable? — while,

> With shudd'ring horror pale, and eyes aghast,
> They view their lamentable lot, and find
> No rest![12]

This they frequently do. A Negro man, on board a vessel of my master, while I belonged to her, having been put in irons for some trifling misdemeanor, and kept in that state for some days, being weary of life, took an opportunity of jumping overboard into the sea; however, he was picked up without being drowned. Another, whose life was also a burden to him, resolved to starve himself to death, and refused to eat any victuals. This procured him a severe flogging; and he also, on the first occasion which offered, jumped overboard at Charleston, but was saved.

Nor is there any greater regard shown to the little property than there is to the persons and lives of the Negroes. I have already related an instance or two of particular oppression out of many which I have witnessed; but the following is frequent in all the islands. The wretched field slaves, after toiling all the day for an unfeeling owner, who gives them but little victuals, steal sometimes a few moments from rest or refreshment to gather some small portion of grass, according as their time will admit. This they commonly tie up in a parcel; either a bit's worth (six pence) or half a bit's worth, and bring it to town, or to the market, to sell. Nothing is more common than for the white people on this occasion to take the grass from them without paying for it; and not only so, but too often also, to my knowledge, our clerks, and many others, at the same time

[12] Milton, *Paradise Lost,* 2.616–18.

have committed acts of violence on the poor, wretched, and helpless females; whom I have seen for hours stand crying to no purpose, and get no redress or pay of any kind. Is not this one common and crying sin enough to bring down God's judgment on the islands? He tells us the oppressor and the oppressed are both in his hands; and if these are not the poor, the broken-hearted, the blind, the captive, the bruised, which our Saviour speaks of, who are they?

One of these depredators once, in St. Eustatius, came on board of our vessel, and bought some fowls and pigs of me; and a whole day after his departure with the things, he returned again and wanted his money back. I refused to give it, and, not seeing my captain on board, he began the common pranks with me; and swore he would even break open my chest and take my money. I therefore expected, as my captain was absent, that he would be as good as his word. And was just proceeding to strike me, when fortunately a British seaman on board, whose heart had not been debauched by a West India climate, interposed and prevented him. But had the cruel man struck me I certainly should have defended myself at the hazard of my life; for what is life to a man thus oppressed? He went away, however, swearing, and threatened that whenever he caught me on shore, he would shoot me, and pay for me afterwards.

The small account in which the life of a Negro is held in the West Indies is so universally known that it might seem impertinent to quote the following extract, if some people had not been hardy enough of late to assert that Negroes are on the same footing in that respect as Europeans. By the 329th Act, page 125, of the Assembly of Barbadoes, it is enacted "That if any Negro, or other slave, under punishment by his master, or his order, for running away, or any other crime or misdemeanor towards his said master, unfortunately shall suffer in life or member, no person whatsoever shall be liable to a fine; but if any person shall, out of *wantonness, or only of bloody-mindedness, or cruel intention, willfully kill a Negro, or other slave, of his own, he shall pay into the public treasury fifteen pounds sterling.*" And it is the same in most, if not all of the West India islands. Is not this one of the many acts of the islands which call loudly for redress? And do not the assembly which enacted it deserve the appellation of savages and brutes rather than of Christians and men? It is an act at once unmerciful, unjust, and unwise; which for cruelty would disgrace an assembly of those who are called barbarians; and for its injustice and *insanity* would shock the morality and common sense of a Samaide or Hottentot.[13]

---

[13] Samoyeds are Mongolians in Siberia; the Hottentots live in southern Africa. Europeans regarded both as barbaric, or uncivilized.

Shocking as this and many more acts of the bloody West India code at first view appear, how is the iniquity of it heightened when we consider to whom it may be extended! Mr. James Tobin, a zealous laborer in the vineyard of slavery, gives an account of a French planter of his acquaintance, in the island of Martinique, who showed him many mulattoes working in the field like beasts of burden; and he told Mr. Tobin these were all the produce of his own loins![14] And I myself have known similar instances. Pray, reader, are these sons and daughters of the French planter less his children by being the progeny of black women? And what must be the virtue of those legislators, and the feelings of those fathers, who estimate the lives of their sons, however begotten, at no more than fifteen pounds; though they should be murdered, as the act says, *out of wantonness and bloody-mindedness!* But is not the slave trade entirely at war with the heart of man? And surely that which is begun by breaking down the barriers of virtue, involves in its continuance destruction to every principle, and buries all sentiment in ruin!

I have often seen slaves, particularly those who were meagre, in different islands, put into scales and weighed, and then sold from three pence to six pence or nine pence a pound. My master, however, whose humanity was shocked at this mode, used to sell such by the lump. And at or after a sale, it was not uncommon to see Negroes taken from their wives, wives taken from their husbands, and children from their parents, and sent off to other islands, and wherever else their merciless lords choose; and probably never more during life see each other! Oftentimes my heart has bled at these partings, when the friends of the departed have been at the waterside, and with sighs and tears, have kept their eyes fixed on the vessel, till it went out of sight.

A poor Creole Negro, I knew well, who, after having been often thus transported from island to island, at last resided in Montserrat. This man used to tell me many melancholy tales of himself. Generally, after he had done working for his master, he used to employ his few leisure moments to go a fishing. When he had caught any fish, his master would frequently take them from him without paying him; and at other times some other white people would serve him in the same manner. One day he said to me, very movingly, "Sometimes when a white man take away my fish, I go to my maser, and he get me my right; and when my maser by strength take

---

[14] James Tobin was an English merchant who lived in Nevis from 1775 to 1783. A defender of slavery, his 1785 *Cursory Remarks* attacked abolitionist James Ramsay's antislavery *Essay on the Treatment and Conversion of African Slaves in the British Sugar Colonies* (London, 1784). His son James Webbe Tobin remained in Nevis and became a corresponding member of the African Institution, a British antislavery group.

away my fishes, what me must do? I can't go to any body to be righted; then," said the poor man, looking up above, "I must look up to God Mighty in the top for right." This artless tale moved me much, and I could not help feeling the just cause Moses had in redressing his brother against the Egyptian.[15] I exhorted the man to look up still to the God on the top, since there was no redress below. Though I little thought then that I myself should more than once experience such imposition, and need the same exhortation hereafter, in my own transactions in the islands, and that even this poor man and I should some time after suffer together in the same manner, as shall be related hereafter.

Nor was such usage as this confined to particular places or individuals, for in all the different islands in which I have been (and I have visited no less than fifteen) the treatment of the slaves was nearly the same; so nearly, indeed, that the history of an island, or even a plantation, with a few such exceptions as I have mentioned, might serve for a history of the whole. Such a tendency has the slave trade to debauch men's minds, and harden them to every feeling of humanity! For I will not suppose that the dealers in slaves are born worse than other men—No; such is the fatality of this mistaken avarice that it corrupts the milk of human kindness and turns it into gall. And, had the pursuits of those men been different, they might have been as generous, as tender-hearted and just, as they are unfeeling, rapacious, and cruel. Surely this traffic cannot be good, which spreads like a pestilence, and taints what it touches! which violates that first natural right of mankind, equality and independency, and gives one man a dominion over his fellows which God could never intend! For it raises the owner to a state as far above man as it depresses the slave below it; and, with all the presumption of human pride, sets a distinction between them, immeasurable in extent, and endless in duration! Yet how mistaken is the avarice even of the planters. Are slaves more useful by being thus humbled to the condition of brutes than they would be if suffered to enjoy the privileges of men? The freedom which diffuses health and prosperity throughout Britain answers you—No. When you make men slaves, you deprive them of half their virtue; you set them, in your own conduct, an example of fraud, rapine, and cruelty, and compel them to live with you in a state of war; and yet you complain that they are not honest or faithful! You stupify them with stripes, and think it necessary to keep them in a state of ignorance. And yet you assert that they are incapable of learning; that their minds are such a barren soil or moor that culture would be lost on them; and that they come from a climate where

[15] Exodus 2:11–12.

nature, though prodigal of her bounties in a degree unknown to yourselves, has left man alone scant and unfinished, and incapable of enjoying the treasures she has poured out for him! An assertion at once impious and absurd. Why do you use those instruments of torture? Are they fit to be applied by one rational being to another? And are ye not struck with shame and mortification, to see the partakers of your nature reduced so low? But, above all, are there no dangers attending this mode of treatment? Are you not hourly in dread of an insurrection? Nor would it be surprising; for when

> ———No peace is given
> To us enslav'd, but custody severe,
> And stripes and arbitrary punishment
> Inflicted—What peace can we return?
> But to our power, hostility and hate;
> Untam'd reluctance, and revenge, though slow.
> Yet ever plotting how the conqueror least
> May reap his conquest, and may least rejoice
> In doing what we most in suffering feel.[16]

But by changing your conduct, and treating your slaves as men, every cause of fear would be banished. They would be faithful, honest, intelligent, and vigorous; and peace, prosperity, and happiness would attend you.

[16] Milton, *Paradise Lost*, 2.332–40.

CHAPTER 6

Some account of Brimstone Hill in Montserrat—Favorable change in the author's situation—He commences merchant with three pence—His various success in dealing in the different islands, and America, and the impositions he meets with in his transactions with Europeans—A curious imposition on human nature—Danger of the surfs in the West Indies—Remarkable instance of kidnapping a free mulatto—The author is nearly murdered by Doctor Perkins in Savannah.

In the preceding chapter I have set before the reader a few of those many instances of oppression, extortion, and cruelty which I have been a witness to in the West Indies; but were I to enumerate them all, the catalogue would be tedious and disgusting. The punishments of the slaves on every trifling occasion are so frequent, and so well known, together with the different instruments with which they are tortured, that it cannot any longer afford novelty to recite them; and they are too shocking to yield delight either to the writer or the reader. I shall therefore hereafter only mention such as incidentally befell myself in the course of my adventures.

In the variety of departments in which I was employed by my master, I had an opportunity of seeing many curious scenes in different islands; but, above all, I was struck with a celebrated curiosity called Brimstone Hill, which is a high and steep mountain, some few miles from the town of Plymouth in Montserrat. I had often heard of some wonders that were to be seen on this hill, and I went once with some white and black people to visit it. When we arrived at the top, I saw under different cliffs great flakes of brimstone, occasioned by the streams of various little ponds, which were then boiling naturally in the earth. Some of these ponds were as white as milk, some quite blue, and many others of different colors. I had taken some potatoes with me, and I put them into different ponds, and in a few minutes they were well boiled. I tasted some of them, but they were very sulphurous; and the silver shoe buckles, and all the other things of that metal we had among us, were, in a little time turned as black as lead.

Sometime in the year 1763, kind Providence seemed to appear rather more favorable to me. One of my master's vessels, a Bermudas sloop, about sixty tons burthen, was commanded by one Captain Thomas Farmer, an Englishman, a very alert and active man, who gained my master a great deal of money by his good management in carrying passengers from one island to another; but very often his sailors used to get drunk and run away from the vessel, which hindered him in his business very much. This man had taken a liking to me, and many times begged of my master to let me go a trip with him as a sailor; but he would tell him he could not spare me, though the vessel sometimes could not go for want of hands, for sailors were generally very scarce in the island. However, at last, from necessity or force, my master was prevailed on, though very reluctantly, to let me go with this captain; but he gave him great charge to take care that I did not run away, for if I did he would make him pay for me. This being the case, the captain had for some time a sharp eye upon me whenever the vessel anchored; and as soon as she returned I was sent for on shore again.

Thus was I slaving, as it were, for life, sometimes at one thing, and sometimes at another: so that the captain and I were nearly the most useful men in my master's employment. I also became so useful to the captain on ship-board, that many times, when he used to ask for me to go with him, though it should be but for twenty-four hours, to some of the islands near us, my master would answer he could not spare me, at which the captain would swear, and would not go the trip, and tell my master I was better to him on board than any three white men he had; for they used to behave ill in many respects, particularly in getting drunk; and then they frequently got the boat stove, so as to hinder the vessel from coming back as soon as she might have done. This my master knew very well; and at last, by the captain's constant entreaties, after I had been several times with him, one day to my great joy, told me the captain would not let him rest, and asked whether I would go aboard as a sailor, or stay on shore and mind the stores, for he could not bear any longer to be plagued in this manner. I was very happy at this proposal, for I immediately thought I might in time stand some chance by being on board to get a little money, or possibly make my escape if I should be used ill. I also expected to get better food, and in greater abundance; for I had oftentimes felt much hunger, though my master treated his slaves, as I have observed, uncommonly well. I therefore, without hesitation, answered him, that I would go and be a sailor if he pleased. Accordingly I was ordered on board directly. Nevertheless, between the vessel and the shore, when she was in port, I had little or no rest, as my master always wished to have me along with him. Indeed he was a very pleasant gentleman, and but for my expectations on ship-board, I should not have thought of leaving him. But the captain liked me also very much, and I was entirely his right-hand man. I did all I could to deserve his favor, and in return I received better treatment from him than any other I believe ever met with in the West Indies in my situation.

After I had been sailing for some time with this captain, at length I endeavored to try my luck, and commence merchant. I had but a very small capital to begin with; for one single half bit, which is equal to three pence in England, made up my whole stock. However, I trusted to the Lord to be with me; and at one of our trips to St. Eustatius, a Dutch island, I bought a glass tumbler with my half bit, and when I came to Montserrat, I sold it for a bit, or six pence. Luckily we made several successive trips to St. Eustatius (which was a general mart for the West Indies, about twenty leagues from Montserrat), and in our next, finding my tumbler so profitable, with this one bit I bought two tumblers more; and when I came back, I sold them for two bits, equal to a shilling sterling. When we went again, I bought with these two bits four more of these glasses, which I sold for four bits on our return to Montserrat. And in our next voyage to St. Eustatius, I bought two glasses with one bit, and with the other three I bought a jug of Geneva,[1] nearly about three pints in measure. When we came to Montserrat, I sold the gin for eight bits, and the tumblers for two, so that my

[1] Gin.

capital now amounted in all to a dollar, well husbanded and acquired in the space of a month or six weeks, when I blessed the Lord that I was so rich. As we sailed to different islands, I laid this money out in various things occasionally, and it used to turn to very good account, especially when we went to Guadeloupe, Grenada, and the rest of the French islands.

Thus was I going all about the islands upwards of four years, and ever trading as I went, during which I experienced many instances of ill usage, and have seen many injuries done to other Negroes in our dealings with whites. And, amidst our recreations, when we have been dancing and merry-making, they, without cause, have molested and insulted us. Indeed, I was more than once obliged to look up to God on high, as I had advised the poor fisherman some time before. And I had not been long trading for myself in the manner I have related above, when I experienced the like trial in company with him as follows: this man being used to the water, was upon an emergency put on board of us by his master, to work as another hand, on a voyage to Santa Cruz; and at our sailing he had brought his little all for a venture, which consisted of six bits' worth of limes and oranges in a bag; I had also my whole stock, which was about twelve bits' worth of the same kind of goods, separate in two bags, for we had heard these fruits sold well in that island. When we came there, in some little convenient time, he and I went ashore with our fruits to sell them; but we had scarcely landed, when we were met by two white men, who presently took our three bags from us. We could not at first guess what they meant to do, and for some time we thought they were jesting with us; but they too soon let us know otherwise, for they took our ventures immediately to a house hard by, and adjoining the fort, while we followed all the way begging of them to give us our fruits, but in vain. They not only refused to return them, but swore at us, and threatened if we did not immediately depart they would flog us well. We told them these three bags were all we were worth in the world, and that we brought them with us to sell when we came from Montserrat, and showed them the vessel. But this was rather against us, as they now saw we were strangers, as well as slaves. They still therefore swore, and desired us to be gone, and even took sticks to beat us; while we, seeing they meant what they said, went off in the greatest confusion and despair.

Thus, in the very minute of gaining more by three times than I ever did by any venture in my life before, was I deprived of every farthing I was worth. An unsupportable misfortune! but how to help ourselves we knew not. In our consternation we went to the commanding officer of the fort, and told him how we had been served by his people, but we obtained not the least redress: he answered our complaints only by a volley of imprecations against us, and immediately took a horse-whip, in order to chastise us so that we were obliged to turn out much faster than we came in.

I now, in the agony of distress and indignation, wished that the ire of God in his forked lightning might transfix these cruel oppressors among the dead. Still however we persevered; went back again to the house, and begged and besought them again and again for our fruits, till at last some other people that were in the house asked if we would be contented if they kept one bag and gave us the other two. We, seeing no remedy whatever, consented to this; and they, observing one bag to have both kinds of fruit in it, which belonged to my companion, kept that; and the other two, which were mine, they gave us back. As soon as I got them, I ran as fast as I could, and got the first Negro man I could to help me off. My companion, however, stayed a little longer to plead; he told them the bag they had was his, and likewise all that he was worth in the world; but this was of no avail, and he was obliged to return without it. The poor old man wringing his hands, cried bitterly for his loss; and, indeed, he then did look up to God on high, which so moved me in pity for him, that I gave him nearly one third of my fruits.

We then proceeded to the markets to sell them; and Providence was more favorable to us than we could have expected, for we sold our fruits uncommonly well; I got for mine about thirty-seven bits. Such a surprising reverse of fortune in so short a space of time seemed like a dream, and proved no small encouragement for me to trust the Lord in any situation. My captain afterwards frequently used to take my part, and get me my right, when I have been plundered or used ill by these tender Christian depredators; among whom I have shuddered to observe the unceasing blasphemous execrations which are wantonly thrown out by persons of all ages and conditions, not only without occasion, but even as if they were indulgencies and pleasure.

At one of our trips to St. Kitts, I had eleven bits of my own; and my friendly captain lent me five more, with which I bought a Bible. I was very glad to get this book, which I scarcely could meet with anywhere. I think there was none sold in Montserrat; and, much to my grief, from being forced out of the *Etna* in the manner I have related, my Bible, and the *Guide to the Indians,* the two books I loved above all others, were left behind.

While I was in this place, St. Kitts, a very curious imposition on human nature took place: a white man wanted to marry in the church a free black woman, that had land and slaves in Montserrat; but the clergyman told him it was against the law of the place to marry a white and a black in the church. The man then asked to be married on the water, to which the parson consented, and the two lovers went in one boat, and the parson and clerk in another, and thus the ceremony was performed. After this, the loving pair came on board our vessel, and my captain treated them extremely well, and brought them safe to Montserrat.

The reader cannot but judge of the irksomeness of this situation to a mind like mine, in being daily exposed to new hardships and impositions, after having seen many better days, and been, as it were, in a state of freedom and plenty; added to which, every part of the world I had hitherto been in, seemed to me a paradise in comparison to the West Indies. My mind was therefore hourly replete with inventions and thoughts of being freed, and, if possible, by honest and honorable means; for I always remembered the old adage, and I trust it has ever been my ruling principle, that "honesty is the best policy"; and likewise that other golden percept— "To do unto all men as I would they should do unto me." However, as I was from early years a predestinarian, I thought whatever fate had determined must ever come to pass; and, therefore, if ever it were my lot to be freed, nothing could prevent me, although I should at present see no means or hope to obtain my freedom; on the other hand, if it were my fate not to be freed, I never should be so, and all my endeavors for that purpose would be fruitless. In the midst of these thoughts, I therefore looked up with prayers anxiously to God for my liberty; and at the same time used every honest means, and did all that was possible on my part to obtain it.

In process of time, I became master of a few pounds, and in a fair way of making more, which my friendly captain knew very well; this occasioned him sometimes to take liberties with me; but whenever he treated me waspishly, I used plainly to tell him my mind, and that I would die before I would be imposed upon as other Negroes were, and that to me life had lost its relish when liberty was gone. This I said, although I foresaw my then well-being or future hopes of freedom (humanly speaking) depended on this man. However, as he could not bear the thoughts of my not sailing with him, he always became mild on my threats. I therefore continued with him; and, from my great attention to his orders and his business, I gained him credit, and through his kindness to me, I at last procured my liberty.

While I thus went on, filled with the thoughts of freedom, and resisting oppression as well as I was able, my life hung daily in suspense, particularly in the surfs I have formerly mentioned, as I could not swim. These are extremely violent throughout the West Indies, and I was ever exposed to their howling rage and devouring fury in all the islands. I have seen them strike and toss a boat right up on end, and maim several on board. Once in the Grenada islands, when I and about eight others were pulling a large boat with two puncheons of water in it, a surf struck us, and drove the boat, and all in it, about half a stone's throw, among some trees, and above the high water mark. We were obliged to get all the assistance we could from the nearest estate to mend the boat, and launch it into the water again. At Montserrat, one night, in pressing hard to get off the shore on board, the punt was overset with us four times; the first time I was very near being drowned; however, the jacket I had on kept me up above water a little space of time, when I called on a man near me, who was a good swimmer, and told him I could not swim; he then made haste to me, and, just as I was sinking, he caught hold of me, and brought me to sounding, and then he went and brought the punt also. As soon as we had turned the water out of her, lest we should be used ill for being absent, we attempted again three times more, and as often the horrid surfs served us as at first; but at last, the fifth time we attempted, we gained our point, at the imminent hazard of our lives.

One day also, at Old Road, in Montserrat, our captain, and three men besides myself, were going in a large canoe in quest of rum and sugar, when a single surf tossed the canoe an amazing distance from the water, and some of us, near a stone's throw from each other. Most of us were very much bruised; so that I and many more often said, and really thought, that there was not such another place under the heavens as this. I longed, therefore, much to leave it, and daily wished to see my master's promise performed of going to Philadelphia.

While we lay in this place, a very cruel thing happened on board our sloop, which filled me with horror; though I found afterwards such practices were frequent. There was a very clever and decent free young mulatto man, who sailed a long time with us; he had a free woman for his wife, by whom he had a child, and she was then living on shore, and all very happy. Our captain and mate, and other people on board, and several elsewhere, even the natives of Bermudas, all knew this young man from a child that he was always free, and no one had ever claimed him as their property. However, as might too often overcomes right in these parts, it happened that a Bermudas captain, whose vessel lay there for a few days in the road, came on board of us, and seeing the mulatto man, whose name was Joseph Clipson, he told him he was not free, and that he had orders from his master to bring him to Bermudas. The poor man could not believe the captain to be in earnest, but he was very soon undeceived, his men laying violent hands on him; and although he showed a certificate of his being born free in St. Kitts, and most people on board knew that he served his time to boat-building, and always passed for a free man, yet he was forcibly taken out of our vessel. He then asked to be carried ashore before the Secretary or Magistrates, and these infernal invaders of human rights promised him he should; but instead of that, they carried him on board of the other vessel. And the next day, without giving the poor man any hearing on shore, or suffering him even to see his wife or child, he was carried away, and probably doomed never more in this world to see them again.

Nor was this the only instance of this kind of barbarity I was a witness to. I have since often seen in Jamaica and other islands, free men, whom I have known in America, thus villainously trepanned and held in bondage. I have heard of two similar practices even in Philadelphia. And were it not for the benevolence of the Quakers in that city, many of the sable race, who now breathe the air of liberty, would, I believe, be groaning indeed under some planter's chains. These things opened my mind to a new scene of horror, to which I had been before a stranger. Hitherto I had thought only slavery dreadful, but the state of a free Negro appeared to me now equally so at least, and in some respects even worse, for they live in constant alarm for their liberty; which is but nominal, for they are universally insulted and plundered, without the possibility of redress; for such is the equity of the West Indian laws, that no free Negro's evidence will be admitted in their courts of justice. In this situation, is it surprising that slaves, when mildly treated, should prefer even the misery of slavery to such a mockery of freedom? I was now completely disgusted with the West Indies, and thought I never should be entirely free until I had left them.

> With thoughts like these, my anxious boding mind
> Recall'd those pleasing scenes I left behind;
> Scenes, where fair liberty, in bright array,
> Makes darkness bright, and e'en illumines day;
> Where, nor complexion, wealth, or station, can
> Protect the wretch who makes a slave of man.

I determined to make every exertion to obtain my freedom, and to return to Old England. For this purpose, I thought a knowledge of navigation might be of use to me; for, though I did not intend to run away unless I should be ill used; yet, in such a case, if I understood navigation, I might attempt my escape in our sloop, which was one of the swiftest sailing vessels in the West Indies, and I could be at no loss for hands to join me: and if I should make this attempt, I had intended to have gone for England; but this, as I said, was only to be in the event of my meeting with any ill usage. I therefore employed the mate of our vessel to teach me navigation, for which I agreed to give him twenty-four dollars, and actually paid him part of the money down; though when the captain, some time after, came to know that the mate was to have such a sum for teaching me, he rebuked him, and said it was a shame for him to take any money from me. However, my progress in this useful art was much retarded by the constancy of our work.

Had I wished to run away, I did not want opportunities, which frequently presented themselves; and particularly at one time, soon after this. When we were at the island of Guadeloupe, there was a large fleet of merchantmen bound for Old France; and seamen then being very scarce, they gave from fifteen to twenty pounds a man for the run. Our mate and all the white sailors left our vessel on this account, and went on board of the French ships. They would have had me also to go with them, for they regarded me, and swore to protect me, if I would go: and, as the fleet was to sail the next day, I really believe I could have got safe to Europe at that time. However, as my master was kind, I would not attempt to leave him; still remembering the old maxim, that "honesty is the best policy," I suffered them to go without me. Indeed my captain was much afraid of my leaving him and the vessel at that time, as I had so fair an opportunity: but, I thank God, this fidelity of mine turned out much to my advantage hereafter, when I did not in the least think of it; and made me so much in favor with the captain, that he used now and then to teach me some parts of navigation himself; but some of our passengers, and others, seeing this, found much fault with him for it, saying it was a very dangerous thing to let a Negro know navigation; thus I was hindered again in my pursuits.

About the latter end of the year 1764, my master bought a larger sloop, called the *Prudence,* about seventy or eighty tons, of which my captain had the command. I went with him in this vessel, and we took a load of new slaves for Georgia and Charleston. My master now left me entirely to the captain, though he still wished me to be with him; but I, who always much wished to lose sight of the West Indies, was not a little rejoiced at the thoughts of seeing any other country. Therefore, relying on the goodness of my captain, I got ready all the little venture I could; and, when the vessel was ready, we sailed to my great joy. When we got to our destined places, Georgia and Charleston, I expected I should have an opportunity of selling my little property to advantage. But here, particularly in Charleston, I met with buyers, white men, who imposed on me as in other places. Notwithstanding, I was resolved to have fortitude, thinking no lot or trial too hard when kind Heaven is the rewarder.

We soon got loaded again, and returned to Montserrat; and there, amongst the rest of the islands, I sold my goods well; and in this manner I continued trading during the year 1764—meeting with various scenes of imposition, as usual. After this, my master fitted out his vessel for Philadelphia, in the year 1765; and during the time we were loading her, and getting ready for the voyage, I worked with redoubled alacrity, from the hope of getting money enough by these voyages to buy my freedom, in time, if it should please God; and also to see the town of Philadelphia, which I had heard a great deal about for some years past. Besides which, I had always longed to prove my master's promise the first day I came to him.

In the midst of these elevated ideas, and while I was about getting my little stock of merchandise in readiness, one Sunday my master sent for me to his house. When I came there I found him and the captain together; and, on my going in, I was struck with astonishment at his telling me he heard that I meant to run away from him when I got to Philadelphia. "And therefore," said he, "I must tell you again, you cost me a great deal of money, no less than forty pounds sterling; and it will not do to lose so much. You are a valuable fellow," continued he, "and I can get any day for you one hundred guineas, from many gentlemen in this island." And then he told me of Captain Doran's brother-in-law, a severe master, who ever wanted to buy me to make me his overseer. My captain also said he could get much more than a hundred guineas for me in Carolina.

This I knew to be a fact; for the gentleman that wanted to buy me came off several times on board of us, and spoke to me to live with him, and said he would use me well. When I asked him what work he would put me to, he said, as I was a sailor, he would make me a captain of one of his rice vessels. But I refused; and fearing at the same time, by a sudden turn I saw in the captain's temper, he might mean to sell me, I told the gentleman I would not live with him on any condition, and that I certainly would run away with his vessel; but he said he did not fear that, as he would catch me again, and then he told me how cruelly he would serve me if I should do so. My captain, however, gave him to understand that I knew something of navigation, so he thought better of it; and, to my great joy, he went away.

I now told my master I did not say I would run away in Philadelphia; neither did I mean it, as he did not use me ill, nor yet the captain; for if they did, I certainly would have made some attempts before now; but as I thought that if it were God's will I ever should be freed, it would be so, and, on the contrary, if it was not his will, it would not happen. So I hoped if ever I were freed, whilst I was used well, it should be by honest means; but as I could not help myself, he must do as he pleased, I could only hope and trust to the God of Heaven; and at that instant my mind was big with inventions and full of schemes to escape. I then appealed to the captain, whether he ever saw any sign of my making the least attempt to run away, and asked him if I did not always come on board according to the time for which he gave me liberty; and, more particularly, when all our men left us at Guadeloupe, and went on board of the French fleet, and advised me to go with them, whether I might not, and that he could not have got me again.

To my no small surprise, and very great joy, the captain confirmed every syllable that I had said, and even more; for he said he had tried different times to see if I would make any attempt of this kind, both at St. Eustatius and in America, and he never found that I made the smallest; but, on the contrary, I always came on board according to his orders; and he did really believe, if I ever meant to run away, that, as I could never have had a better opportunity, I would have done it the night the mate and all the people left our vessel at Guadeloupe. The captain then informed my master, who had been thus imposed on by our mate (though I did not know who was my enemy), the reason the mate had for imposing this lie upon him; which was, because I had acquainted the captain of the provisions the mate had given away or taken out of the vessel. This speech of the captain was like life to the dead to me, and instantly my soul glorified God; and still more so, on hearing my master immediately say that I was a sensible fellow, and he never did intend to use me as a common slave; and that but for the entreaties of the captain, and his character of me, he would not have let me go from the shores about as I had done. That also, in so doing, he thought by carrying one little thing or other to different places to sell, I might make money. That he also intended to encourage me in this, by crediting me with half a puncheon of rum and half a hogshead of sugar at a time; so that, from being careful, I might have money enough, in some time, to purchase my freedom; and, when that was the case, I might depend upon it he would let me have it for forty pounds sterling money, which was only the same price he gave for me.

This sound gladdened my poor heart beyond measure; though indeed it was no more than the very idea I had formed in my mind of my master long before, and I immediately made him this reply: "Sir, I always had that very thought of you, indeed I had, and that made me so diligent in serving you." He then gave me a large piece of silver coin, such as I never had seen or had before, and told me to get ready for the voyage, and he would credit me with a tierce of sugar, and another of rum; he also said that he had two amiable sisters in Philadelphia, from whom I might get some necessary things. Upon this my noble captain desired me to go aboard; and, knowing the African metal, he charged me not to say any thing of this matter to anybody; and he promised that the lying mate should not go with him any more. This was a change indeed: in the same hour to feel the most exquisite pain, and in the turn of a moment the fullest joy. It caused in me such sensations as I was only able to express in my looks; my heart was so overpowered with gratitude, that I could have kissed both of their feet. When I left the room, I immediately went, or rather flew, to the vessel; which being loaded, my master, as good as his word, trusted me with a tierce of rum, and another of sugar, when we sailed, and arrived safe at the elegant town of Philadelphia. I sold my goods here pretty well; and in this charming place I found everything plentiful and cheap.

While I was in this place, a very extraordinary occurrence befell me. I had been told one evening of a *wise* woman, a Mrs. Davis, who revealed secrets, foretold events, &c. I put little faith in this story at first, as I could not conceive that any mortal could foresee the future disposals of Providence, nor did I believe in any other revelation than that of the Holy Scriptures; however, I was greatly astonished at seeing this woman in a dream that night, though a person I never before beheld in my life. This made such an impression on me that I could not get the idea the next day out of my mind, and I then became as anxious to see her as I was before indifferent. Accordingly in the evening, after we left off working, I enquired where she lived, and being directed to her, to my inexpressible surprise, beheld the very woman in the very same dress she appeared to me to wear in the vision. She immediately told me I had dreamed of her the preceding night; related to me many things that had happened with a correctness that astonished me, and finally told me I should not be long a slave: this was the more agreeable news, as I believed it the more readily from her having so faithfully related the past incidents of my life. She said I should be twice in very great danger of my life within eighteen months, which, if I escaped, I should afterwards go on well. So, giving me her blessing, we parted. After staying here sometime till our vessel was loaded, and I had bought in my little traffic, we sailed from this agreeable spot for Montserrat, once more to encounter the raging surfs.

We arrived safe at Montserrat, where we discharged our cargo; and soon after that, we took slaves on board for St. Eustatius, and from thence to Georgia. I had always exerted myself, and did double work, in order to make our voyages as short as possible; and from thus overworking myself while we were at Georgia, I caught a fever and ague.[2] I was very ill for eleven days, and near dying; eternity was now exceedingly impressed on my mind, and I feared very much that awful event. I prayed the Lord, therefore, to spare me; and I made a promise in my mind to God, that I

---

[2] A sickness marked by fever and alternating chills and sweating.

would be good if ever I should recover. At length, from having an eminent doctor to attend me, I was restored again to health; and soon after, we got the vessel loaded, and set off for Montserrat.

During the passage, as I was perfectly restored, and had much business of the vessel to mind, all my endeavors to keep up my integrity, and perform my promise to God, began to fail; and, in spite of all I could do, as we drew nearer and nearer to the islands, my resolutions more and more declined, as if the very air of that country or climate seemed fatal to piety. When we were safe arrived at Montserrat, and I had got ashore, I forgot my former resolutions. Alas! how prone is the heart to leave that God it wishes to love! and how strongly do the things of this world strike the senses and captivate the soul!

After our vessel was discharged, we soon got her ready, and took in, as usual, some of the poor oppressed natives of Africa, and other Negroes; we then set off again for Georgia and Charleston. We arrived at Georgia, and, having landed part of our cargo, proceeded to Charleston with the remainder. While we were there, I saw the town illuminated; the guns were fired, and bonfires and other demonstrations of joy shown, on account of the repeal of the Stamp Act.[3] Here I disposed of some goods on my own account; the white men buying them with smooth promises and fair words, giving me, however, but very indifferent payment. There was one gentleman particularly, who bought a puncheon of rum of me, which gave me a great deal of trouble; and, although I used the interest of my friendly captain, I could not obtain anything for it; for, being a Negro man, I could not oblige him to pay me. This vexed me much, not knowing how to act; and I lost some time in seeking after this Christian; and though, when the Sabbath came (which the Negroes usually make their holiday), I was much inclined to go to public worship, I was obliged to hire some black men to help to pull a boat across the water to go in quest of this gentleman. When I found him, after much entreaty, both from myself and my worthy captain, he at last paid me in dollars; some of them, however, were copper, and of consequence of no value; but he took advantage of my being a Negro man, and obliged me to put up with those or none, although I objected to them. Immediately after, as I was trying to pass them in the market, amongst other white men, I was abused for offering to

---

[3] To pay for the Seven Years' War, the British Parliament imposed this tax on the American colonies. All newspapers, printed sheets, and stationery had to have a revenue stamp affixed as proof of payment. The mainland colonists insisted that Parliament did not have the right to tax them and often protested violently throughout 1765. Parliament repealed the stamp tax (definite news of the repeal reached the colonies in May 1766) but did not give up the principle that Parliament could tax the American colonies.

pass bad coin; and, though I showed them the man I got them from, I was within one minute of being tied up and flogged without either judge or jury; however, by the help of a good pair of heels, I ran off, and so escaped the bastinadoes I should have received. I got on board as fast as I could, but still continued in fear of them until we sailed, which I thank God we did not long after; and I have never been amongst them since.

We soon came to Georgia, where we were to complete our landing, and here worse fate than ever attended me; for one Sunday night, as I was with some Negroes in their master's yard, in the town of Savannah, it happened that their master, one Doctor Perkins, who was a very severe and cruel man, came in drunk; and not liking to see any strange Negroes in his yard, he and a ruffian of a white man, he had in his service, beset me in an instant, and both of them struck me with the first weapons they could get hold of. I cried out as long as I could for help and mercy; but, though I gave a good account of myself, and he knew my captain, who lodged hard by him, it was to no purpose. They beat and mangled me in a shameful manner, leaving me near dead. I lost so much blood from the wounds I received, that I lay quite motionless, and was so benumbed that I could not feel anything for many hours. Early in the morning they took me away to the jail.

As I did not return to the ship all night, my captain, not knowing where I was, and being uneasy that I did not then make my appearance, made enquiry after me; and having found where I was, immediately came to me. As soon as the good man saw me so cut and mangled, he could not forbear weeping; he soon got me out of jail to his lodgings, and immediately sent for the best doctors in the place, who at first declared it as their opinion that I could not recover. My captain on this went to all the lawyers in the town for their advice, but they told him they could do nothing for me as I was a Negro. He then went to Doctor Perkins, the hero who had vanquished me, and menaced him, swearing he would be revenged on him, and challenged him to fight. But cowardice is ever the companion of cruelty—and the Doctor refused. However, by the skilfulness of one Dr. Brady of that place, I began at last to amend; but, although I was so sore and bad with the wounds I had all over me that I could not rest in any posture, yet I was in more pain on account of the captain's uneasiness about me, than I otherwise should have been. The worthy man nursed and watched me all the hours of the night; and I was, through his attention and that of the doctor, able to get out of bed in about sixteen or eighteen days. All this time I was very much wanted on board, as I used frequently to go up and down the river for rafts, and other parts of our cargo, and stow

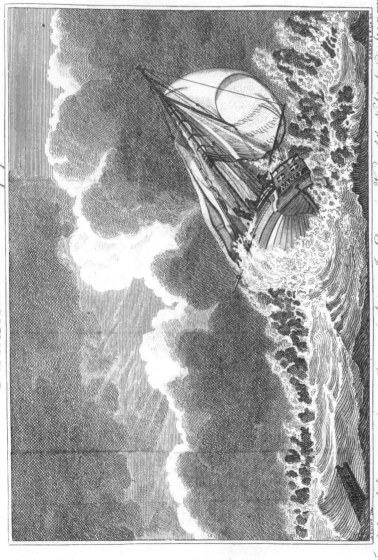

BAHAMA BANKS. 1767.

This engraving depicts the wreck of the slave ship *Nancy* on the Bahama Banks in 1767.

them, when the mate was sick or absent. In about four weeks, I was able to go on duty, and in a fortnight after, having got in all our lading,[4] our vessel set sail for Montserrat; and in less than three weeks we arrived there safe towards the end of the year. This ended my adventures in 1765, for I did not leave Montserrat again till the beginning of the following year.

[4] Cargo.

CHAPTER 7

The author's disgust at the West Indies—Forms schemes to obtain his freedom—Ludicrous disappointment he and his Captain met with in Georgia—At last, by several successful voyages, he acquires a sum of money sufficient to purchase it—Applies to his master, who accepts it, and grants his manumission, to his great joy—He afterwards enters as a freeman on board one of Mr. King's ships, and sails for Georgia—Impositions on free Negroes, as usual—His venture of turkies—Sails for Montserrat, and on his passage his friend, the Captain, falls ill and dies.

Every day now brought me nearer my freedom, and I was impatient till we proceeded again to sea, that I might have an opportunity of getting a sum large enough to purchase it. I was not long ungratified; for, in the beginning of the year 1766, my master bought another sloop, named the *Nancy,* the largest I had ever seen. She was partly laden, and was to proceed to Philadelphia; our captain had his choice of three, and I was well pleased he chose this, which was the largest; for, from his having a large vessel, I had more room, and could carry a larger quantity of goods with me. Accordingly, when we had delivered our old vessel, the *Prudence,* and completed the lading of the *Nancy,* having made near three hundred per cent by four barrels of pork I brought from Charleston, I laid in as large a cargo as I could, trusting to God's providence to prosper my undertaking. With these views I sailed for Philadelphia. On our passage, when we drew near the land, I was for the first time surprised at the sight of some whales, having never seen any such large sea monsters before; and as we sailed by the land, one morning, I saw a puppy whale close by the vessel; it was about the length of a wherry boat, and it followed us all the day till we got within the Capes. We arrived safe, and in good time at Philadelphia, and I sold my goods there chiefly to the Quakers. They always appeared to be a very honest, discreet sort of people, and never attempted to impose on me; I therefore liked them, and ever after chose to deal with them in preference to any others.

One Sunday morning, while I was here, as I was going to church, I chanced to pass a meetinghouse. The doors being open, and the house full of people, it excited my curiosity to go in. When I entered the house, to my great surprise, I saw a very tall woman standing in the midst of them, speaking in an audible voice something which I could not understand. Having never seen anything of this kind before, I stood and stared about me for some time, wondering at this odd scene. As soon as it was over, I took an opportunity to make inquiry about the place and people, when I was informed they were called Quakers. I particularly asked what that woman I saw in the midst of them had said, but none of them were pleased to satisfy me; so I quitted them, and soon after, as I was returning, I came to a church crowded with people; the church-yard was full likewise, and a number of people were even mounted on ladders looking in at the windows. I thought this a strange sight, as I had never seen churches, either in England or the West Indies, crowded in this manner before. I therefore made bold to ask some people the meaning of all this, and they told me the Rev. Mr. George Whitfield[1] was preaching. I had often heard of this gentleman, and had wished to see and hear him; but I never before had an opportunity. I now therefore resolved to gratify myself with the sight, and pressed in amidst the multitude. When I got into the church, I saw this pious man exhorting the people with the greatest fervor and earnestness, and sweating as much as I ever did while in slavery on Montserrat beach. I was very much struck and impressed with this; I thought it strange I had never seen divines exert themselves in this manner before, and was no longer at a loss to account for the thin congregations they preached to.

When we had discharged our cargo here, and were loaded again, we left this fruitful land once more, and set sail for Montserrat. My traffic had hitherto succeeded so well with me, that I thought, by selling my goods when we arrived at Montserrat, I should have enough to purchase my freedom. But as soon as our vessel arrived there, my master came on board, and gave orders for us to go to St. Eustatius, and discharge our cargo there, and from thence proceed for Georgia. I was much disappointed at this; but thinking, as usual, it was of no use to encounter with the decrees of fate, I submitted without repining, and we went to St.

---

[1] George Whitefield (1714–1770), English clergyman, proponent of the Great Awakening. Equiano and Whitefield were never in Philadelphia at the same time, but both were in Savannah in February 1765, when Whitefield preached a "solemn and affectionate farewell" to a "very crowded" congregation, which had come to thank him for his many services to the colony. (*Georgia Gazette,* February 21, 1765.)

Eustatius. After we had discharged our cargo there, we took in a live cargo (as we call a cargo of slaves). Here I sold my goods tolerably well; but, not being able to lay out all my money in this small island to as much advantage as in many other places, I laid out only part, and the remainder I brought away with me net. We sailed from hence for Georgia, and I was glad when we got there, though I had not much reason to like the place from my last adventure in Savannah; but I longed to get back to Montserrat and procure my freedom, which I expected to be able to purchase when I returned. As soon as we arrived here, I waited on my careful doctor, Mr. Brady, to whom I made the most grateful acknowledgements in my power, for his former kindness and attention during my illness.

While we were here, an odd circumstance happened to the captain and me, which disappointed us both a great deal. A silversmith, whom we had brought to this place some voyage before, agreed with the captain to return with us to the West Indies, and promised at the same time to give the captain a great deal of money, having pretended to take a liking to him, and being, as we thought, very rich. But while we stayed to load our vessel, this man was taken ill in a house where he worked, and in a week's time became very bad. The worse he grew the more he used to speak of giving the captain what he had promised him, so that he expected something considerable from the death of this man, who had no wife or child, and he attended him day and night. I used also to go with the captain, at his own desire, to attend him; and especially when we saw there was no appearance of his recovery; and, in order to recompense me for my trouble, the captain promised me ten pounds, when he should get the man's property. I thought this would be of great service to me, although I had nearly money enough to purchase my freedom, if I should get safe this voyage to Montserrat. In this expectation I laid out above eight pounds of my money for a suit of superfine clothes to dance in at my freedom, which I hoped was then at hand. We still continued to attend this man, and were with him even on the last day he lived, till very late at night, when we went on board. After we were got to bed, about one or two o'clock in the morning, the captain was sent for, and informed the man was dead. On this he came to my bed, and, waking me, informed me of it, and desired me to get up and procure a light, and immediately go with him. I told him I was very sleepy, and wished he would take somebody else with him; or else, as the man was dead, and could want no further attendance, to let all things remain as they were till the next morning.

"No, no," said he, "we will have the money tonight, I cannot wait till tomorrow, so let us go." Accordingly I got up and struck a light, and away we both went and saw the man as dead as we could wish. The captain said he would give him a grand burial, in gratitude for the promised treasure; and desired that all the things belonging to the deceased might be brought forth. Among others, there was a nest of trunks of which he had kept the keys, whilst the man was ill, and when they were produced we opened them with no small eagerness and expectation; and as there was a great number within one another, with much impatience we took them one out of the other. At last, when we came to the smallest, and had opened it, we saw it was full of papers, which we supposed to be notes, at the sight of which our hearts leapt for joy; and that instant the captain, clapping his hands, cried out, "Thank God, here it is."

But when we took up the trunk, and began to examine the supposed treasure, and long looked-for bounty (alas! alas! how uncertain and deceitful are all human affairs!); what had we found? while we thought we were embracing a substance, we grasped an empty nothing. The whole amount that was in the nest of trunks, was only one dollar and a half; and all that the man possessed would not pay for his coffin. Our sudden and exquisite joy was now succeeded by as sudden and exquisite pain; and my captain and I exhibited, for some time, most ridiculous figures—pictures of chagrin and astonishment! We went away greatly mortified, and left the deceased to do as well as he could for himself, as we had taken so good care of him when alive for nothing.

We set sail once more for Montserrat, and arrived there safe, but much out of humor with our friend the silversmith. When we had unladen the vessel, and I had sold my venture, finding myself master of about forty-seven pounds—I consulted my true friend, the captain, how I should proceed in offering my master the money for my freedom. He told me to come on a certain morning, when he and my master would be at breakfast together. Accordingly, on that morning I went, and met the captain there, as he had appointed. When I went in I made my obeisance to my master, and with my money in my hand, and many fears in my heart, I prayed him to be as good as his offer to me, when he was pleased to promise me my freedom as soon as I could purchase it. This speech seemed to confound him, he began to recoil, and my heart that instant sunk within me. "What," said he, "give you your freedom? Why, where did you get the money? Have you got forty pounds sterling?" "Yes, sir," I answered. "How did you get it?" replied he. I told him, very honestly. The captain then said he knew I got the money honestly, and with much industry, and that I was particularly careful. On which my master replied, I got money much faster than he did; and said he would not have made me the promise he did if he had thought I should have got the money so soon. "Come, come," said my worthy captain, clapping my master on the back, "Come, Robert (which was his name), I think you must let him have his freedom; you have laid your money out very well; you have received a very good interest for it all this time, and here is now the principal at last. I know Gustavus has earned you more than a hundred a year, and he will save you money, as he will not leave you. Come, Robert, take the money."

My master then said he would not be worse than his promise; and, taking the money, told me to go to the Secretary at the Register Office, and get my manumission[2] drawn up. These words of my master were like a voice from heaven to me. In an instant all my trepidation was turned into unutterable bliss; and I most reverently bowed myself with gratitude, unable to express my feelings, but by the overflowing of my eyes, and a heart replete with thanks to God, while my true and worthy friend, the captain, congratulated us both with a peculiar degree of heart-felt pleasure. As soon as the first transports of my joy were over, and that I had expressed my thanks to these my worthy friends, in the best manner I was able, I rose with a heart full of affection and reverence, and left the room, in order to obey my master's joyful mandate of going to the Register Office. As I was leaving the house I called to mind the words of the Psalmist, in the 126th Psalm,[3] and like him, "I glorified God in my heart, in whom I trusted." These words had been impressed on my mind from the very day I was forced from Deptford to the present hour, and I now saw them, as I thought, fulfilled and verified. My imagination was all rapture as I flew to the Register Office; and, in this respect, like the apostle Peter[4] (whose deliverance from prison was so sudden and extraordinary that he thought he was in a vision), I could scarcely believe I was awake. Heavens! who could do justice to my feelings at this moment! Not conquering heroes themselves, in the midst of a triumph—Not the tender mother who has just regained her long lost infant, and presses it to her heart—Not the weary hungry mariner, at the sight of the desired friendly port—Not the lover, when he once more embraces his beloved mistress, after she has been ravished from his arms! All within my breast was tumult, wildness, and delirium! My feet scarcely touched the ground, for they were winged with joy; and, like Elijah, as he rose to Heaven, they "were with lightning sped as I went on." Everyone I met I told of my happiness, and blazed about the virtue of my amiable master and captain.

When I got to the office and acquainted the Register with my errand, he congratulated me on the occasion, and told me he would draw up my

[2] Formal emancipation from slavery.
[3] Psalm 126, "Thanksgiving for Return from Captivity."
[4] Acts 12:9. [Equiano's note.]

manumission for half price, which was a guinea. I thanked him for his kindness; and, having received it, and paid him, I hastened to my master to get him to sign it, that I might be fully released. Accordingly he signed the manumission that day; so that, before night, I, who had been a slave in the morning, trembling at the will of another, was become my own master, and completely free. I thought this was the happiest day I had ever experienced; and my joy was still heightened by the blessings and prayers of many of the sable race, particularly the aged, to whom my heart had ever been attached with reverence.

As the form of my manumission has something peculiar in it, and expresses the absolute power and dominion one man claims over his fellow, I shall beg leave to present it before my readers at full length.

MONTSERRAT.

To all men unto whom these presents shall come: I, Robert King, of the parish of St. Anthony, in the said island, merchant, send greeting: Know ye, that I the aforesaid Robert King, for and in consideration of the sum of seventy pounds current money of the said island, to me in hand paid, and to the intent that a Negro man-slave, named Gustavus Vassa, shall and may become free, having manumitted, emancipated, enfranchised, and set free, and by these presents do manumit, emancipate, enfranchise, and set free, the aforesaid Negro man-slave, named Gustavus Vassa, for ever; hereby giving, granting, and releasing unto him, the said Gustavus Vassa, all right, title, dominion, sovereignty, and property, which, as lord and master over the aforesaid Gustavus Vassa, I had, or now have, or by any means whatsoever I may or can hereafter possibly have over him the aforesaid Negro, for ever. In witness whereof, I the above said Robert King have unto these presents set my hand and seal this tenth day of July, in the year of our Lord one thousand seven hundred and sixty-six.

ROBERT KING

Signed, sealed, and delivered in the presence of Terry Legay, Montserrat.

Registered the within manumission at full length, this eleventh day of July 1766, in liber. D.

TERRY LEGAY, Register

In short, the fair as well as the black people immediately styled me by a new appellation, to me the most desirable in the world, which was freeman; and at the dances I gave, my Georgia super-fine blue clothes made no indifferent appearance, as I thought. Some of the sable females, who formerly stood aloof, now began to relax and appear less coy; but my heart was still fixed on London, where I hoped to be ere long. So that my worthy captain and his owner, my late master, finding that the bent of my mind was towards London, said to me, "We hope you won't leave us, but that you will still be with the vessels." Here gratitude bowed me down; and none but the generous mind can judge of my feelings, struggling between inclination and duty. However, notwithstanding my wish to be in London, I obediently answered my benefactors, that I would go in the vessel, and not leave them; and from that day I was entered on board as an able-bodied sailor, at thirty-six shillings per month, besides what perquisites I could make.

My intention was to make a voyage or two, entirely to please these my honored patrons; but I determined that the year following, if it pleased God, I would see Old England once more, and surprise my old master, Captain Pascal, who was hourly in my mind; for I still loved him, notwithstanding his usage of me, and pleased myself with thinking what he would say, when he saw what the Lord had done for me in so short a time, instead of being, as he might perhaps suppose, under the cruel yoke of some planter. With these kind of reveries I used often to entertain myself, and shorten the time till my return; and now, being as in my original free African state, I embarked on board the *Nancy*, after having got all things ready for our voyage. In this state of serenity, we sailed for St. Eustatius; and having smooth seas and calm weather, we soon arrived there. After taking our cargo on board, we proceeded to Savannah, in Georgia, in August, 1766. While we were there, as usual, I used to go for the cargo up the rivers in boats; and on this business have been frequently beset by alligators, which were very numerous on that coast; and shot many of them when they have been near getting into our boats, which we have with great difficulty sometimes prevented, and have been very much frightened at them. I have seen a young one sold in Georgia alive for six pence.

During our stay at this place, one evening, a slave belonging to Mr. Read, a merchant of Savannah, came near our vessel, and began to use me very ill. I entreated him, with all the patience I was master of, to desist, as I knew there was little or no law for a free Negro here; but the fellow, instead of taking my advice, persevered in his insults, and even struck me. At this I lost all temper, and fell on him and beat him soundly. The next morning his master came to our vessel as we lay along side the wharf, and desired me to come ashore, that he might have me flogged all round the town, for beating his Negro slave. I told him he had insulted me, and given the provocation, by first striking me. I had told my captain also the whole affair that morning, and wished him to have gone along with me to Mr. Read, to prevent bad consequences; but he said that it did not signify, and if Mr. Read said any thing, he would make matters up, and desired me to go to work, which I accordingly did. The captain being on board when Mr. Read came and applied to him to deliver me up, he said he knew nothing of the matter, I was a free man. I was astonished and frightened at this, and thought I had better keep where I was than go ashore and be flogged round the town, without judge or jury. I therefore refused to stir; and Mr. Read went away, swearing he would bring all the constables in town, for he would have me out of the vessel. When he was gone, I thought his threat might prove too true to my sorrow; and as I was confirmed in this belief, as well by the many instances I had seen of the treatment of free Negroes, as from a fact that had happened within my own knowledge here a short time before.

There was a free black man, a carpenter, that I knew, who, for asking the gentleman that he worked for, for the money he had earned, was put into jail: and afterwards this oppressed man was sent from Georgia, with false accusations, of an intention to set the gentleman's house on fire, and run away with his slaves. I was therefore much embarrassed, and very apprehensive of a flogging at least. I dreaded, of all things, the thoughts of being striped, as I never in my life had the marks of any violence of that kind. At that instant a rage seized my soul, and for a little I determined to resist the first man that should offer to lay violent hands on me, or basely use me without a trial; for I would sooner die like a free man, than suffer myself to be scourged by the hands of ruffians, and my blood drawn like a slave. The captain and others, more cautious, advised me to make haste and conceal myself; for they said Mr. Read was a very spiteful man, and he would soon come on board with constables and take me.

At first I refused this counsel, being determined to stand my ground; but at length, by the prevailing entreaties of the captain and Mr. Dixon, with whom he lodged, I went to Mr. Dixon's house, which was a little out of town, at a place called Yea-ma-chra.[5] I was but just gone, when Mr. Read, with the constables, came for me, and searched the vessel; but, not finding me there, he swore he would have me dead or alive. I was secreted about five days; however, the good character which my captain always gave me, as well as some other gentlemen who also knew me, procured me some friends. At last some of them told my captain that he did not use me well, in suffering me thus to be imposed upon, and said they would see me redressed, and get me on board some other vessel.

My captain, on this, immediately went to Mr. Read, and told him, that ever since I eloped from the vessel, his work had been neglected, and he could not go on with her loading, himself and mate not being well; and, as I

---

[5] A Creek Indian village on the bluffs above the English settlement at Savannah.

had managed things on board for them, my absence must retard his voyage, and consequently hurt the owner; he therefore begged of him to forgive me, as he said he never heard any complaint of me before, during the several years I had been with him. After repeated entreaties, Mr. Read said I might go to hell, and that he would not meddle with me; on which my captain came immediately to me at his lodging, and telling me how pleasantly matters had gone on, desired me to go on board.

Some of my other friends then asked him if he had got the constable's warrant from them; the captain said, No. On this I was desired by them to stay in the house; and they said they would get me on board of some other vessel before the evening. When the captain heard this, he became almost distracted. He went immediately for the warrant, and, after using every exertion in his power, he at last got it from my hunters; but I had all the expenses to pay.

After I had thanked all my friends for their kindness, I went on board again to my work, of which I had always plenty. We were in haste to complete our lading, and were to carry twenty head of cattle with us to the West Indies, where they are a very profitable article. In order to encourage me in working, and to make up for the time I had lost, my captain promised me the privilege of carrying two bullocks of my own with me; and this made me work with redoubled ardor. As soon as I had got the vessel loaded, in doing which I was obliged to perform the duty of the mate as well as my own work, and that the bullocks were near coming on board, I asked the captain leave to bring my two, according to his promise; but to my great surprise, he told me there was no room for them. I then asked him to permit me to take one; but he said he could not. I was a good deal mortified at this usage, and told him I had no notion that he intended thus to impose on me; nor could I think well of any man that was so much worse than his word. On this we had some disagreement, and I gave him to understand that I intended to leave the vessel. At this he appeared to be very much dejected; and our mate, who had been very sickly, and whose duty had long devolved upon me, advised him to persuade me to stay; in consequence of which, he spoke very kindly to me, making many fair promises, telling me, that, as the mate was so sickly, he could not do without me; and that, as the safety of the vessel and cargo depended greatly upon me, he therefore hoped that I would not be offended at what had passed between us, and swore he would make up all matters when we arrived in the West Indies; so I consented to slave on as before.

Soon after this, as the bullocks were coming on board, one of them ran at the captain, and butted him so furiously in the breast, that he never recovered of the blow. In order to make me some amends for his treatment about the bullocks, the captain now pressed me very much to take some turkeys, and other fowls with me, and gave me liberty to take as many as I could find room for; but I told him he knew very well I had never carried any turkeys before, as I always thought they were such tender birds that they were not fit to cross the seas. However, he continued to press me to buy them for once; and what seemed very surprising to me, the more I was against it, the more he urged my taking them, insomuch that he ensured me from all losses that might happen by them, and I was prevailed on to take them; but I thought this very strange, as he had never acted so with me before. This, and not being able to dispose of my paper money any other way, induced me at length to take four dozen. The turkeys, however, I was so dissatisfied about, that I determined to make no more voyages to this quarter, nor with this captain; and was very apprehensive that my free voyage would be the worst I had ever made.

We set sail for Montserrat. The captain and mate had been both complaining of sickness when we sailed, and as we proceeded on our voyage they grew worse. This was about November, and we had not been long at sea before we began to meet with strong northerly gales and rough seas; and in about seven or eight days all the bullocks were near being drowned, and four or five of them died. Our vessel, which had not been tight at first, was much less so now. And, though we were but nine in the whole, including five sailors and myself, yet we were obliged to attend to the pumps every half or three quarters of an hour. The captain and mate came on deck as often as they were able, which was now but seldom; for they declined so fast, that they were not well enough to make observations above four or five times the whole voyage. The whole care of the vessel rested therefore upon me, and I was obliged to direct her by mere dint of reason, not being able to work a traverse. The captain was now very sorry he had not taught me navigation, and protested, if ever he should get well again, he would not fail to do so; but in about seventeen days his illness increased so much, that he was obliged to keep his bed, continuing sensible, however, till the last, constantly having the owner's interest at heart; for this just and benevolent man ever appeared much concerned about the welfare of what he was intrusted with.

When this dear friend found the symptoms of death approaching, he called me by my name; and, when I came to him, he asked (with almost his last breath) if he had ever done me any harm? "God forbid I should think so," replied I, "I should then be the most ungrateful of wretches to the best of benefactors." While I was thus expressing my affection and sorrow by his bed side, he expired without saying another word; and the day following we committed his body to the deep. Every man on board loved him, and regretted his death; but I was exceedingly affected at it, and found that I did not know, till he was gone, the strength of my regard for him. Indeed, I had every reason in the world to be attached to him; for, besides that he was in general mild, affable, generous, faithful, benevolent, and just, he was to me a friend and father; and had it pleased Providence, that he had died about five months before, I verily believe I should not have obtained my freedom when I did; and it is not improbable that I might not have been able to get it at any rate afterwards.

The captain being dead, the mate came on the deck, and made such observations as he was able, but to no purpose. In the course of a few days more, the few bullocks that remained were found dead; but the turkeys I had, though on the deck, and exposed to so much wet and bad weather, did well, and I afterwards gained near three hundred per cent on the sale of them; so that in the event it proved a happy circumstance for me that I had not bought the bullocks I intended, for they must have perished with the rest; and I could not help looking on this otherwise trifling circumstance as a particular providence of God, and was thankful accordingly. The care of the vessel took up all my time, and engaged my attention entirely. As we were now out of the variable winds, I thought I should not be much puzzled to hit upon the islands. I was persuaded I steered right for Antigua, which I wished to reach, as the nearest to us; and in the course of nine or ten days we made the island, to our great joy; and the day after, we came safe to Montserrat.

Many were surprised when they heard of my conducting the sloop into the port, and I now obtained a new appellation, and was called Captain. This elatcd me not a little, and it was quite flattering to my vanity to be thus styled by as high a title as any freeman in this place possessed. When the death of the captain became known, he was much regretted by all who knew him, for he was a man universally respected. At the same time the sable captain lost no fame; for the success I had met with, increased the affection of my friends in no small measure.

CHAPTER 8

The author, to oblige Mr. King, once more embarks for Georgia in one of his vessels—A new captain is appointed—They sail, and steer a new course—Three remarkable dreams—The vessel is shipwrecked on the Bahama Bank, but the crew are preserved, principally by means of the author—He sets out from the island with the captain, in a small boat, in quest of a ship—Their distress—Meet with a wrecker—Sail for Providence—Are overtaken again by a terrible storm, and all are near perishing—Arrive at New Providence—The author, after some time, sails from thence to Georgia—Meets with another storm, and is obliged to put back and refit—Arrives at Georgia—Meets new impositions—Two white men attempt to kidnap him—Officiates as a person at a funeral ceremony—Bids adieu to Georgia, and sails for Martinique.

As I had now, by the death of my captain, lost my great benefactor and friend, I had little inducement to remain longer in the West Indies, except my gratitude to Mr. King, which I thought I had pretty well discharged in bringing back his vessel safe, and delivering his cargo to his satisfaction. I began to think of leaving this part of the world, of which I had been long tired, and returning to England, where my heart had always been, but Mr. King still pressed me very much to stay with his vessel; and he had done so much for me that I found myself unable to refuse his requests, and consented to go another voyage to Georgia, as the mate, from his ill state of health, was quite useless in the vessel. Accordingly a new captain was appointed, whose name was William Phillips, an old acquaintance of mine; and, having refitted our vessel, and taken several slaves on board, we set sail for St. Eustatius, where we stayed but a few days; and on the 30th of January, 1767, we steered for Georgia. Our new captain boasted strangely of his skill in navigation and conducting a vessel; and in consequence of this he steered a new course, several points more to the westward than we ever did before; this appeared to me very extraordinary.

On the fourth of February, which was soon after we had got into our new course, I dreamt the ship was wrecked amidst the surfs and rocks, and that I was the means of saving everyone on board; and on the night following I dreamed the very same dream. These dreams, however, made no impression on my mind; and the next evening, it being my watch below, I was pumping the vessel, a little after eight o'clock, just before I went off the deck, as is the custom; and being weary with the duty of the day, and tired at the pump (for we made a good deal of water), I began to express my impatience, and uttered with an oath, "Damn the vessel's bottom out." But my conscience instantly smote me for the expression.

When I left the deck I went to bed, and had scarcely fallen asleep, when I dreamed the same dream again about the ship as I had dreamed the two preceding nights. At twelve o'clock the watch was changed; and, as I had always the charge of the captain's watch, I then went upon deck. At half after one in the morning, the man at the helm saw something under the lee-beam that the sea washed against, and he immediately called to me that there was a grampus, and desired me to look at it. Accordingly I stood up and observed it for some time; but, when I saw the sea wash up against it again and again, I said it was not a fish but a rock. Being soon certain of this, I went down to the captain, and, with some confusion, told him the danger we were in, and desired him to come upon deck immediately. He said it was very well, and I went up again. As soon as I was upon deck, the wind, which had been pretty high, having abated a little, the vessel began to be carried sideways towards the rock, by means of the current. Still the captain did not appear. I therefore went to him again, and told him the vessel was then near a large rock, and desired he would come up with all speed. He said he would, and I returned to the deck.

When I was upon the deck again, I saw we were not above a pistol shot from the rock, and I heard the noise of the breakers all around us. I was exceedingly alarmed at this, and the captain having not yet come on the deck, I lost all patience; and, growing quite enraged, I ran down to him again, and asked him why he did not come up, and what he could mean by all this? "The breakers," said I, "are round us, and the vessel is almost on the rock." With that he came on the deck with me, and we tried to put the vessel about, and get her out of the current, but all to no purpose, the wind being very small. We then called all hands up immediately; and after a little we got up one end of a cable, and fastened it to the anchor. By this time the surf was foamed round us, and made a dreadful noise on the breakers; and the very moment we let the anchor go, the vessel struck against the rocks. One swell now succeeded another, as it were one wave calling on its fellow; the roaring of the billows increased, and, with one single heave of the swells, the sloop was pierced and transfixed among the rocks! in a moment a scene of horror presented itself to my mind, such as I never had conceived or experienced before. All my sins stared me in the face; and especially, I thought that God had hurled his direful vengeance on my guilty head for cursing the vessel on which my life depended. My spirits at this forsook me, and I expected every moment to go to the bottom. I determined if I should still be saved, that I would never swear again. And in the midst of my distress, while the dreadful surfs were dashing with unremitting fury among the rocks, I remembered the Lord, though fearful that I was undeserving of forgiveness, and I thought that as he had often delivered he might yet deliver; and, calling to mind the many mercies he had shown me in times past, they gave me some small hope that he might still help me.

I then began to think how we might be saved; and I believe no mind was ever like mine so replete with inventions, and confused with schemes, though how to escape death I knew not. The captain immediately ordered the hatches to be nailed down on the slaves in the hold, where there were about twenty, all of whom must unavoidably have perished if he had been obeyed. When he desired the man to nail down the hatches, I thought that my sin was the cause of this, and that God would charge me with these people's blood. This thought rushed upon my mind that instant with such violence, that it quite overpowered me, and I fainted. I recovered just as the people were about to nail down the hatches; perceiving which, I desired them to stop. The captain then said it must be done. I asked him why? He said that everyone would endeavor to get into the boat, which was but small, and thereby we should be drowned; for it would not have carried above ten at the most. I could no longer refrain my emotion, and told him he deserved drowning for not knowing how to navigate the vessel; and I believe the people would have tossed him overboard if I had given them the least hint of it. However, the hatches were not nailed down; and, as none of us could leave the vessel then on account of the darkness, and as we knew not where to go, and were convinced besides that the boat could not survive the surfs, we all said we would remain on the dry part of the vessel, and trust to God till daylight appeared, when we should know better what to do.

I then advised to get the boat prepared against morning, and some of us began to set about it; but others abandoned all care of the ship and themselves, and fell to drinking. Our boat had a piece out of her bottom near two feet long, and we had no materials to mend her; however, necessity being the mother of invention, I took some pump leather and nailed it to the broken part, and plastered it over with tallow-grease. And, thus prepared, with the utmost anxiety of mind, we watched for daylight, and thought every minute an hour till it appeared. At last it saluted our longing eyes, and kind Providence accompanied its approach with what was no small comfort to us, for the dreadful swells began to subside; and the next thing that we discovered to raise our drooping spirits, was a small key or desolate island, about five or six miles off. But a barrier soon presented itself; for there was not water enough for our boat to go over the reefs, and this threw us again into a sad consternation; but there was no alternative, we were therefore obliged to put but few in the boat at once. And, what was still worse, all of us were frequently under the necessity of getting out to drag and lift it over the reefs. This cost us much labor and fatigue; and, what was yet more distressing, we could not avoid having our legs cut and torn very much with the rocks. There were only four people that would work with me at the oars, and they consisted of three black men and a Dutch Creole sailor; and, though we went with the boat five times that day, we had no others to assist us. But, had we not worked in this manner, I really believe the people could not have been saved; for not one of the white men did anything to preserve their lives. Indeed, they soon got so drunk that they were not able, but lay about the deck like swine, so that we were at last obliged to lift them into the boat, and carry them on shore by force. This want of assistance made our labor intolerably severe; insomuch, that, by going on shore so often that day, the skin was partly stript off my hands.

However, we continued all the day to toil and strain our exertions, till we had brought all on board safe to the shore, so that out of thirty-two people we lost not one.

My dream now returned upon my mind with all its force. It was fulfilled in every part, for our danger was the same I had dreamt of; and I could not help looking on myself as the principal instrument in effecting our deliverance; for, owing to some of our people getting drunk, the rest of us were obliged to double our exertions. And it was fortunate we did, for in a very little time longer the patch of leather on the boat would have been worn out, and she would have been no longer fit for service. Situated as we were, who could think that men should be so careless of the danger they were in? for, if the wind had but raised the swell as it was when the vessel struck, we must have bid a final farewell to all hopes of deliverance; and, though I warned the people who were drinking, and entreated them to embrace the moment of deliverance, nevertheless they persisted, as if not possessed of the least spark of reason. I could not help thinking, that if any of these people had been lost, God would charge me with their lives; which, perhaps, was one cause of my laboring so hard for their preservation. And, indeed, every one of them afterwards seemed so sensible of the service I had rendered them, that while we were on the key I was a kind of chieftain amongst them. I brought some limes, oranges, and lemons ashore; and, finding it to be a good soil where we were, I planted several of them as a token to anyone that might be cast away hereafter. This key, as we afterwards found, was one of the Bahama islands, which consist of a cluster of large islands with smaller ones or keys, as they are called, interspersed among them. It was about a mile in circumference, with a white sandy beach running in a regular order along it.

On that part of it where we first attempted to land, there stood some very large birds, called flamingoes. These, from the reflection of the sun, appeared to us at a little distance as large as men; and when they walked backwards and forwards, we could not conceive what they were. Our captain swore they were cannibals. This created a great panic among us, and we held a consultation how to act. The captain wanted to go to a key that was within sight, but a great way off; but I was against it, as in so doing we should not be able to save all the people. "And therefore," said I, "let us go on shore here, and perhaps these cannibals may take to the water." Accordingly we steered towards them; and when we approached them, to our very great joy and no less wonder, they walked off, one after the other very deliberately; and at last they took flight and relieved us entirely from our fears. About the key there were turtles and several sorts of fish in such abundance that we caught them without bait, which was a great relief to us after the salt provisions on board. There was also a large rock on the beach, about ten feet high, which was in the form of a punch-bowl at the top; this we could not help thinking Providence had ordained to supply us with rain water; and it was something singular, that, if we did not take the water when it rained, in some little time after, it would turn as salt as sea water.

Our first care after refreshment was to make ourselves tents to lodge in, which we did as well as we could with some sails we had brought from the ship. We then began to think how we might get from this place, which was quite uninhabited; and we determined to repair our boat, which was very much shattered, and to put to sea in quest of a ship or some inhabited island. It took us up, however, eleven days before we could get the boat ready for sea in the manner we wanted it, with a sail and other necessaries. When we had got all things prepared, the captain wanted me to stay on shore while he went to sea in quest of a vessel to take all the people off the key. But this I refused; and the captain and myself, with five more, set off in the boat towards New Providence.[1] We had no more than two musket loads of gun-powder with us, if anything should happen, and our stock of provisions consisted of three gallons of rum, four of water, some salt beef, and some biscuit; and in this manner we proceeded to sea.

On the second day of our voyage, we came to an island called Abaco, the largest of the Bahama islands. We were much in want of water, for by this time our water was expended, and we were exceedingly fatigued in pulling two days in the heat of the sun; and it being late in the evening, we hauled the boat ashore to try for water, and remain during the night. When we came ashore we searched for water, but could find none. When it was dark, we made a fire around us for fear of the wild beasts, as the place was an entire thick wood, and we took it by turns to watch. In this situation we found very little rest, and waited with impatience for the morning. As soon as the light appeared we set off again with our boat, in hopes of finding assistance during the day. We were now much dejected and weakened by

---

[1] New Providence Island, site of Nassau.

pulling the boat; for our sail was of no use, and we were almost famished for want of fresh water to drink. We had nothing left to eat but salt beef, and that we could not use without water. In this situation we toiled all day in sight of the island, which was very long; in the evening, seeing no relief, we made shore again, and fastened our boat. We then went to look for fresh water, being quite faint for the want of it; and we dug and searched about for some all the remainder of the evening, but could not find one drop, so that our dejection at this period became excessive, and our terror so great, that we expected nothing but death to deliver us. We could not touch our beef, which was salt as brine, without fresh water, and we were in the greatest terror from the apprehension of wild beasts.

When unwelcome night came, we acted as on the night before; and the next morning we set off again from the island in hopes of seeing some vessel. In this manner we toiled as well as we were able till four o'clock, during which we passed several keys, but could not meet with a ship; and, still famishing with thirst, went ashore on one of those keys again, in hopes of finding some water. Here we found some leaves with a few drops of water in them, which we lapped with much eagerness; we then dug in several places, but without success. As we were digging holes in search of water, there came forth some very thick and black stuff; but none of us could touch it, except the poor Dutch Creole, who drank above a quart of it as eagerly as if it had been wine. We tried to catch fish, but could not; and we now began to repine at our fate, and abandon ourselves to despair, when, in the midst of our murmuring, the captain all at once cried out, "A sail! a sail! a sail!" This gladdening sound was like a reprieve to a convict, and we all instantly returned to look at it; but in a little time some of us began to be afraid it was not a sail. However, at a venture, we embarked and steered after it; and in half an hour to our unspeakable joy, we plainly saw that it was a vessel. At this our drooping spirits revived, and we made towards her with all the speed imaginable. When we came near to her, we found she was a little sloop, about the size of a Gravesend hoy, and quite full of people; a circumstance which we could not make out the meaning of. Our captain, who was a Welshman, swore that they were pirates, and would kill us. I said, be that as it might, we must board her if we were to die by it; and if they should not receive us kindly, we must oppose them as well as we could, for there was no alternative between their perishing and ours. This counsel was immediately taken, and I really believe that the captain, myself, and the Dutchman would then have faced twenty men. We had two cutlasses and a musket, that I brought in the boat; and in this situation, we rowed alongside, and immediately boarded her. I believe there were about forty hands on board; but how great was our surprise, as soon as we got on board, to find that the major part of them were in the same predicament as ourselves.

They belonged to a whaling schooner that was wrecked two days before us, about nine miles to the north of our vessel. When she was wrecked, some of them had taken to their boats, and had left some of their people and property on the key, in the same manner as we had done; and were going like us to New Providence in quest of a ship, when they met with this little sloop, called a wrecker, their employment in those seas being to look after wrecks. They were then going to take the remainder of the people belonging to the schooner; for which the wrecker was to have all things belonging to the vessel, and likewise their people's help to get what they could out of her, and were then to carry the crew to New Providence.

We told the people of the wrecker the condition of our vessel, and we made the same agreement with them as the schooner's people; and, on their complying, we begged of them to go to our key directly, because our people were in want of water. They agreed, therefore, to go along with us first; and in two days we arrived at the key, to the inexpressible joy of the people that we had left behind, as they had been reduced to great extremities for want of water in our absence. Luckily for us, the wrecker had now more people on board than she could carry or victual for any moderate length of time; they therefore hired the schooner's people to work on the wreck, and we left them our boat, and embarked for New Providence.

Nothing could have been more fortunate than our meeting with this wrecker, for New Providence was at such a distance that we never could have reached it in our boat. The island of Abaco was much longer than we expected; and it was not till after sailing for three or four days that we got safe to the farther end of it, towards New Providence. When we arrived there we watered, and got a good many lobsters and other shell-fish; which proved a great relief to us, as our provisions and water were almost exhausted. We then proceeded on our voyage; but the day after we left the island, late in the evening, and whilst we were yet amongst the Bahama keys, we were overtaken by a violent gale of wind, so that we were obliged to cut away the mast. The vessel was very near foundering; for she parted from her anchors, and struck several times on the shoals. Here we expected every minute that she would have gone to pieces, and each moment to be our last; so much so, that my old captain and sickly, useless mate, and several others, fainted; and death stared us in the face on every side.

All the swearers on board now began to call on the God of Heaven to assist them: and, sure enough, beyond our comprehension he did assist us, and in a miraculous manner delivered us! In the very height of our extremity the wind lulled for a few minutes; and, although the swell was high beyond expression, two men, who were expert swimmers, attempted to go to the buoy of the anchor, which we still saw on the water, at some distance, in a little punt that belonged to the wrecker, which was not large enough to carry more than two. She filled at different times in their endeavors to get into her alongside of our vessel; and they saw nothing but death before them, as well as we; but they said they might as well die that way as any other. A coil of very small rope, with a little buoy, was put in along with them; and, at last, with great hazard, they got the punt clear from the vessel; and these two intrepid water heroes paddled away for life towards the buoy of the anchor. Our eyes were fixed on them all the time, expecting every minute to be their last; and the prayers of all those that remained in their senses were offered up to God, on their behalf, for a speedy deliverance, and for our own, which depended on them; and he heard and answered us! These two men at last reached the buoy; and, having fastened the punt to it, they tied one end of their rope to the small buoy that they had in the punt, and sent it adrift towards the vessel. We on board, observing this, threw out boat-hooks and leads fastened to lines, in order to catch the buoy; at last we caught it, and fastened a hawser to the end of the small rope; we then gave them a sign to pull, and they pulled the hawser to them, and fastened it to the buoy, which being done we hauled for our lives; and, through the mercy of God, we got again from the shoals into the deep water, and the punt got safe to the vessel. It is impossible for any to conceive our heart-felt joy at this second deliverance from ruin, but those who have suffered the same hardships. Those whose strength and senses were gone came to themselves, and were now as elated as they were before depressed. Two days after this the wind ceased, and the water became smooth. The punt then went on shore, and we cut down some trees; and having found our mast and mended it, we brought it on board, and fixed it up. As soon as we had done this, we got up the anchor, and away we went once more for New Providence, which in three days more we reached safe, after having been above three weeks in a situation in which we did not expect to escape with life. The inhabitants here were very kind to us; and, when they learned our situation, shewed us a great deal of hospitality and friendship. Soon after this every one of our old fellow sufferers that were free parted from us, and shaped their course where their inclination led them. One merchant, who had a large sloop, seeing our condition, and knowing we wanted to go to Georgia, told four of us that his vessel was going there; and, if we would work on board and load her, he would give us our passage free. As we could not get any wages whatever, and found it very hard to get off the place, we were obliged to consent to his proposal; and we went on board and helped to load the sloop, though we had only our victuals allowed us. When she was entirely loaded, he told us she was going to Jamaica first, where we must go if we went in her. This, however, I refused; but my fellow sufferers not having any money to help themselves with, necessity obliged them to accept of the offer, and to steer that course, though they did not like it.

We stayed in New Providence about seventeen or eighteen days, during which time I met with many friends, who gave me encouragement to stay there with them, but I declined it; though, had not my heart been fixed on England, I should have stayed, as I liked the place extremely, and there were some free black people here who were very happy, and we passed our time pleasantly together, with the melodious sound of the catguts, under the lime and lemon trees. At length Captain Phillips hired a sloop to carry him and some of the slaves that he could not sell to Georgia; and I agreed to go with him in this vessel, meaning now to take my farewell of that place. When the vessel was ready we all embarked; and I took my leave of New Providence, not without regret. We sailed about four o'clock in the morning with a fair wind, for Georgia; and about eleven o'clock the same morning, a sudden and short gale sprung up and blew away most of our sails; and, as we were still among the keys, in a very few minutes it dashed the sloop against the rocks. Luckily for us the water was deep; and the sea was not so angry, but that, after having for some time labored hard, and being many in number, we were saved, through God's mercy; and, by using our greatest exertions, we got the vessel off. The next day we returned to Providence, where we soon got her again refitted. Some of the people swore that we had spells set upon us by somebody in Montserrat; and others that we had witches and wizards amongst the poor helpless slaves; and that we never should arrive safe at Georgia. But these things did not deter me; I said, "Let us again face the winds and seas, and swear not, but trust to God, and he will deliver us." We therefore once more set sail; and with hard labor, in seven days' time, we arrived safe at Georgia.

After our arrival we went up to the town of Savannah; and the same evening I went to a friend's house to lodge, whose name was Mosa, a black man. We were very happy at meeting each other; and after supper we had a light till it was between nine and ten o'clock at night. About that time the watch or patrol came by, and, discerning a light in the house, they knocked at the door; we opened it, and they came in and sat down and drank some punch with us; they also begged some limes of me, as they understood I had some, which I readily gave them. A little after this they told me I must go to the watch house with them; this surprised me a good deal, after our kindness to them; and I asked them, Why so? They said that all Negroes who had a light in their houses after nine o'clock were to be taken into custody, and either pay some dollars or be flogged. Some of those people knew that I was a free man; but, as the man of the house was not free, and had his master to protect him, they did not take the same liberty with him they did with me. I told them that I was a free man, and just arrived from Providence; that we were not making any noise, and that I was not a stranger in that place, but was very well known there: "Besides," said I, "what will you do with me?" "That you shall see," replied they, "but you must go to the watch house with us." Now, whether they meant to get money from me or not I was at a loss to know, but I thought immediately of the oranges and limes at Santa Cruz; and seeing that nothing would pacify them I went with them to the watch house, where I remained during the night. Early the next morning these imposing ruffians flogged a Negro man and woman that they had in the watch house, and then they told me that I must be flogged too. I asked why? and if there was any law for free men? and told them if there was I would have it put in force against them. But this only exasperated them the more, and instantly swore they would serve me as Doctor Perkins had done; and were going to lay violent hands on me; when one of them more humane than the rest, said that as I was a free man they could not justify striping me by law. I then immediately sent for Doctor Brady, who was known to be an honest and worthy man; and on his coming to my assistance they let me go.

This was not the only disagreeable incident I met with while I was in this place; for one day, while I was a little way out of the town of Savannah, I was beset by two white men, who meant to play their usual tricks with me in the way of kidnapping. As soon as these men accosted me, one of them said to the other, "This is the very fellow we are looking for, that you lost," and the other swore I was the identical person. On this they made up to me, and were about to handle me; but I told them to be still and keep off, for I had seen those kind of tricks played upon other free blacks, and they must not think to serve me so. At this they paused a little, and one said to the other—it will not do; and the other answered that I talked too good English. I replied, I believed I did; and I had also with me a revengeful stick equal to the occasion; and my mind was likewise good. Happily, however, it was not used; and after we had talked together a little in this manner the rogues left me.

I stayed in Savannah some time, anxiously trying to get to Montserrat once more, to see Mr. King, my old master, and then to take a final farewell of the American quarter of the globe. At last I met with a sloop called the *Speedwell,* Captain John Bunton, which belonged to Grenada and was bound to Martinique, a French island, with a cargo of rice, and I shipped myself on board of her.

Before I left Georgia, a black woman who had a child lying dead, being very tenacious of the church burial service, and not able to get any white person to perform it, applied to me for that purpose. I told her I was no parson; and besides, that the service over the dead did not affect the soul. This however did not satisfy her; she still urged me very hard: I therefore complied with her earnest entreaties, and at last consented to act the parson for the first time in my life. As she was much respected, there was a great company both of white and black people at the grave. I then accordingly assumed my new vocation, and performed the funeral ceremony to the satisfaction of all present; after which, I bade adieu to Georgia, and sailed for Martinique.

CHAPTER 9

The author arrives at Martinique—Meets with new difficulties—Gets to Montserrat, where he takes leave of his old master, and sails for England— Meets Capt. Pascal—Learns the French horn—Hires himself with Doctor Irving, where he learns to freshen sea water—Leaves the Doctor, and goes a voyage to Turkey and Portugal; and afterwards goes a voyage to Grenada, and another to Jamaica—Returns to the Doctor, and they embark together on a voyage to the North Pole, with the Hon. Captain Phipps—Some account of that voyage, and the dangers the author was in—He returns to England.

I thus took a final leave of Georgia, for the treatment I had received in it disgusted me very much against the place; and when I left it and sailed for Martinique I determined never more to revisit it. My new captain conducted his vessel safer than any former one; and, after an agreeable voyage, we got safe to our intended port. While I was on this island I went about a good deal, and found it very pleasant; in particular, I admired the town of St. Pierre, which is the principal one in the island, and built more like an European town than any I had seen in the West Indies. In general also, slaves were better treated, had more holidays, and looked better than those in the English islands. After we had done our business here, I wanted my discharge, which was necessary; for it was then the month of May, and I wished much to be at Montserrat to bid farewell to

Mr. King, and all my other friends there, in time to sail for Old England in the July fleet. But, alas! I had put a great stumbling block in my own way, by which I was near losing my passage that season to England.

I had lent my captain some money which I now wanted to enable me to prosecute my intentions. This I told him; but when I applied for it, though I urged the necessity of my occasion, I met with so much shuffling from him, that I began at last to be afraid of losing my money, as I could not recover it by law; for I have already mentioned that throughout the West Indies no black man's testimony is admitted, on any occasion, against any white person whatever, and therefore my own oath would have been of no use. I was obliged, therefore, to remain with him till he might be disposed to return it to me. Thus we sailed from Martinique for the Grenadas,[1] I frequently pressing the captain for my money to no purpose; and to render my condition worse, when we got there, the captain and his owners quarrelled, so that my situation became daily more irksome: for besides that, we on board had little or no victuals allowed us, and I could not get my money nor wages, as I could then have gotten my passage free to Montserrat had I been able to accept it. The worst of all was, that it was growing late in July, and the ships in the islands must sail by the 26th of that month. At last, however, with a great many entreaties, I got my money from the captain, and took the first vessel I could meet with for St. Eustatius. From thence I went in another to Basse Terre in St. Kitts, where I arrived on the 19th of July.

On the 22d, having met with a vessel bound to Montserrat, I wanted to go in her; but the captain and others would not take me on board until I should advertise myself, and give notice of my going off the island. I told them of my haste to be in Montserrat, and that the time then would not admit of advertising, it being late in the evening, and the vessel about to sail; but he insisted it was necessary, and otherwise he said he would not take me. This reduced me to great perplexity; for if I should be compelled to submit to this degrading necessity, which every black freeman is under, of advertising himself like a slave, when he leaves an island, and which I thought a gross imposition upon any freeman, I feared I should miss that opportunity of going to Montserrat, and then I could not get to England that year. The vessel was just going off, and no time could be lost; I immediately therefore set about with a heavy heart, to try who I could get to befriend me in complying with the demands of the captain. Luckily I found in a few minutes, some gentlemen of Montserrat whom I knew; and having told them my situation, I requested their friendly assistance in

[1] The Grenadines.

helping me off the island. Some of them, on this, went with me to the captain, and satisfied him of my freedom; and, to my very great joy, he desired me to go on board.

We then set sail, and the next day, 23d, I arrived at the wished-for place, after an absence of six months, in which I had more than once experienced the delivering hand of Providence, when all human means of escaping destruction seemed hopeless. I saw my friends with a gladness of heart which was increased by my absence and the dangers I had escaped, and I was received with great friendship by them all, but particularly by Mr. King, to whom I related the fate of his sloop, the *Nancy*, and the causes of her being wrecked. I now learned with extreme sorrow that his house was washed away during my absence, by the bursting of the pond at the top of a mountain that was opposite the town of Plymouth. It swept great part of the town away, and Mr. King lost a great deal of property from the inundation, and nearly his life.[2] When I told him I intended to go to London that season, and that I had come to visit him before my departure, the good man expressed a great deal of affection for me, and sorrow that I should leave him, and warmly advised me to stay there, insisting, as I was much respected by all the gentlemen in the place, that I might do very well, and in a short time have land and slaves of my own. I thanked him for this instance of his friendship; but, as I wished very much to be in London, I declined remaining any longer there, and begged he would excuse me. I then requested he would be kind enough to give me a certificate of my behavior while in his service, which he very readily complied with, and gave me the following:

MONTSERRAT, JULY 26, 1767.

The bearer hereof, Gustavus Vassa, was my slave for upwards of three years, during which he has always behaved himself well, and discharged his duty with honesty and assiduity.

ROBERT KING

TO ALL WHOM THIS MAY CONCERN.

Having obtained this, I parted from my kind master, after many sincere professions of gratitude and regard, and prepared for my departure for London.

I immediately agreed to go with one Capt. John Hamer, for seven guineas (the passage to London) on board a ship called the *Andromache;*

---

[2] In 1767 Fort Ghaut, a reservoir near Plymouth, Montserrat, overflowed, destroying many houses, including Robert King's, and threatening the whole town.

and on the 24th and 25th, I had free dances, as they are called, with some of my countrymen, previous to my setting off; after which I took leave of all my friends, and on the 26th I embarked for London, exceedingly glad to see myself once more on board of a ship; and still more so, in steering the course I had long wished for. With a light heart I bade Montserrat farewell, and have never had my feet on it since; and with it I bade adieu to the sound of the cruel whip, and all other dreadful instruments of torture; adieu to the offensive sight of the violated chastity of the sable females, which has too often accosted my eyes; adieu to oppressions (although to me less severe than most of my countrymen); and adieu to the angry, howling, dashing surfs. I wished for a grateful and thankful heart to praise the Lord God on high for all his mercies! in this ecstasy, I steered the ship all night.

We had a most prosperous voyage, and, at the end of seven weeks, arrived at Cherry Garden stairs. Thus were my longing eyes once more gratified with the sight of London, after having been absent from it above four years. I immediately received my wages, and I never had earned seven guineas so quick in my life before; I had thirty-seven guineas in all, when I got cleared from the ship. I now entered upon a scene quite new to me, but full of hope. In this situation my first thoughts were to look out for some of my former friends, and amongst the first of those were the Miss Guerins. As soon, therefore, as I had regaled myself I went in quest of those kind ladies, whom I was very impatient to see; and with some difficulty and perseverance, I found them at May's-hill, Greenwich. They were most agreeably surprised to see me, and I quite overjoyed at meeting with them. I told them my history, at which they expressed great wonder, and freely acknowledged it did their cousin, Captain Pascal, no honor. He then visited there frequently; and I met him four or five days after in Greenwich park.

When he saw me he appeared a good deal surprised, and asked me how I came back? I answered, "In a ship." To which he replied dryly, "I suppose you did not walk back to London on the water." As I saw, by his manner, that he did not seem to be sorry for his behavior to me, and that I had not much reason to expect any favor from him, I told him that he had used me very ill, after I had been such a faithful servant to him for so many years; on which, without saying any more, he turned about and went away. A few days after this I met Capt. Pascal at Miss Guerin's house, and asked him for my prize money. He said there was none due to me; for, if my prize money had been £10,000 he had a right to it all. I told him I was informed otherwise: on which he bade me defiance; and in a bantering tone, desired me to commence a law-suit against him for it: "There are lawyers enough," said he, "that will take the cause in hand, and you had better try it." I told him then that I would try it, which enraged him very much; however, out of regard to the ladies, I remained still, and never made any farther demand of my right.

Some time afterwards these friendly ladies asked me what I meant to do with myself, and how they could assist me. I thanked them, and said, if they pleased, I would be their servant; but if not, I had thirty-seven guineas, which would support me for some time, I would be much obliged to them to recommend me to some person who would teach me a business whereby I might earn my living. They answered me very politely, that they were sorry it did not suit them to take me as their servant, and asked me what business I should like to learn? I said, hair dressing. They then promised to assist me in this; and soon after they recommended me to a gentleman, whom I had known before, one Capt. O'Hara, who treated me with much kindness, and procured me a master, a hair dresser, in Coventry court Haymarket, with whom he placed me. I was with this man from September till the February following. In that time we had a neighbor in the same court who taught the French horn. He used to blow it so well that I was charmed with it, and agreed with him to teach me to blow it. Accordingly he took me in hand, and began to instruct me, and I soon learned all the three parts. I took great delight in blowing on this instrument, the evenings being long; and besides that I was fond of it, I did not like to be idle, and it filled up my vacant hours innocently. At this time also I agreed with the Rev. Mr. Gregory, who lived in the same court, where he kept an academy and an evening school, to improve me in arithmetic. This he did as far as barter and alligation; so that all the time I was there I was entirely employed.

In February 1768 I hired myself to Dr. Charles Irving, in Pallmall, so celebrated for his successful experiments in making sea water fresh; and here I had plenty of hair dressing to improve my hand. This gentleman was an excellent master; he was exceedingly kind and good tempered; and allowed me in the evenings to attend my schools, which I esteemed a great blessing; therefore I thanked God and him for it, and used all my diligence to improve the opportunity. This diligence and attention recommended me to the notice and care of my three preceptors, who, on their parts, bestowed a great deal of pains in my instruction, and besides, were all very kind to me. My wages, however, which were by two-thirds less than ever I had in my life (for I had only £12 per annum), I soon found would not be sufficient to defray this extraordinary expense of masters, and my own necessary expenses; my old thirty-seven guineas had by this time worn all away to one. I thought it best, therefore, to try the sea again in quest of more money, as I had been bred to it, and had hitherto found the profession of it successful. I had also a very great desire to see Turkey, and I now determined to gratify it. Accordingly, in the month of May, 1768, I told the doctor my wish to go to sea again, to which he made no opposition; and we parted on friendly terms.

The same day I went into the city in quest of a master. I was extremely fortunate in my inquiry, for I soon heard of a gentleman who had a ship going to Italy and Turkey, and he wanted a man who could dress hair well. I was overjoyed at this and went immediately on board of his ship, as I had been directed, which I found to be fitted up with great taste, and I already foreboded no small pleasure in sailing in her. Not finding the gentleman on board, I was directed to his lodgings, where I met with him the next day, and gave him a specimen of my dressing. He liked it so well that he hired me immediately, so that I was perfectly happy; for the ship, master, and voyage, were entirely to my mind. The ship was called the *Delaware,* and my master's name was John Jolly, a neat, smart, good humored man, just such an one as I wished to serve.

We sailed from England in July following, and our voyage was extremely pleasant. We went to Villa Franca, Nice, and Leghorn; and in all these places I was charmed with the richness and beauty of the countries, and struck with the elegant buildings with which they abound. We had always in them plenty of extraordinary good wines and rich fruits, which I was very fond of; and I had frequent occasions of gratifying both my taste and curiosity; for my captain always lodged on shore in those places, which afforded me opportunities to see the country around. I also learned navigation of the mate, which I was very fond of. When we left Italy we had delightful sailing among the Archipelago islands, and from thence to Smyrna in Turkey. This is a very ancient city; the houses are built of stone, and most of them have graves adjoining to them; so that they sometimes present the appearance of church-yards. Provisions are very plentiful in this city, and good wine less than a penny a pint. The grapes, pomegranates, and many other fruits, were also the richest and largest I ever tasted. The natives are well looking and strong made, and treated me always with great civility. In general I believe they are fond of black people; and several of them gave me pressing invitations to stay amongst them, although they keep the franks, or Christians, separate, and do not suffer them to dwell immediately amongst them. I was astonished in not seeing women in any of their shops, and very rarely any in the streets; and whenever I did they were covered with a veil from head to foot, so that I could not see their faces, except when any of them out of curiosity uncovered them to look at me, which they sometimes did. I was surprised to see how the Greeks are, in some measure, kept under by the Turks, as the Negroes are in the West Indies by the white people. The less refined

Greeks, as I have already hinted, dance here in the same manner as we do in our nation. On the whole, during our stay here, which was about five months, I liked the place and the Turks extremely well. I could not help observing one very remarkable circumstance there: the tails of the sheep are flat and so very large that I have known the tail even of a lamb to weigh from eleven to thirteen pounds. The fat of them is very white and rich, and is excellent in puddings, for which it is much used. Our ship being at length richly loaded with silk and other articles, we sailed for England.

In May 1769, soon after our return from Turkey, our ship made a delightful voyage to Oporto, in Portugal, where we arrived at the time of the carnival. On our arrival, there were sent on board of us thirty-six articles to observe with very heavy penalties if we should break any of them; and none of us even dared to go on board any other vessel or on shore, till the Inquisition[3] had sent on board and searched for everything illegal, especially Bibles. Such as were produced, and certain other things, were sent on shore till the ships were going away; and any person, in whose custody a Bible was found concealed, was to be imprisoned and flogged, and sent into slavery for ten years. I saw here many very magnificent sights, particularly the garden of Eden, where many of the clergy and laity went in procession in their several orders with the host, and sung Te Deum. I had a great curiosity to go into some of their churches, but could not gain admittance, without using the necessary sprinkling of holy water at my entrance. From curiosity, and a wish to be holy, I therefore complied with this ceremony, but its virtues were lost upon me, for I found myself nothing the better for it. This place abounds with plenty of all kinds of provisions. The town is well built and pretty, and commands a fine prospect. Our ship having taken in a load of wine, and other commodities, we sailed for London, and arrived in July following.

Our next voyage was to the Mediterranean. The ship was again got ready, and we sailed in September for Genoa. This is one of the finest cities I ever saw; some of the edifices were of beautiful marble, and made a most noble appearance; and many had very curious fountains before them. The churches were rich and magnificent, and curiously adorned, both in the inside and out. But all this grandeur was, in my eyes, disgraced by the galley slaves, whose condition, both there and in other parts of Italy, is truly piteous and wretched. After we had stayed there some weeks, during which we bought many different things we wanted, and got them very cheap, we sailed to Naples, a charming city, and remarkably clean.

---

[3] Roman Catholic ecclesiastical tribunal that punished heretics and suppressed heretical literature, including Protestant Bibles.

The bay is the most beautiful I ever saw; the moles for shipping are excellent. I thought it extraordinary to see grand operas acted here on Sunday nights, and even attended by their majesties. I too, like these great ones, went to those sights, and vainly served God in the day, while I thus served mammon[4] effectually at night. While we remained here, there happened an eruption of Mount Vesuvius, of which I had a perfect view. It was extremely awful; and we were so near that the ashes from it, used to be thick on our deck. After we had transacted our business at Naples, we sailed with a fair wind, once more for Smyrna, where we arrived in December. A seraskier, or officer, took a liking to me here, and wanted me to stay, and offered me two wives; however, I refused the temptation, thinking one was as much as some could manage, and more than others would venture on. The merchants here travel in caravans or large companies. I have seen many caravans from India, with some hundreds of camels, laden with different goods. The people of these caravans are quite brown. Among other articles, they brought with them a great quantity of locusts, which are a kind of pulse, sweet and pleasant to the palate, and in shape resembling French beans, but longer. Each kind of goods is sold in a street by itself, and I always found the Turks very honest in their dealings. They let no Christians into their mosques or churches, for which I was very sorry; as I was always fond of going to see the different modes of worship of the people wherever I went. The plague broke out while we were in Smyrna, and we stopped taking goods into the ship till it was over. She was then richly laden, and we sailed in about March 1770 for England. One day in our passage, we met with an accident, which was near burning the ship. A black cook, in melting some fat, overset the pan into the fire under the deck, which immediately began to blaze, and the flame went up very high under the foretop. With the fright, the poor cook became almost white, and altogether speechless. Happily, however, we got the fire out, without doing much mischief. After various delays in this passage, which was tedious, we arrived in Standgate creek in July; and, at the latter end of the year, some new event occurred, so that my noble captain, the ship, and I, all separated.

In April 1771, I shipped myself as steward, with Captain William Robertson, of the ship *Grenada Planter,* once more to try my fortune in the West Indies; and we sailed from London for Madeira, Barbadoes, and the Grenadas. When we were at this last place, having some goods to sell, I met once more with my former kind of West India customers.

A white man, an islander, bought some goods of me, to the amount of

---

[4] Material wealth or goods. See Matthew 6:24: "No one can serve two masters. . . . You cannot serve God and mammon."

some pounds, and made me many fair promises as usual, but without any intention of paying me. He had likewise bought goods from some more of our people, whom he intended to serve in the same manner; but he still amused us with promises. However, when our ship was loaded, and near sailing, this honest buyer discovered no intention or sign of paying for anything he had bought of us; but on the contrary, when I asked him for my money, he threatened me and another black man he had bought goods of, so that we found we were like to get more blows than payment. On this, we went to complain to one Mr. M'Intosh, a justice of the peace; we told his worship of the man's villainous tricks, and begged that he would be kind enough to see us redressed; but being Negroes, although free, we could not get any remedy; and our ship being then just upon the point of sailing, we knew not how to help ourselves, though we thought it hard to lose our property in this manner. Luckily for us, however, this man was also indebted to three white sailors, who could not get a farthing from him; they therefore readily joined us, and we all went together in search of him. When we found where he was, I took him out of a house and threatened him with vengeance; on which, finding he was likely to be handled roughly, the rogue offered each of us some small allowance, but nothing near our demands. This exasperated us much more; and some were for cutting his ears off; but he begged hard for mercy, which was at last granted him, after we had entirely stripped him. We then let him go, for which he thanked us, glad to get off so easily, and ran into the bushes, after having wished us a good voyage. We then repaired on board, and shortly after set sail for England. I cannot help remarking here, a very narrow escape we had from being blown up, owing to a piece of negligence of mine. Just as our ship was under sail, I went down under the cabin, to do some business, and had a lighted candle in my hand, which, in my hurry, without thinking, I held in a barrel of gunpowder. It remained in the powder until it was near catching fire, when fortunately, I observed it, and snatched it out in time, and providentially no harm happened; but I was so overcome with terror that I immediately fainted at this deliverance.

In twenty-eight days' time, we arrived in England, and I got clear of this ship. But, being still of a roving disposition, and desirous of seeing as many different parts of the world as I could, I shipped myself soon after, in the same year, as steward on board of a fine large ship, called the *Jamaica*, Capt. David Watt; and we sailed from England in December 1771, for Nevis and Jamaica. I found Jamaica to be a very fine, large island, well peopled, and the most considerable of the West India islands. There was a vast number of Negroes here, whom I found as usual, exceedingly imposed upon by the white people, and the slaves punished as in the other islands. There are Negroes whose business is to flog slaves; they go about to different people for employment, and the usual pay is from one to four bits. I saw many cruel punishments inflicted on the slaves, in the short time I stayed here. In particular, I was present when a poor fellow was tied up and kept hanging by the wrists, at some distance from the ground, and then some half hundred weights were fixed to his ankles, in which posture he was flogged unmercifully. There was also, as I heard, two different masters noted for cruelty on the island, who had staked up two Negroes naked, and in two hours the vermin stung them to death. I heard a gentleman, I well knew, tell my captain, that he passed sentence on a Negro man to be burnt alive for attempting to poison an overseer.

I pass over numerous other instances, in order to relieve the reader, by a milder scene of roguery. Before I had been long on the island, one Mr. Smith, at Port Morant, bought goods of me to the amount of twenty-five pounds sterling; but when I demanded payment from him, he was going each time to beat me, and threatened that he would put me in jail. One time he would say I was going to set his house on fire; at another, he would swear I was going to run away with his slaves. I was astonished at this usage, from a person who was in the situation of a gentleman, but I had no alternative, and was, therefore, obliged to submit.

When I came to Kingston, I was surprised to see the number of Africans who were assembled together on Sundays, particularly at a large commodious place, called Spring Path. Here each different nation of Africa meet and dance after the manner of their own country. They still retain most of their native customs; they bury their dead, and put victuals, pipes, and tobacco, and other things, in the grave with the corpse, in the same manner as in Africa.

Our ship having got her loading, we sailed for London, where we arrived in the August following. On my return to London, I waited on my old and good master, Dr. Irving, who made me an offer of his service again. Being now tired of the sea, I gladly accepted it. I was very happy in living with this gentleman once more, during which time we were daily employed in reducing old Neptune's dominions, by purifying the briny element and making it fresh.[5] Thus I went on till May 1773, when I was roused by the sound of fame, to seek new adventures, and find, towards the North Pole, what our Creator never intended we should, a passage to India.

An expedition was now fitting out to explore a north-east passage, conducted by the Honorable Constantine John Phipps, since Lord Mul-

---

[5] Constantine John Phipps, *A Voyage towards the North Pole Undertaken by His Majesty's Command, 1773* (London, 1774), includes a diagram and description of Doctor Irving's still.

grave, in his Majesty's sloop-of-war, the *Race Horse*. My master being anxious for the reputation of this adventure, we therefore prepared everything for our voyage, and I attended him on board the *Race Horse*, the 24th day of May, 1773. We proceeded to Sheerness, where we were joined by his Majesty's sloop, the *Carcass*, commanded by Captain Lutwidge. On the 4th of June, we sailed towards our destined place, the Pole; and on the 15th of the same month, we were off Shetland.

On this day I had a great and unexpected deliverance, from an accident which was near blowing up the ship and destroying the crew, which made me ever after, during the voyage, uncommonly cautious. The ship was so filled that there was very little room on board for anyone, which placed me in a very awkward situation. I had resolved to keep a journal of this singular and interesting voyage; and I had no other place for this purpose but a little cabin, or the doctor's store-room, where I slept. This little place was stuffed with all manner of combustibles, particularly with tow[6] and aquafortis,[7] and many other dangerous things. Unfortunately, it happened in the evening, as I was writing my journal, that I had occasion to take the candle out of the lanthorn,[8] and a spark having touched a single thread of the tow, all the rest caught the flame, and immediately the whole was in a blaze. I saw nothing but present death before me, and expected to be the first to perish in the flames. In a moment the alarm was spread, and many people who were near, ran to assist in putting out the fire. All this time, I was in the very midst of the flames; my shirt and the handkerchief on my neck, were burnt, and I was almost smothered with the smoke. However, through God's mercy, as I was nearly giving up all hopes, some people brought blankets and mattresses, and threw them on the flames, by which means in a short time the fire was put out. I was severely reprimanded and menaced by such of the officers who knew it, and strictly charged never more to go there with a light; and, indeed, even my own fears made me give heed to this command for a little time; but at last, not being able to write my journal in any other part of the ship, I was tempted again to venture by stealth, with a light in the same cabin, though not without considerable fear and dread on my mind.

On the 20th of June, we began to use Dr. Irving's apparatus for making salt water fresh; I used to attend the distillery: I frequently purified from twenty-six to forty gallons a day. The water thus distilled was perfectly pure, well tasted, and free from salt, and was used on various occasions on board the ship. On the 28th of June, being in latitude 78, we made

[6] Rope.
[7] Nitric acid.
[8] Lantern.

Greenland, where I was surprised to see the sun did not set. The weather now became extremely cold; and as we sailed between north and east, which was our course, we saw many very high and curious mountains of ice; and also a great number of very large whales, which used to come close to our ship, and blow the water up to a very great height in the air. One morning we had vast quantities of sea horses about the ship, which neighed exactly like any other horses.[9] We fired some harpoon guns amongst them, in order to take some, but we could not get any. The 30th, the captain of a Greenland ship came on board, and told us of three ships that were lost in the ice; however, we still held on our course, till July the 11th, when we were stopt by one compact and impenetrable body of ice. We ran along it from east to west about ten degrees; and on the 27th, we got as far north as 80°37'; and in 19 or 20 degrees, east longitude from London.

On the 29th and 30th of July, we saw one continued plain of smooth, unbroken ice, bounded only by the horizon; and we fastened to a piece of ice that was eight yards eleven inches thick. We had generally sunshine, and constant daylight; which gave cheerfulness and novelty to the whole of this striking, grand, and uncommon scene; and, to heighten it still more, the reflection of the sun from the ice gave the clouds a most beautiful appearance. We killed many different animals at this time, and among the rest nine bears. Though they had nothing in their paunches but water, yet they were all very fat. We used to decoy them to the ship sometimes by burning feathers or skins. I thought them coarse eating, but some of the ship's company relished them very much. Some of our people, once in the boat, fired at and wounded a sea horse, which dived immediately, and in a little time after, brought up with it a number of others. They all joined in an attack upon the boat, and were with difficulty prevented from staving or oversetting her; but a boat from the *Carcass* having come to assist ours, and joined it, they dispersed, after having wrested an oar from one of the men. One of the ship's boats had before been attacked in the same manner, but happily no harm was done. Though we wounded several of these animals we never got but one.

We remained hereabouts until the 1st of August, when the two ships got completely fastened in the ice, occasioned by the loose ice that set in from the sea. This made our situation very dreadful and alarming; so that on the 7th day, we were in very great apprehension of having the ships squeezed to pieces. The officers now held a council to know what was best

---

[9] Walruses. The Russian word *morse* was corrupted by the sailors to "sea horse." (Phipps, *Voyage*, 184.)

for us to do in order to save our lives; and it was determined that we should endeavor to escape by dragging our boats along the ice towards the sea, which, however, was farther off than any of us thought. This determination filled us with extreme dejection, and confounded us with despair, for we had very little prospect of escaping with life. However, we sawed some of the ice about the ships, to keep it from hurting them, and thus kept them in a kind of pond. We then began to drag the boats as well as we could towards the sea; but, after two or three days' labor, we made very little progress, so that some of our hearts totally failed us; and I really began to give up myself for lost, when I saw our surrounding calamities. While we were at this hard labor, I once fell into a pond we had made amongst some loose ice, and was very near being drowned; but providentially some people were near who gave me immediate assistance, and thereby I escaped drowning.

Our deplorable condition, which kept up the constant apprehension of our perishing in the ice, brought me gradually to think of eternity, in such a manner as I never had done before. I had the fears of death hourly upon me, and shuddered at the thoughts of meeting the grim king of terrors in the natural state I then was in, and was exceedingly doubtful of a happy eternity if I should die in it. I had no hopes of my life being prolonged for any time; for we saw that our existence could not be long on the ice after leaving the ships, which were now out of sight, and some miles from the boats. Our appearance now became truly lamentable; pale dejection seized every countenance; many, who had been before blasphemers, in this our distress, began to call on the good God of Heaven for his help; and in the time of our utter need he heard us, and against hope or human probability, delivered us! It was the eleventh day of the ships' being thus fastened, and the fourth of our drawing the boats in this manner, that the wind changed to the E. N. E. The weather immediately became mild, and the ice broke towards the sea, which was to the S. W. of us. Many of us on this got on board again, and with all our might we hove the ships into every open water we could find, and made all the sail on them in our power; and now, having a prospect of success, we made signals for the boats, and the remainder of the people.

This seemed to us like a reprieve from death, and happy was the man who could first get on board of any ship, or the first boat he could meet. We then proceeded in this manner, till we got into the open water again, which we accomplished in about thirty hours, to our infinite joy and gladness of heart. As soon as we were out of danger, we came to anchor and refitted; and on the 19th of August, we sailed from this uninhabited extremity of the world, where the inhospitable climate affords neither food nor shelter, and not a tree or a shrub of any kind grows amongst its barren rocks; but all is one desolate and expanded waste of ice, which even the constant beams of the sun for six months in the year cannot penetrate or dissolve.

The sun now being on the decline, the days shortened as we sailed to the southward; and, on the 28th, in latitude 73, it was dark by ten o'clock at night. September 10th, in latitude 58, 59, we met a very severe gale of wind and high seas, and shipped a great deal of water in the space of ten hours. This made us work exceedingly hard at all our pumps a whole day; and one sea, which struck the ship with more force than anything I ever met with of the kind before, laid her under water for some time, so that we thought she would have gone down. Two boats were washed from the booms, and the long-boat from the chucks; all other moveable things on the decks were also washed away, among which were many curious things, of different kinds, which we had brought from Greenland; and we were obliged, in order to lighten the ship, to toss some of our guns overboard. We saw a ship at the same time, in very great distress, and her masts were gone; but we were unable to assist her. We now lost sight of the *Carcass*, till the 26th, when we saw land about Orfordness, of which place she joined us. From thence we sailed for London, and on the 30th came up to Deptford.

And thus ended our Arctic voyage, to the no small joy of all on board, after having been absent four months, in which time, at the imminent hazard of our lives, we explored nearly as far towards the Pole as 81 degrees north, and 20 degrees east longitude; being much farther, by all accounts, than any navigator had ever ventured before; in which we fully proved the impracticability of finding a passage that way to India.

CHAPTER 10

The author leaves Doctor Irving, and engages on board a Turkey ship— Account of a black man's being kidnapped on board and sent to the West Indies, and the author's fruitless endeavors to procure his freedom—Some account of the manner of the author's conversion to the faith of Jesus Christ.

Our voyage to the North Pole being ended, I returned to London with Doctor Irving, with whom I continued for some time, during which I began seriously to reflect on the dangers I had escaped, particularly those of my last voyage, which made a lasting impression on my mind, and by the grace of God proved afterwards a mercy to me; it caused me to reflect deeply on my eternal state, and to seek the Lord with full purpose of heart ere it was too late. I rejoiced greatly; and heartily thanked the Lord for directing me to London, where I was determined to work out my own salvation, and in so doing procure a title to heaven; being the result of a mind blinded by ignorance and sin.

In process of time I left my master, Doctor Irving, the purifier of waters. I lodged in Coventry court, Haymarket, where I was continually oppressed and much concerned about the salvation of my soul, and was determined (in my own strength) to be a first-rate Christian. I used every means for this purpose; and, not being able to find any person amongst those with whom I was then acquainted that acquiesced with me in point of religion, or, in scripture language, that would show me any good, I was much dejected, and knew not where to seek relief; however, I first frequented the neighboring churches, St. James's and others, two or three times a day, for many weeks; still I came away dissatisfied: something was wanting that I could not obtain, and I really found more heart-felt relief in reading my Bible at home than in attending the church; and, being resolved to be saved, I pursued other methods. First I went among the Quakers, where the word of God was neither read or preached, so that I remained as much in the dark as ever. I then searched into the Roman Catholic principles, but was not in the least edified. I at length had recourse to the Jews, which availed me nothing, as the fear of eternity daily harassed my mind, and I knew not where to seek shelter from the wrath to come. However, this was my conclusion, at all events, to read the four evangelists, and whatever sect or party I found adhering thereto, such I would join.

Thus I went on heavily, without any guide to direct me the way that leadeth to eternal life. I asked different people questions about the manner of going to heaven, and was told different ways. Here I was much staggered, and could not find any at that time more righteous than myself, or indeed so much inclined to devotion. I thought we should not all be saved (this is agreeable to the holy scriptures) nor would all be damned. I found none among the circle of my acquaintance that kept wholly the Ten Commandments. So righteous was I in my own eyes, that I was convinced I excelled many of them in that point, by keeping eight out of ten; and finding those who in general termed themselves Christians not so honest or so good in their morals as the Turks, I really thought the Turks were in a safer way of salvation than my neighbors; so that between hopes and fears I went on, and the chief comforts I enjoyed were in the musical French horn, which I then practised, and also dressing of hair. Such was my situation some months, experiencing the dishonesty of many people here. I determined at last to set out for Turkey, and there to end my days.

It was now early in the spring, 1774. I sought for a master, and found a Captain John Hughes, commander of a ship called *Anglicanai,* fitting out in the river Thames, and bound to Smyrna, in Turkey. I shipped myself with him as a steward; at the same time I recommended to him a very clever black man, John Annis, as a cook. This man was on board the ship near two months doing his duty; he had formerly lived many years with Mr. William Kirkpatrick, a gentleman of the island of St. Kitts, from whom he parted by consent, though he afterwards tried many schemes to inveigle the poor man. He had applied to many captains who traded to St. Kitts to trepan him; and when all their attempts and schemes of kidnapping proved abortive, Mr. Kirkpatrick came to our ship at Union Stairs, on Easter Monday, April the fourth, with two wherry boats and six men, having learned that the man was on board, and tied, and forcibly took him away from the ship, in the presence of the crew and the chief mate, who had detained him after he had information to come away. I believe this was a combined piece of business; but, be that as it may, it certainly reflected great disgrace on the mate and captain also, who, although they had desired the oppressed man to stay on board, yet this vile act on the man who had served him, he did not in the least assist to recover or pay me a farthing of his wages, which was about five pounds.

I proved the only friend he had, who attempted to regain him his liberty if possible, having known the want of liberty myself. I sent as soon as I could to Gravesend, and got knowledge of the ship in which he was; but unluckily she had sailed the first tide after he was put on board. My intention was then immediately to apprehend Mr. Kirkpatrick, who was about setting off for Scotland; and, having obtained a habeas corpus[1] for him and got a tipstaff[2] to go with me to St. Paul's churchyard, where he lived, he, suspecting something of this kind, set a watch to look out.

My being known to them obliged me to use the following deception: I whitened my face, that they might not know me; and this had the desired effect. He did not go out of his house that night, and next morning I contrived a well plotted stratagem, notwithstanding he had a gentleman in his house to personate him. My direction to the tipstaff, who got admittance into the house, was to conduct him to a judge, according to the writ. When he came there, his plea was, that he had not the body in custody, on which he was admitted to bail.

---

[1] *Habeas corpus ad subjiciendum,* a writ, or document, questioning whether someone is being legally imprisoned or held by another person.
[2] An officer.

I proceeded immediately to that well-known philanthropist, Granville Sharp, Esq., who received me with the utmost kindness, and gave me every instruction that was needful on the occasion.[3] I left him in full hope that I should gain the unhappy man his liberty, with the warmest sense of gratitude towards Mr. Sharp, for his kindness; but alas! my attorney proved unfaithful; he took my money, lost me many months' employ, and did not do the least good in the cause; and when the poor man arrived at St. Kitts, he was, according to custom, staked to the ground with four pins through a cord, two on his wrists, and two on his ankles, was cut and flogged most unmercifully and afterwards loaded cruelly with irons about his neck. I had two very moving letters from him, while he was in this situation, and made attempts to go after him at a great hazard, but was sadly disappointed. I also was told of it by some very respectable families now in London, who saw him in St. Kitts, in the same state, in which he remained till kind death released him out of the hands of his tyrants.

During this disagreeable business I was under strong convictions of sin, and thought that my state was worse than any man's; my mind was unaccountably disturbed; I often wished for death, though at the same time convinced I was altogether unprepared for that awful summons. Suffering much by villains in the late cause, and being much concerned about the state of my soul, these things (but particularly the latter) brought me very low, so that I became a burden to myself and viewed all things around me as emptiness and vanity, which could give no satisfaction to a troubled conscience.

I was again determined to go to Turkey, and resolved, at that time, never more to return to England. I engaged as a steward on board a Turkeyman (the *Wester Hall,* Captain Lina) but was prevented by means of my late captain, Mr. Hughes, and others. All this appeared to be against me, and the only comfort I then experienced was in reading the Holy Scriptures, where I saw that "there is no new thing under the sun" (Eccles. 1:9); and what was appointed for me I must submit to. Thus I continued to travel in much heaviness, and frequently murmured against the Almighty, particularly in his providential dealings; and, awful to think! I began to blaspheme, and wished often to be anything but a human being.

In these severe conflicts the Lord answered me by awful "visions of the night, when deep sleep falleth upon men, in slumberings upon the bed" (Job 33:15). He was pleased, in much mercy, to give me to see, and in some measure understand, the great and awful scene of the judgment day, that "no unclean person, no unholy thing, can enter into the king-

[3]British abolitionist Granville Sharp (1735–1813) had been rescuing blacks from being shipped to the West Indies since the 1760s.

dom of God" (Eph. 5:5). I would then, if it had been possible, have changed my nature with the meanest worm on the earth; and was ready to say to the mountains and rocks "fall on me" (Rev. 6:16), but all in vain. I then in the greatest agony requested the divine Creator that he would grant me a small space of time to repent of my follies and vile iniquities, which I felt were grievous. The Lord, in his manifold mercies, was pleased to grant my request, and, being yet in a state of time, the sense of God's mercies were so great on my mind when I awoke that my strength entirely failed me for many minutes, and I was exceedingly weak. This was the first spiritual mercy I ever was sensible of, and being on praying ground, as soon as I recovered a little strength, and got out of bed and dressed myself, I invoked heaven, from my inmost soul, and fervently begged that God would never again permit me to blaspheme his most holy name. The Lord, who is long-suffering and full of compassion to such poor rebels as we are, condescended to hear and answer. I felt that I was altogether unholy, and saw clearly what a bad use I had made of the faculties I was endowed with: they were given me to glorify God with; I thought, therefore, I had better want them here, and enter into life eternal, than abuse them and be cast into hell fire. I prayed to be directed, if there were any holier than those with whom I was acquainted, that the Lord would point them out to me. I appealed to the Searcher of hearts, whether I did not wish to love him more, and serve him better. Notwithstanding all this, the reader may easily discern, if a believer, that I was still in nature's darkness. At length I hated the house in which I lodged, because God's most holy name was blasphemed in it; then I saw the word of God verified, *viz.*, "Before they call, I will answer; and while they are yet speaking, I will hear."[4]

I had a great desire to read the Bible the whole day at home; but not having a convenient place for retirement, I left the house in the day, rather than stay amongst the wicked ones; and that day, as I was walking, it pleased God to direct me to a house where there was an old sea-faring man, who experienced much of the love of God shed abroad in his heart. He began to discourse with me; and, as I desired to love the Lord, his conversation rejoiced me greatly; and, indeed, I had never heard before the love of Christ to believers set forth in such a manner, and in so clear a point of view. Here I had more questions to put to the man than his time would permit him to answer; and in that memorable hour there came in a dissenting minister; he joined our discourse, and asked me some few questions; among others, where I heard the Gospel preached? I knew not

[4] Isaiah 65:24.

what he meant by hearing the Gospel; I told him I had read the Gospel; and he asked where I went to church, or whether I went at all or not? To which I replied, "I attended St. James's, St. Martin's, and St. Ann's Soho." "So," said he, "you are a churchman?" I answered, I was. He then invited me to a love-feast at his chapel that evening. I accepted the offer, and thanked him; and soon after he went away, I had some further discourse with the old Christian, added to some profitable reading, which made me exceedingly happy. When I left him he reminded me of coming to the feast; I assured him I would be there.

Thus we parted, and I weighed over the heavenly conversation that passed between these two men, which cheered my then heavy and drooping spirit more than anything I had met with for many months. However, I thought the time long in going to my supposed banquet. I also wished much for the company of these friendly men; their company pleased me much; and I thought the gentleman very kind in asking me, a stranger, to a feast; but how singular did it appear to me, to have it in a chapel!

When the wished-for hour came I went, and happily the old man was there, who kindly seated me, as he belonged to the place. I was much astonished to see the place filled with people, and no signs of eating and drinking. There were many ministers in the company. At last they began by giving out hymns, and between the singing, the ministers engaged in prayer; in short, I knew not what to make of this sight, having never seen anything of the kind in my life before now. Some of the guests began to speak their experience, agreeable to what I read in the Scriptures; much was said by every speaker of the providence of God, and his unspeakable mercies, to each of them. This I knew in a great measure, and could most heartily join them. But when they spoke of a future state, they seemed to be altogether certain of their calling and election of God; and that no one could ever separate them from the love of Christ, or pluck them out of his hands. This filled me with utter consternation, intermingled with admiration.

I was so amazed as not to know what to think of the company; my heart was attracted, and my affections were enlarged. I wished to be as happy as them, and was persuaded in my mind that they were different from the world "that lieth in wickedness" (I John 5:19). Their language and singing, &c., did well harmonize; I was entirely overcome, and wished to live and die thus. Lastly, some persons in the place produced some neat baskets full of buns, which they distributed about; and each person communicated with his neighbor, and sipped water out of different mugs, which they handed about to all who were present.

This kind of Christian fellowship I had never seen, nor ever thought of seeing on earth; it fully reminded me of what I had read in the Holy Scriptures, of the primitive Christians, who loved each other and broke bread, in partaking of it, even from house to house. This entertainment (which lasted about four hours) ended in singing and prayer. It was the first soul feast I ever was present at. This last twenty-four hours produced me things, spiritual and temporal, sleeping and waking, judgment and mercy, that I could not but admire the goodness of God, in directing the blind, blasphemous sinner in the path that he knew not of, even among the just; and, instead of judgment, he has shewed mercy, and will hear and answer the prayers and supplications of every returning prodigal:

> O! to grace how great a debtor
> Daily I'm constrained to be![5]

After this I was resolved to win Heaven if possible; and if I perished I thought it should be at the feet of Jesus, in praying to him for salvation. After having been an eye-witness to some of the happiness which attended those who feared God, I knew not how, with any kind of propriety, to return to my lodgings, where the name of God was continually profaned, at which I felt the greatest horror; I paused in my mind for some time, not knowing what to do; whether to hire a bed elsewhere, or go home again. At last fearing an evil report might arise, I went home, with a farewell to card playing and vain jesting, &c. I saw that time was very short, eternity long, and very near; and I viewed those persons alone blessed who were found ready at midnight call, or when the judge of all, both quick and dead, cometh.

The next day I took courage, and went to Holborn, to see my new and worthy acquaintance, the old man, Mr. C——; he, with his wife, a gracious woman, were at work, at silk weaving; they seemed mutually happy, and both quite glad to see me, and I more so to see them. I sat down and we conversed much about soul matters, &c. Their discourse was amazingly delightful, edifying, and pleasant. I knew not at last how to leave this agreeable pair, till time summoned me away. As I was going they lent me a little book, entitled *The Conversion of an Indian*. It was in questions and answers. The poor man came over the sea to London to inquire after the Christian's God, who (through rich mercy) he found and had not his journey in vain. The above book was of great use to me, and at that time was a means of strengthening my faith; however, in parting, they both invited me to call on them when I pleased.

This delighted me, and I took care to make all the improvement from it I

[5]Robert Robinson (1735–1790), Hymn 686, "Come, Thou Fount of Every Blessing." (*The Hymnal 1982, according to the Use of the Episcopal Church* [New York: Church Pension Fund, 1985].)

could; and so far I thanked God for such company and desires. I prayed that the many evils I felt within might be done away, and that I might be weaned from my former carnal acquaintances. This was quickly heard and answered, and I was soon connected with those whom the scripture calls the excellent of the earth. I heard the gospel preached, and the thoughts of my heart and actions were laid open by the preachers, and the way of salvation by Christ alone was evidently set forth. Thus I went on happily for near two months; and I once heard, during this period, a reverend gentleman, Mr. G——, speak of a man who had departed this life in full assurance of his going to glory.

I was much astonished at the assertion; and did very deliberately inquire how he could get at this knowledge. I was answered fully, agreeable to what I read in the oracles of truth; and was told also that if I did not experience the new birth and the pardon of my sins, through the blood of Christ, before I died, I could not enter the kingdom of heaven. I knew not what to think of this report, as I thought I kept eight commandments out of ten; then my worthy interpreter told me I did not do it, nor could I; and he added, that no man ever did or could keep the commandments, without offending in one point. I thought this sounded very strange, and puzzled me much for many weeks: for I thought it a hard saying.

I then asked my friend Mr. L——d, who was a clerk in a chapel, why the commandments of God were given, if we could not be saved by them? To which he replied, "The law is a schoolmaster to bring us to Christ," who alone could and did keep the commandments, and fulfilled all their requirements for his elect people, even those to whom he had given a living faith, and the sins of those chosen vessels *were already* atoned for and forgiven them whilst living; and if I did not experience the same before my exit, the Lord would say at that great day to me, "Go, ye cursed," &c., &c., for God would appear faithful in his judgments to the wicked, as he would be faithful in shewing mercy to those who were ordained to it before the world was; therefore Christ Jesus seemed to be all in all to that man's soul.

I was much wounded at this discourse, and brought into such a dilemma as I never expected. I asked him, if *he* was to die that moment, whether he was sure to enter the kingdom of God? and added, "Do you *know* that your sins are forgiven you?" He answered in the affirmative. Then confusion, anger, and discontent seized me, and I staggered much at this sort of doctrine; it brought me to a stand, not knowing which to believe, whether salvation by works, or by faith only in Christ. I requested him to tell me how I might know when my sins were forgiven me. He assured me he could not, and that none but God alone could do this. I told him it was very mysterious; but he said it was really matter of fact, and quoted many portions of scripture immediately to the point, to which I could make no reply. He then desired me to pray to God to shew me these things. I answered, that I prayed to God every day. He said, "I perceive you are a churchman." I answered, I was. He then entreated me to beg of God to shew me the true state of my soul. I thought the prayer very short and odd; so we parted for that time. I weighed all these things well over, and could not help thinking how it was possible for a man to know that his sins were forgiven him in this life. I wished that God would reveal this self-same thing unto me.

In a short time after this I went to Westminster chapel; the Rev. Mr. P—— preached from Lam. 3:39.[6] It was a wonderful sermon; he clearly shewed that a living man had no cause to complain for the punishments of his sins; he evidently justified the Lord in all his dealings with the sons of men; he also shewed the justice of God in the eternal punishment of the wicked and impenitent. The discourse seemed to me like a two-edged sword, cutting all ways; it afforded me much joy, intermingled with many fears about my soul; and when it was ended, he gave it out that he intended, the ensuing week, to examine all those who meant to attend the Lord's table.

Now I thought much of my good works, and at the same time was doubtful of my being a proper object to receive the sacrament; I was full of meditation till the day of examining. However, I went to the chapel, and, though much distressed, I addressed the reverend gentleman, thinking if I was not right, he would endeavor to convince me of it. When I conversed with him, the first thing he asked me was, what I knew of Christ? I told him I believed in him, and had been baptized in his name. "Then," said he, "when were you brought to the knowledge of God? and how were you convinced of sin?" I knew not what he meant by these questions; I told him I kept eight commandments out of ten; but that I sometimes swore on board ship, and sometimes when on shore, and broke the Sabbath. He then asked me if I could read? I answered, "Yes." "Then," said he, "do you not read in the Bible, he that offends in one point is guilty of all?" I said, "Yes." Then he assured me, that one sin unatoned for was as sufficient to damn a soul as one leak was to sink a ship. Here I was struck with awe; for the minister exhorted me much, and reminded me of the shortness of time, and the length of eternity, and that no unregenerate soul, or anything unclean, could enter the kingdom of Heaven.

He did not admit me as a communicant, but recommended me to read

[6] "Wherefore doth a living man complain, a man for the punishment of his sins?"

the scriptures and hear the word preached, not to neglect fervent prayer to God, who has promised to hear the supplications of those who seek him in godly sincerity; so I took my leave of him, with many thanks, and resolved to follow his advice, so far as the Lord would condescend to enable me. During this time I was out of employ, nor was I likely to get a situation suitable for me, which obliged me to go once more to sea. I engaged as steward of a ship called the *Hope*, Captain Richard Strange, bound from London to Cadiz in Spain. In a short time after I was on board, I heard the name of God much blasphemed, and I feared greatly lest I should catch the horrible infection. I thought if I sinned again after having life and death set evidently before me, I should certainly go to hell. My mind was uncommonly chagrined, and I murmured much at God's providential dealings with me, and was discontented with the commandments, that I could not be saved by what I had done; I hated all things, and wished I had never been born; confusion seized me, and I wished to be annihilated.

One day I was standing on the very edge of the stern of the ship, thinking to drown myself; but this scripture was instantly impressed on my mind—"That no murderer hath eternal life abiding in him" (I John 3:15). Then I paused and thought myself the unhappiest man living. Again I was convinced that the Lord was better to me than I deserved, and I was better off in the world than many. After this I began to fear death; I fretted, mourned, and prayed, till I became a burden to others, but more so to myself. At length I concluded to beg my bread on shore rather than go again to sea amongst a people who feared not God, and I entreated the captain three different times to discharge me; he would not, but each time gave me greater and greater encouragement to continue with him, and all on board shewed me very great civility: notwithstanding all this I was unwilling to embark again. At last some of my religious friends advised me, by saying it was my lawful calling, consequently it was my duty to obey, and that God was not confined to place, &c., &c. particularly Mr. G——S——, the governor of Tothil-fields, Bridewell, who pitied my case, and read the eleventh chapter of the Hebrews to me, with exhortations. He prayed for me, and I believed that he prevailed on my behalf, as my burden was then greatly removed, and I found a heartfelt resignation to the will of God. The good man gave me a pocket Bible and Alleine's *Alarm to the Unconverted*. We parted, and the next day I went on board again. We sailed for Spain, and I found favor with the captain. It was the fourth of the month of September when we sailed from London; we had a delightful voyage to Cadiz, where we arrived the twenty-third of the same month. The place is strong, commands a fine prospect, and is very rich.

The Spanish galleons frequent that port, and some arrived whilst we were there. I had many opportunities of reading the scriptures. I wrestled hard with God in fervent prayer, who had declared in his word that he would hear the groanings and deep sighs of the poor in spirit. I found this verified to my utter astonishment and comfort in the following manner.

On the morning of the 6th of October (I pray you to attend), all that day, I thought I should either see or hear something supernatural. I had a secret impulse on my mind of something that was to take place, which drove me continually for that time to a throne of grace. It pleased God to enable me to wrestle with him, as Jacob did: I prayed that if sudden death were to happen, and I perished, it might be at Christ's feet.

In the evening of the same day, as I was reading and meditating on the fourth chapter of Acts, twelfth verse,[7] under the solemn apprehensions of eternity, and reflecting on my past actions, I began to think I had lived a moral life, and that I had a proper ground to believe I had an interest in the divine favor; but still meditating on the subject, not knowing whether salvation was to be had partly for our own good deeds or solely as the sovereign gift of God; in this deep consternation the Lord was pleased to break in upon my soul with his bright beams of heavenly light; and in an instant, as it were, removing the veil, and letting light into a dark place, I saw clearly with an eye of faith, the crucified Saviour bleeding on the cross on mount Calvary; the scriptures became an unsealed book; I saw myself a condemned criminal under the law, which came with its full force to my conscience, and when "the commandment came sin revived, and I died." I saw the Lord Jesus Christ in his humiliation, loaded and bearing my reproach, sin, and shame. I then clearly perceived that by the deeds of the law no flesh living could be justified. I was then convinced that by the first Adam sin came, and by the second Adam (the Lord Jesus Christ) all that are saved must be made alive. It was given me at that time to know what it was to be born again (John 3:5). I saw the eighth chapter to the Romans, and the doctrines of God's decrees, verified agreeable to his eternal, everlasting, and unchangeable purposes. The word of God was sweet to my taste, yea, sweeter than honey and the honeycomb. Christ was revealed to my soul as the chiefest among ten thousand. These heavenly moments were really as life to the dead, and what John calls an earnest of the Spirit.[8] This was indeed unspeakable, and I firmly believe undeniable by many.

---

[7] "And there is salvation in no one else, for there is no other name under heaven given among men by which we must be saved."

[8] John 16:13, 14, &c. [Equiano's note.]

Now every leading providential circumstance that happened to me, from the day I was taken from my parents to that hour, was then in my view, as if it had but just then occurred. I was sensible of the invisible hand of God, which guided and protected me, when in truth I knew it not: still the Lord pursued me, although I slighted and disregarded it; this mercy melted me down. When I considered my poor wretched state I wept, seeing what a great debtor I was to sovereign free grace. Now the Ethiopian was willing to be saved by Jesus Christ, the sinner's only surety, and also to rely on none other person or thing for salvation. Self was obnoxious, and good works he had none, for it is God that worketh in us both to will and to do.

Oh! the amazing things of that hour can never be told—it was joy in the Holy Ghost! I felt an astonishing change; the burden of sin, the gaping jaws of hell, and the fears of death, that weighed me down before, now lost their horror; indeed I thought death would now be the best earthly friend I ever had. Such were my grief and joy as I believe are seldom experienced. I was bathed in tears, and said, What am I that God should thus look on me, the vilest of sinners? I felt a deep concern for my mother and friends, which occasioned me to pray with fresh ardor; and in the abyss of thought, I viewed the unconverted people of the world in a very awful state, being without God and without hope.

It pleased God to pour out on me the spirit of prayer and the grace of supplication, so that in loud acclamations I was enabled to praise and glorify his most holy name. When I got out of the cabin, and told some of the people what the Lord had done for me, alas! who could understand me or believe my report! None but to whom the arm of the Lord was revealed. I became a barbarian to them in talking of the love of Christ: his name was to me as ointment poured forth, indeed it was sweet to my soul, but to them a rock of offense. I thought my case singular, and every hour a day until I came to London, for I much longed to be with some to whom I could tell of the wonders of God's love towards me, and join in prayer to him whom my soul loved and thirsted after. I had uncommon commotions within, such as few can tell aught about.

Now the Bible was my only companion and comfort; I prized it much, with many thanks to God that I could read it for myself, and was not left to be tossed about or led by man's devices and notions. The worth of a soul cannot be told. May the Lord give the reader an understanding in this. Whenever I looked in the Bible I saw things new, and many texts were immediately applied to me with great comfort, for I knew that to me was the word of salvation sent. Sure I was that the Spirit which indited the word opened my heart to receive the truth of it as it is in Jesus—that the same Spirit enabled me to act in faith upon the promises that were precious to me, and enabled me to believe to the salvation of my soul. By free grace I was persuaded that I had a part in the first resurrection, and was enlightened with the "light of the living" (Job 33:30). I wished for a man of God with whom I might converse: my soul was like the chariots of Amminadib (Canticles 6:12).

These, among others, were the precious promises that were so powerfully applied to me. "All things whatsoever ye shall ask in prayer, believing, ye shall receive" (Mat. 21:22). "Peace I leave with you, my peace I give unto you" (John 14:27). I saw the blessed Redeemer to be the fountain of life, and the well of salvation. I experienced him to be all in all; he had brought me by a way that I knew not, and he had made crooked paths straight. Then in his name I set up my Ebenezer, saying, Hitherto he hath helped me: and could say to the sinners about me, Behold what a Saviour I have! Thus I was, by the teaching of that all-glorious Deity, the great One in Three, and Three in One, confirmed in the truths of the Bible, those oracles of everlasting truth, on which every soul living must stand or fall eternally, agreeable to Acts 4:12. "Neither is there salvation in any other, for there is none other name under heaven given among men whereby we must be saved, but only Christ Jesus." May God give the reader a right understanding in these facts! "To him that believeth, all things are possible, but to them that are unbelieving nothing is pure" (Titus 1:15).

During this period we remained at Cadiz until our ship got laden. We sailed about the fourth of November; and, having a good passage, we arrived in London the month following, to my comfort, with heartfelt gratitude to God for his rich and unspeakable mercies.

On my return I had but one text which puzzled me, or that the devil endeavored to buffet me with, *viz.*, Rom. 11:6, and, as I had heard of the Rev. Mr. Romaine, and his great knowledge in the scriptures, I wished much to hear him preach.[9] One day I went to Blackfriars church, and, to my great satisfaction and surprise, he preached from that very text. He very clearly shewed the difference between human works and free election, which is according to God's sovereign will and pleasure. These glad tidings set me entirely at liberty, and I went out of the church rejoicing, seeing my spots were those of God's children. I went to Westminster Chapel, and saw some of my old friends, who were glad when they perceived the wonderful change that the Lord had wrought in me, particu-

---

[9] "But if it is by grace, it is no more of works: otherwise grace is no more grace." William Romaine (1714–1795) was one of the most controversial preachers of salvation through faith alone.

larly Mr. G—— S——, my worthy acquaintance, who was a man of a choice spirit and had great zeal for the Lord's service. I enjoyed his correspondence till he died, in the year 1784. I was again examined at that same chapel, and was received into church fellowship amongst them. I rejoiced in spirit, making melody in my heart to the God of all my mercies. Now my whole wish was to be dissolved, and to be with Christ—but, alas! I must wait mine appointed time.

MISCELLANEOUS VERSES:

OR,

Reflections on the state of my mind during my first Convictions, of the necessity of believing the Truth, and experiencing the inestimable benefits of Christianity.

Well may I say my life has been
One scene of sorrow and of pain;
From early days I griefs have known,
And as I grew my griefs have grown:

Dangers were always in my path;
And fear of wrath, and sometimes death:
While pale dejection in me reign'd,
I often wept, by grief constrained.

When taken from my native land,
By an unjust and cruel band,
How did uncommon dread prevail!
My sighs no more I could conceal.

To ease my mind I often strove,
And tried my trouble to remove;
I sung, and utter'd sighs between—
Assay'd to stifle guilt with sin.

But O! not all that I could do
Would stop the current of my woe:
Conviction still my vileness shew'd;
How great my guilt—how lost to good.

"Prevented that I could not die,
Nor could to one sure refuge fly:
An orphan state I had to mourn—
Forsook by all, and left forlorn."

Those who beheld my downcast mien,
Could not guess at my woes unseen;
They by appearance could not know
The troubles that I waded through.

Lust, anger, blasphemy, and pride,
With legions of such ills beside,
"Troubled my thoughts," while doubts and fears,
Clouded and darken'd most my years.

"Sighs now no more would be confin'd—
They breath'd the trouble of my mind:"
I wish'd for death, but check the word,
And often pray'd unto the Lord.

Unhappy more than some on earth,
I thought the place that gave me birth—
Strange thoughts oppress'd—while I replied
"Why not in Ethiopia died?"

And why thus spar'd when nigh to hell?—
God only knew—I could not tell!
"A tott'ring fence a bowing wall,"
"I thought myself ere since the fall."

Oft times I mus'd, and night despair,
While birds melodious fill'd the air:
"Thrice happy songsters, ever free,"
How blest were they, compar'd to me!

Thus all things added to my pain,
While grief compell'd me to complain!
When sable clouds began to rise
My mind grew darker than the skies.

The English nation call'd to leave,
How did my breast with sorrows heave!
I long'd for rest—cried, "Help me Lord;
Some mitigation, Lord, afford!"

Yet on, dejected, still I went—
Heart-throbbing woes within me pent;
Nor land, nor sea, could comfort give,
Nor aught my anxious mind relieve.

Weary with troubles yet unknown
To all but God and self alone,
Numerous months for peace I strove,
Numerous foes I had to prove.

Inur'd to dangers, griefs, and woes,
Train'd up 'midst perils, death, and foes,
I said, "Must it thus ever be?
No quiet is permitted me."

Hard hap, and more than heavy lot!
I pray'd to God "Forget me not—
What thou ordain'st help me to bear;
But O! deliver from despair!"

Strivings and wrestling seem'd in vain;
Nothing I did could ease my pain:
Then gave I up my work and will,
Confess'd and owned my doom was hell!

Like some poor pris'ner at the bar,
Conscious of guilt, of sin and fear,
Arraign'd, and self-condemned, I stood—
"Lost in the world and in my blood!"

Yet here, 'midst blackest clouds confin'd,
A beam from Christ, the day star shin'd:
Surely, thought I, if Jesus please,
He can at once sign my release.

I, ignorant of his righteousness,
Set up my labors in its place;
"Forgot for why his blood was shed,
And pray'd and fasted in its stead."

He died for sinners—I am one!
Might not his blood for me atone?
Tho' I am nothing else but sin,
Yet surely he can make me clean!

Thus light came in, and I believed;
Myself forgot, and help receiv'd!
My Saviour then I know I found,
For, eas'd from guilt no more I groan'd.

O, happy hour, in which I ceas'd
To mourn, for then I found a rest!
My soul and Christ were now as one—
Thy light, O Jesus, in me shone!

Bless'd be thy name, for now I know
I and my works can nothing do;
"The Lord alone can ransom man—
For this the spotless Lamb was slain!"

When sacrifices, works, and pray'r,
Prov'd vain, and ineffectual were—
"Lo, then I come!" the Saviour cried,
And bleeding, bow'd his head, and died!

He died for all who ever saw
No help in them, nor by the law:
I this have seen: and gladly own
"Salvation is by Christ alone!"[10]

[10] Acts 4:12. [Equiano's note.]

CHAPTER 11

The author embarks on board a ship bound for Cadiz—Is near being ship-wrecked—Goes to Malaga—Remarkable fine cathedral there—The author disputes with a popish priest—Picking up eleven miserable men at sea in returning to England—Engages again with Doctor Irving to accompany him to Jamaica and the Mosquito Shore—Meets with an Indian Prince on board—The author attempts to instruct him in the truths of the Gospel—Frustrated by the bad example of some in the ship—They arrive on the Mosquito Shore with some slaves they purchased at Jamaica, and begin to cultivate a plantation—Some account of the manners and customs of the Mosquito Indians—Successful device of the author's to quell a riot among them—Curious entertainment given by them to Doctor Irving and the author, who leaves the shore and goes to Jamaica—Is barbarously treated by a man with whom he engaged for his passage—Escapes and goes to the Mosquito admiral, who treats him kindly—He gets another vessel and goes on board—Instances of bad treatment—Meets Dr. Irving—Gets to Jamaica—Is cheated by his captain—Leaves the Doctor and goes for England.

When our ship was got ready for sea again, I was entreated by the captain to go in her once more; but as I felt myself now as happy as I could wish to be in this life, I for some time refused; however, the advice of my friends at last prevailed; and, in full resignation to the will of God, I again embarked for Cadiz, in March 1775. We had a very good passage, without any material accident, until we arrived off the Bay of Cadiz, when one Sunday, just as we were going into the harbor, the ship struck against a rock and knocked off a garboard plank, which is the next to the keel. In an instant all hands were in the greatest confusion, and began with loud cries to call on God to have mercy on them. Although I could not swim, and saw no way of escaping death, I felt no dread in my then situation, having no desire to live. I even rejoiced in spirit, thinking this death would be sudden glory. But the fulness of time was not yet come.

The people near to me were much astonished in seeing me thus calm and resigned; but I told them of the peace of God, which, through sovereign grace I enjoyed, and these words were that instant in my mind:

Christ is my pilot wise, my compass is his word:
My soul each storm defies, while I have such a Lord.
I trust his faithfulness and power,
To save me in the trying hour.
Though rocks and quicksands deep through all my passage lie,
Yet Christ shall safely keep and guide me with his eye,
How can I sink with such a prop,
That bears the world and all things up.

At this time there were many large Spanish flukers or passage vessels, full of people crossing the channel; who seeing our condition, a number of them came alongside of us. As many hands as could be employed began to work; some at our three pumps, and the rest unloading the ship as fast as possible. There being only a single rock called the Porpus on which we struck, we soon got off of it, and providentially it was then high water, we therefore ran the ship ashore at the nearest place to keep her from sinking. After many tides, with a great deal of care and industry, we got her repaired again. When we had dispatched our business at Cadiz we went to Gibraltar, and from thence to Malaga, a very pleasant and rich city, where there is one of the finest cathedrals I had ever seen. It had been above fifty years in building, as I heard, though it was not then quite finished; great parts of the inside, however, were completed and highly decorated with the richest marble columns and many superb paintings; it was lighted occasionally by an amazing number of wax tapers of different sizes, some of which were as thick as a man's thigh: these, however, were only used on some of their grand festivals.

I was very much shocked at the custom of bull-baiting, and other diversions which prevailed here on Sunday evenings, to the great scandal of Christianity and morals. I used to express my abhorrence of it to a priest whom I met with. I had frequent contests about religion with the reverend father, in which he took great pains to make a proselyte of me to his church; and I no less to convert him to mine. On these occasions I used to produce my Bible, and shew him in what points his church erred. He then said he had been in England, and that every person there read the Bible, which was very wrong; but I answered him that Christ desired us to search the scriptures. In his zeal for my conversion, he solicited me to go to one of the universities in Spain, and declared that I should have my education free; and told me, if I got myself made a priest, I might in time become even pope; and that Pope Benedict was a black man.[1] As I was ever desirous of learning, I paused for some time upon this temptation; and thought by being crafty I might catch some with guile; but I began to think that it would be only hypocrisy in me to embrace his offer, as I could not in conscience conform to the opinions of his church. I was therefore enabled to regard the word of God, which says, "Come out from amongst them," and refused Father Vincent's offer. So we parted without conviction on either side.

Having taken at this place some fine wines, fruits, and money, we proceeded to Cadiz, where we took about two tons more of money, &c., and then sailed for England in the month of June. When we were about the north latitude 42, we had contrary wind for several days and the ship did not make in that time above six or seven miles strait course. This made the captain exceeding fretful and peevish, and I was very sorry to hear God's most holy name often blasphemed by him. One day as he was in that impious mood, a young gentleman on board who was a passenger, reproached him, and said he acted wrong; for we ought to be thankful to God for all things, as we were not in want of anything on board; and though the wind was contrary for us, yet it was fair for some others, who, perhaps stood in more need of it than we. I immediately seconded this young gentleman with some boldness, and said we had not the least cause to murmur, for that the Lord was better to us than we deserved, and that he had done all things well. I expected that the captain would be very angry with me for speaking, but he replied not a word. However, before that time on the following day, being the 21st of June, much to our great joy and astonishment, we saw the providential hand of our benign Creator, whose ways with his blind creatures are past finding out. The preceding night I dreamed that I saw a boat immediately off the starboard main shrouds; and exactly at half past one o'clock, the following day at noon, while I was below, just as we had dined in the cabin, the man at the helm cried out, A boat! which brought my dream that instant into my mind; I was the first man that jumped on the deck, and looking from the shrouds onward, according to my dream, I descried a little boat at some distance; but as the

[1] St. Benedict the Black (1526–1589) was not a pope. The son of African slaves living on Sicily, he entered a religious order near Palermo. Beatified in 1743 and canonized in 1807, Benedict is Palermo's protector saint and the patron saint of African Americans.

waves were high, it was as much as we could do sometimes to discern her; we however stopped the ship's way, and the boat, which was extremely small, came alongside with eleven miserable men, whom we took on board immediately. To all human appearance, these people must have perished in the course of one hour or less; the boat being small, it barely contained them. When we took them up they were half drowned, and had no victuals, compass, water, or any other necessary whatsoever, and had only one bit of an oar to steer with, and that right before the wind; so that they were obliged to trust entirely to the mercy of the waves. As soon as we got them all on board, they bowed themselves on their knees, and, with hands and voices lifted up to heaven, thanked God for their deliverance; and I trust that my prayers were not wanting amongst them at the same time. This mercy of the Lord quite melted me, and I recollected his words which I saw thus verified in the 107th Psalm, "O give thanks unto the Lord, for he is good, for his mercy endureth for ever. Hungry and thirsty, their souls fainted in them. They cried unto the Lord in their trouble, and he delivered them out of their distresses. And he led them forth by the right way, that they might go to a city of habitation. O that men would praise the Lord for his goodness, and for his wonderful works to the children of men! For he satisfieth the longing soul, and filleth the hungry soul with goodness.

"Such as sit in darkness and in the shadow of death:

"Then they cried unto the Lord in their trouble, and he saved them out of their distresses. They that go down to the sea in ships, that do business in great waters: these see the works of the Lord and his wonders in the deep. Whoso is wise and will observe these things, even they shall understand the loving kindness of the Lord."

The poor distressed captain said, "that the Lord is good, for, seeing that I am not fit to die, he therefore gave me a space of time to repent." I was very glad to hear this expression, and took an opportunity when convenient, of talking to him on the providence of God. They told us they were Portuguese, and were in a brig loaded with corn, which shifted that morning at five o'clock, owing to which the vessel sunk that instant with two of the crew; and how these eleven got into the boat (which was lashed to the deck) not one of them could tell. We provided them with every necessary, and brought them all safe to London; and I hope the Lord gave them repentance unto life eternal.

I was happy once more amongst my friends and brethren, till November, when my old friend, the celebrated Doctor Irving, bought a remarkable fine sloop, about 150 tons. He had a mind for a new adventure in cultivating a plantation at Jamaica, and the Mosquito shore;[2] asked me to go with him, and said that he would trust me with his estate in preference to anyone. By the advice, therefore, of my friends, I accepted of the offer, knowing that the harvest was fully ripe in those parts, and hoped to be an instrument under God, of bringing some poor sinner to my well beloved master, Jesus Christ. Before I embarked, I found with the Doctor four Mosquito Indians, who were chiefs in their own country, and were brought here by some English traders for some selfish ends. One of them was the Mosquito king's son; a youth of about eighteen years of age; and whilst he was here he was baptized by the name of George. They were going back at the government's expense, after having been in England about twelve months, during which they learned to speak pretty good English. When I came to talk to them about eight days before we sailed I was very much mortified in finding that they had not frequented any churches since they were here, to be baptized, nor was any attention paid to their morals. I was very sorry for this mock Christianity, and had just an opportunity to take some of them once to church before we sailed. We embarked in the month of November 1775, on board of the sloop *Morning Star*, Captain David Miller, and sailed for Jamaica.

In our passage, I took all the pains that I could to instruct the Indian prince in the doctrines of Christianity, of which he was entirely ignorant; and, to my great joy he was quite attentive, and received with gladness the truths that the Lord enabled me to set forth to him. I taught him in the compass of eleven days all the letters, and he could even put two or three of them together and spell them. I had Fox's *Martyrology*,[3] with cuts, and he used to be very fond of looking into it, and would ask many questions about the papal cruelties he saw depicted there, which I explained to him. I made such progress with this youth, especially in religion, that when I used to go to bed at different hours of the night, if he was in his bed, he would get up on purpose to go to prayer with me, without any other clothes than his shirt; and before he would eat any of his meals among the

---

[2] England had been trying to plant colonies on the Nicaragua coast since the seventeenth century but had been vigorously checked by Spain. The English allied themselves with the Zambo-Mosquito people, descendants of indigenous Sumu Indians and escaped slaves, some the survivors of a 1641 shipwreck. Hostile to Spain, the Zambo-Mosquito were courted by England, and the British governor at Jamaica gave three of the Mosquito chiefs the titles of king, admiral, and governor. The Spanish could never subdue the Mosquitos, though they drove out the British in 1779. (Linda A. Newson, *Indian Survival in Colonial Nicaragua* [Norman: University of Oklahoma Press, 1987]; Wallace Brown, "The Mosquito Shore and the Bay of Honduras during the Era of the American Revolution," *Belizean Studies* 18 [1990].)

[3] John Foxe (1516–1587) originally published his *Book of Martyrs* in 1558.

gentlemen in the cabin, he would first come to me to pray as he called it. I was well pleased at this, and took great delight in him, and used much supplication to God for his conversion. I was in full hope of seeing daily every appearance of that change which I could wish; not knowing the devices of satan, who had many of his emissaries to sow his tares[4] as fast as I sowed the good seed, and pull down as fast as I built up.

Thus we went on nearly four-fifths of our passage, when satan at last got the upper hand. Some of his messengers, seeing this poor heathen much advanced in piety, began to ask him whether I had converted him to Christianity, laughed and made their jest at him, for which I rebuked them as much as I could; but this treatment caused the prince to halt between two opinions. Some of the true sons of Belial,[5] who did not believe that there was any hereafter, told him never to fear the devil, for there was none existing; and if ever he came to the prince, they desired he might be sent to them. Thus they teased the poor innocent youth, so that he would not learn his book any more! He would not drink nor carouse with these ungodly actors, nor would he be with me, even at prayers. This grieved me very much. I endeavored to persuade him as well as I could, but he would not come; and entreated him very much to tell me his reasons for acting thus.

At last he asked me, "How comes it that all the white men on board who can read and write, and observe the sun, and know all things, yet swear, lie, and get drunk, only excepting yourself?" I answered him, the reason was, that they did not fear God; and that if any one of them died so they could not go to, or be happy with God. He replied, that if these persons went to hell he would go to hell too. I was sorry to hear this; and, as he sometimes had the toothache, and also some other persons in the ship at the same time, I asked him if their toothache made his easy: he said, No. Then I told him if he and these people went to hell together, their pains would not make his any lighter. This answer had great weight with him; it depressed his spirits much; and he became ever after, during the passage, fond of being alone.

When we were in the latitude of Martinique, and near making the land, one morning we had a brisk gale of wind, and, carrying too much sail, the main-mast went over the side. Many people were then all about the deck, and the yards, masts, and rigging came tumbling all about us, yet there was not one of us in the least hurt although some were within a hair's breadth of being killed; and, particularly, I saw two men who, by the providential hand of God, were most miraculously preserved from being

4 Weeds.
5 Satan.

smashed to pieces. On the fifth of January we made Antigua and Montserrat, and ran along the rest of the islands; and on the fourteenth we arrived at Jamaica.

One Sunday, while we were there, I took the Mosquito Prince George to church, where he saw the sacrament administered. When we came out we saw all kinds of people, almost from the church door for the space of half a mile down to the waterside, buying and selling all kinds of commodities: and these acts afforded me great matter of exhortation to this youth, who was much astonished. Our vessel being ready to sail for the Mosquito shore, I went with the Doctor on board a Guinea-man, to purchase some slaves to carry with us, and cultivate a plantation; and I chose them all my own countrymen. On the 12th of February we sailed from Jamaica, and on the eighteenth arrived at the Mosquito shore, at a place called Dupeupy.[6] All our Indian guests now, after I had admonished them, and a few cases of liquor given them by the Doctor, took an affectionate leave of us, and went ashore, where they were met by the Mosquito king, and we never saw one of them afterwards. We then sailed to the southward of the shore, to a place called Cape Gracias á Dios, where there was a large lagoon or lake, which received the emptying of two or three very fine large rivers, and abounded much in fish and land tortoise. Some of the native Indians came on board of us here; and we used them well, and told them we were come to dwell amongst them, which they seemed pleased at.

So the Doctor and I, with some others, went with them ashore; and they took us to different places to view the land, in order to choose a place to make a plantation of. We fixed on a spot near a river's bank, in a rich soil; and, having got our necessaries out of the sloop, we began to clear away the woods, and plant different kinds of vegetables, which had a quick growth. While we were employed in this manner, our vessel went northward to Black River to trade. While she was there, a Spanish *guarda costa*[7] met with and took her. This proved very hurtful, and a great embarrassment to us. However, we went on with the culture of the land. We used to make fires every night all around us, to keep off wild beasts, which, as soon as it was dark, set up a most hideous roaring. Our habitation being far up in the woods, we frequently saw different kinds of animals; but none of them ever hurt us, except poisonous snakes, the bite of which the Doctor used to cure by giving to the patient as soon as possible, about half a

---

[6] Possibly Tuapi, where the British had named a local Mosquito chief the governor. The Mosquito king, also appointed by the British, generally lived part of the year at Sandy Bay, the rest of the year on the Rio Segovia, at Cape Gracias a Dios.

[7] Coast guard boat.

tumbler of strong rum, with a good deal of Cayenne pepper in it. In this manner he cured two natives and one of his own slaves.

The Indians were exceedingly fond of the Doctor, and they had good reason for it; for I believe they never had such an useful man amongst them. They came from all quarters to our dwelling; and some *woolwow* or flat-headed Indians, who lived fifty or sixty miles above our river, and this side of the South Sea, brought us a good deal of silver in exchange for our goods.[8] The principal articles we could get from our neighboring Indians were turtle oil and shells, little silk grass, and some provisions; but they would not work at anything for us, except fishing; and a few times they assisted to cut some trees down, in order to build us houses; which they did exactly like the Africans, by the joint labor of men, women, and children. I do not recollect any of them to have had more than two wives. These always accompanied their husbands when they came to our dwelling, and then they generally carried whatever they brought to us, and always squatted down behind their husbands. Whenever we gave them anything to eat, the men and their wives eat separate. I never saw the least sign of incontinence amongst them. The women are ornamented with beads, and fond of painting themselves; the men also paint, even to excess, both their faces and shirts: their favorite color is red. The women generally cultivate the ground, and the men are all fishermen and canoe makers.

Upon the whole, I never met any nation that were so simple in their manners as these people, or had so little ornament in their houses. Neither had they, as I ever could learn, one word expressive of an oath. The worst word I ever heard amongst them when they were quarreling, was one that they had got from the English, which was "you rascal." I never saw any mode of worship among them; but in this they were not worse than their European brethren or neighbors, for I am sorry to say that there was not one white person in our dwelling, nor anywhere else, that I saw, in different places I was at on the shore, that was better or more pious than those unenlightened Indians; but they either worked or slept on Sundays: and to my sorrow, working was too much Sunday's employment with ourselves, so much so, that in some length of time we really did not know one day from another. This mode of living laid the foundation of my decamping at last.

The natives are well made and warlike; and they particularly boast of having never been conquered by the Spaniards. They are great drinkers of strong liquors when they can get them. We used to distil rum from

---

[8] The Woolwa, or Ulua Indians lived in the interior of Nicaragua, along the Grande, Segovia, and Escondido rivers. (Newson, *Indian Survival*, 35.)

pineapples, which were very plentiful here, and then we could not get them away from our place. Yet they seemed to be singular, in point of honesty, above any other nation I was ever amongst. The country being hot, we lived under an open shed, where we had all kinds of goods, without a door or a lock to any article; yet we slept in safety, and never lost anything, or were disturbed. This surprised us a good deal; and the Doctor, myself, and others, used to say if we were to lie in that manner in Europe we should have our throats cut the first night. The Indian Governor goes once in a certain time all about the province or district, and has a number of men with him as attendants and assistants. He settles all the differences among the people, like the judge here, and is treated with very great respect. He took care to give us timely notice before he came to our habitation, by sending his stick as a token, for rum, sugar, and gunpowder, which we did not refuse sending; and at the same time we made the utmost preparation to receive his honor and his train.

When he came with his tribe, and all our neighboring chieftains, we expected to find him a grave, reverend judge, solid and sagacious; but instead of that, before he and his gang came in sight, we heard them very clamorous; and they even had plundered some of our good neighboring Indians, having intoxicated themselves with our liquor. When they arrived we did not know what to make of our new guests, and would gladly have dispensed with the honor of their company. However, having no alternative, we feasted them plentifully all the day till the evening, when the Governor, getting quite drunk, grew very unruly, and struck one of our most friendly chiefs who was our nearest neighbor, and also took his gold-laced hat from him. At this a great commotion took place; and the Doctor interfered to make peace, as we could all understand one another, but to no purpose; and at last they became so outrageous that the Doctor, fearing he might get into trouble, left the house, and made the best of his way to the nearest wood, leaving me to do as well as I could among them. I was so enraged with the Governor that I could have wished to have seen him tied fast to a tree and flogged for his behavior; but I had not people enough to cope with his party. I therefore thought of a stratagem to appease the riot. Recollecting a passage I had read in the life of Columbus, when he was amongst the Indians in Mexico or Peru, where on some occasion, he frightened them by telling them of certain events in the Heavens, I had recourse to the same expedient; and it succeeded beyond my most sanguine expectations. When I had formed my determination, I went in the midst of them and, taking hold of the Governor, I pointed up to the Heavens. I menaced him and the rest; I told them God lived there, and that he was angry with them, and they must not quarrel so; that they were all brothers, and if they did not leave off, and go away quietly, I would take the book (pointing to the Bible), read, and *tell* God to make them dead. This operated on them like magic. The clamor immediately ceased, and I gave them some rum and a few other things, after which they went away peaceably; and the Governor afterwards gave our neighbor, who was called Captain Plasmahy, his hat again. When the Doctor returned, he was exceedingly glad at my success in thus getting rid of our troublesome guests.

The Mosquito people within our vicinity, out of respect to the Doctor, myself, and his people, made entertainments of the grand kind, called in their tongue *tourrie* or *dryckbot*. The English of this expression is, a feast of drinking about, of which it seems a corruption of language. The drink consisted of pineapples roasted, and casades chewed or beaten in mortars; which, after lying some time, ferments, and becomes so strong as to intoxicate, when drunk in any quantity. We had timely notice given to us of the entertainment. A white family, within five miles of us, told us how the drink was made, and I and two others went before the time to the village, where the mirth was appointed to be held, and there we saw the whole art of making the drink, and also the kind of animals that were to be eaten there. I cannot say the sight of either the drink or the meat were enticing to me. They had some thousands of pineapples roasting, which they squeezed, dirt and all, into a canoe they had there for the purpose. The casade drink was in beef barrels, and other vessels, and looked exactly like hog-wash. Men, women and children, were thus employed in roasting the pineapples, and squeezing them with their hands. For food they had many land torpins or tortoises, some dried turtle, and three large alligators alive, and tied fast to the trees. I asked the people what they were going to do with these alligators; and I was told they were to be eaten. I was much surprised at this, and went home, not a little disgusted at the preparations.

When the day of the feast was come, we took some rum with us, and went to the appointed place, where we found a great assemblage of these people, who received us very kindly. The mirth had begun before we came, and they were dancing with music; and the musical instruments were nearly the same as those of any other sable people, but, as I thought, much less melodious than any other nation I ever knew. They had many curious gestures in dancing, and a variety of motions and postures of their bodies, which to me were in no wise attracting. The males danced by themselves, and the females also by themselves, as with us. The Doctor shewed his people the example, by immediately joining the women's party, though not by their choice. On perceiving the women disgusted, he joined the males. At night there were great illuminations, by setting fire to many pine trees, while the dryckbot went round merrily by calabashes or gourds; but the liquor might more justly be called eating than drinking. One Owden, the oldest father in the vicinity, was dressed in a strange and terrifying form. Around his body were skins adorned with different kinds of feathers, and he had on his head a very large and high head-piece, in the form of a grenadier's cap, with prickles like a porcupine; and he made a certain noise which resembled the cry of an alligator. Our people skipped amongst them out of complaisance, though some could not drink of their *tourrie;* but our rum met with customers enough, and was soon gone. The alligators were killed and some of them roasted. Their manner of roasting is by digging a hole in the earth, and filling it with wood, which they burn to coal, and then they lay sticks across, on which they set the meat. I had a raw piece of the alligator in my hand; it was very rich: I thought it looked like fresh salmon, and it had a most fragrant smell, but I could not eat any of it. This merry-making at last ended without the least discord in any person in the company, although it was made up of different nations and complexions.

The rainy season came on here about the latter end of May, which continued till August very heavily; so that the rivers were overflowed, and our provisions then in the ground were washed away. I thought this was in some measure a judgment upon us for working on Sundays, and it hurt my mind very much. I often wished to leave this place and sail for Europe; for our mode of procedure and living in this heathenish form was very irksome to me. The word of God saith, "What does it avail a man if he gain the whole world, and lose his own soul?" This was much and heavily impressed on my mind; and, though I did not know how to speak to the Doctor for my discharge, it was disagreeable for me to stay any longer. But about the middle of June I took courage enough to ask him for it. He was very unwilling at first to grant my request; but I gave him so many reasons for it, that at last he consented to my going, and gave me the following certificate of my behavior.

> The bearer, Gustavus Vassa, has served me several years with strict honesty, sobriety, and fidelity. I can therefore with justice recommend him for these qualifications; and indeed in every respect I consider him as an excellent servant. I do hereby certify that he always behaved well, and that he is perfectly trustworthy.
>
> *CHARLES IRVING*
>
> MOSQUITO SHORE, JUNE 15, 1776.

Though I was much attached to the Doctor, I was happy when he consented. I got everything ready for my departure, and hired some

Indians, with a large canoe, to carry me off. All my poor countrymen, the slaves, when they heard of my leaving them, were very sorry, as I had always treated them with care and affection, and did everything I could to comfort the poor creatures, and render their condition easy. Having taken leave of my old friends and companions, on the 18th of June, accompanied by the Doctor, I left that spot of the world, and went southward above twenty miles along the river. There I found a sloop, the captain of which told me he was going to Jamaica. Having agreed for my passage with him and one of the owners, who was also on board, named Hughes, the Doctor and I parted, not without shedding tears on both sides.

The vessel then sailed along the river till night, when she stopped in a lagoon within the same river. During the night a schooner belonging to the same owners came in, and, as she was in want of hands, Hughes, the owner of the sloop asked me to go in the schooner as a sailor, and said he would give me wages. I thanked him; but I said I wanted to go to Jamaica. He then immediately changed his tone, and swore, and abused me very much, and asked how I came to be freed. I told him, and said that I came into that vicinity with Dr. Irving, whom he had seen that day. This account was of no use; he still swore exceedingly at me, and cursed the master for a fool that sold me my freedom, and the Doctor for another in letting me go from him. Then he desired me to go in the schooner, or else I should not go out of the sloop as a freeman. I said this was very hard, and begged to be put on shore again; but he swore that I should not. I said I had been twice amongst the Turks, yet had never seen any such usage with them, and much less could I have expected anything of this kind among the Christians. This incensed him exceedingly; and with a volley of oaths and imprecations, he replied, "Christians! damn you, you are one of St. Paul's men; but by G——, except you have St. Paul's or St. Peter's faith, and walk upon the water to the shore, you shall not go out of the vessel," which I now learnt was going amongst the Spaniards towards Cartagena, where he swore he would sell me. I simply asked him what right he had to sell me? but, without another word, he made some of his people tie ropes round each of my ankles, and also to each wrist, and another rope around my body, and hoisted me up without letting my feet touch or rest upon anything. Thus I hung, without any crime committed, and without judge or jury; merely because I was a free man, and could not by the law get any redress from a white person in those parts of the world. I was in great pain from my situation, and cried and begged very hard for some mercy, but all in vain. My tyrant, in a great rage, brought a musket out of the cabin and loaded it before me and the crew, and swore that he would shoot me if I cried any more. I had now no alternative; I therefore remained silent, seeing not one white man on board who said a word on my behalf. I hung in that manner from between ten and eleven o'clock at night till about one in the morning, when, finding my cruel abuser fast asleep, I begged some of his slaves to slack the rope that was round my body, that my feet might rest on something. This they did at the risk of being cruelly used by their master, who beat some of them severely at first for not tying me when he commanded them. Whilst I remained in this condition, till between five and six o'clock next morning, I trust I prayed to God to forgive this blasphemer who cared not what he did; but when he got up out of his sleep in the morning was of the very same temper and disposition as when he left me at night. When they got up the anchor, and the vessel was getting under way, I once more cried and begged to be released; and now, being fortunately in the way of their hoisting the sails, they released me.

When I was let down, I spoke to one Mr. Cox, a carpenter whom I knew on board, on the impropriety of this conduct. He also knew the Doctor, and the good opinion he ever had of me. This man then went to the captain, and told him not to carry me away in that manner: that I was the Doctor's steward, who regarded me very highly, and would resent this usage when he should come to know it. On which he desired a young man to put me ashore in a small canoe I brought with me. This sound gladdened my heart, and I got hastily into the canoe and set off, whilst my tyrant was down in the cabin; but he soon spied me out, when I was not above thirty or forty yards from the vessel, and running upon the deck with a loaded musket in his hand, he presented it at me, and swore heavily and dreadfully, that he would shoot me that instant, if I did not come back on board. As I knew the wretch would have done as he said, without hesitation I put back to the vessel again; but, as the good Lord would have it, just as I was alongside he was abusing the captain for letting me go from the vessel, which the captain returned, and both of them soon got into a very great heat. The young man that was with me now got out of the canoe; the vessel was sailing on fast with a smooth sea: and I then thought it was neck or nothing, so at that instant I set off again, for my life, in the canoe, towards the shore; and fortunately the confusion was so great amongst them on board, that I got out of the musket shot unnoticed, while the vessel sailed on with a fair wind a different way; so that they could not overtake me without tacking: but even before that could be done I should have been on shore, which I soon reached, with many thanks to God for this unexpected deliverance.

I then went and told the other owner, who lived near that shore (with whom I had agreed for my passage), of the usage I had met with. He was very much astonished and appeared sorry for it. After treating me with kindness, he gave me some refreshment, and three heads of roasted Indian corn, for a voyage of about 18 miles south to look for another vessel. He then directed me to an Indian chief of a district, who was also the Mosquito admiral, and had once been at our dwelling;[9] after which I set off with the canoe across a large lagoon alone (for I could not get anyone to assist me), though I was much jaded, and had pains in my bowels, by means of the rope I had hung by the night before. I was therefore at different times unable to manage the canoe, for the paddling was very laborious. However, a little before dark I got to my destined place, where some of the Indians knew me and received me kindly. I asked for the admiral, and they conducted me to his dwelling. He was glad to see me, and refreshed me with such things as the place afforded; and I had a hammock to sleep in. They acted towards me more like Christians than those whites I was amongst the last night, though they had been baptized. I told the admiral I wanted to go to the next port to get a vessel to carry me to Jamaica, and requested him to send the canoe back which I then had, for which I was to pay him. He agreed with me, and sent five able Indians with a large canoe to carry my things to my intended place, about fifty miles; and we set off the next morning. When we got out of the lagoon and went along shore, the sea was so high that the canoe was oftentimes very near being filled with water. We were obliged to go ashore and drag across different necks of land; we were also two nights in the swamps, which swarmed with mosquito flies, and they proved troublesome to us. This tiresome journey of land and water ended, however, on the third day, to my great joy; and I got on board of a sloop commanded by one Captain Jenning. She was then partly loaded, and he told me he was expecting daily to sail for Jamaica; and having agreed with me to work my passage, I went to work accordingly.

I was not many days on board before we sailed; but to my sorrow and disappointment, though used to such tricks, we went to the southward along the Mosquito shore, instead of steering for Jamaica. I was compelled to assist in cutting a great deal of mahogany wood on the shore as we coasted along it, and load the vessel with it, before she sailed. This fretted me much; but, as I did not know how to help myself among these deceivers, I thought patience was the only remedy I had left, and even that was forced. There was much hard work and little victuals on board; except by good luck we happened to catch turtles. On this coast there was also a particular kind of fish called manatee, which is most excellent eating, and

[9]The Mosquito admiral lived at Laguna de las Perlas.

the flesh is more like beef than fish; the scales are as large as a shilling, and the skin thicker than I ever saw that of any other fish. Within the brackish waters along shore there were likewise vast numbers of alligators, which made the fish scarce. I was on board this sloop sixteen days, during which, in our coasting, we came to another place, where there was a smaller sloop called the *Indian Queen,* commanded by one John Baker. He also was an Englishman, and had been a long time along the shore trading for turtle shells and silver, and had got a good quantity of each on board. He wanted some hands very much; and, understanding I was a free man, and wanted to go to Jamaica, he told me if he could get one or two, that he would sail immediately for that island: he also pretended to shew me some marks of attention and respect, and promised to give me forty-five shillings sterling a month if I would go with him. I thought this much better than cutting wood for nothing. I therefore told the other captain that I wanted to go to Jamaica in the other vessel; but he would not listen to me; and, seeing me resolved to go in a day or two, he got the vessel to sail, intending to carry me away against my will. This treatment mortified me extremely. I immediately, according to an agreement I had made with the captain of the *Indian Queen,* called for her boat, which was lying near us, and it came alongside; and, by the means of a North Pole shipmate which I met with in the sloop I was in, I got my things into the boat, and went on board the *Indian Queen,* July the 10th.

A few days after I was there, we got all things ready and sailed: but again, to my great mortification, this vessel still went to the south, nearly as far as Cartagena, trading along the coast, instead of going to Jamaica, as the captain had promised me; and, what was worst of all, he was a very cruel and bloody-minded man, and was a horrid blasphemer. Among others, he had a white pilot, one Stoker, whom he beat often as severely as he did some Negroes he had on board. One night in particular, after he had beaten this man most cruelly, he put him into the boat, and made two Negroes row him to a desolate key, or small island, and he loaded two pistols, and swore bitterly that he would shoot the Negroes if they brought Stoker on board again. There was not the least doubt but that he would do as he said, and the two poor fellows were obliged to obey the cruel mandate; but, when the captain was asleep, the two Negroes took a blanket and carried it to the unfortunate Stoker, which I believe was the means of saving his life from the annoyance of insects. A great deal of entreaty was used with the captain the next day, before he would consent to let Stoker come on board; and when the poor man was brought on board he was very ill, from his situation during the night, and he remained so till he was drowned a little time after.

As we sailed southward we came to many uninhabited islands, which were overgrown with fine large cocoanuts. As I was very much in want of provisions, I brought a boat load of them on board, which lasted me and others for several weeks, and afforded us many a delicious repast in our scarcity. One day, before this, I could not help observing the providential hand of God, that ever supplies all our wants, though in the way and manner we know not. I had been a whole day without food, and made signals for boats to come off, but in vain. I therefore earnestly prayed to God for relief in my need; and at the close of the evening I went off the deck. Just as I laid down I heard a noise on the deck, and, not knowing what it meant, I went directly on the deck again, when what should I see but a fine large fish about seven or eight pounds, which had jumped aboard! I took it, and admired, with thanks, the good hand of God; and, what I considered as not less extraordinary, the captain, who was very avaricious, did not attempt to take it from me, there being only him and I on board; for the rest were all gone ashore trading. Sometimes the people did not come off for some days; this used to fret the captain, and then he would vent his fury on me by beating me, or making me feel in other cruel ways.

One day especially, in his wild, wicked, and mad career, after striking me several times with different things, and once across my mouth, even with a red burning stick out of the fire, he got a barrel of gunpowder on the deck, and swore that he would blow up the vessel. I was then at my wit's end, and earnestly prayed to God to direct me. The head was out of the barrel; and the captain took a lighted stick out of the fire to blow himself and me up, because there was a vessel then in sight coming in, which he supposed was a Spaniard, and he was afraid of falling into their hands. Seeing this I got an axe, unnoticed by him, and placed myself between him and the powder, having resolved in myself as soon as he attempted to put the fire in the barrel to chop him down that instant. I was more than an hour in this situation; during which he struck me often, still keeping the fire in his hand for this wicked purpose. I really should have thought myself justifiable in any other part of the world if I had killed him, and prayed to God, who gave me a mind which rested solely on himself. I prayed for resignation, that his will might be done: and the following two portions of his holy word, which occurred to my mind, buoyed up my hope, and kept me from taking the life of this wicked man. "He hath determined the times before appointed, and set bounds to our habitations" (Acts 17:26). And, "Who is there among you that feareth the Lord, that obeyeth the voice of his servant, that walketh in darkness and hath no light? let him trust in the name of the Lord, and stay upon his God" (Isaiah 50:10). And this by the grace of God I was enabled to do. I found him a present help in the time of need, and the captain's fury began to subside as the night approached: but I found,

> That he who cannot stem his anger's tide
> Doth a wild horse without a bridle ride.

The next morning we discovered that the vessel which had caused such a fury in the captain was an English sloop. They soon came to an anchor where we were, and, to my no small surprise, I learned that Doctor Irving was on board of her, on his way from the Mosquito shore to Jamaica. I was for going immediately to see this old master and friend, but the captain would not suffer me to leave the vessel. I then informed the Doctor, by letter, how I was treated, and begged that he would take me out of the sloop; but he informed me that it was not in his power, as he was a passenger himself; but he sent me some rum and sugar for my own use. I now learned that after I had left the estate which I managed for this gentleman on the Mosquito shore, during which the slaves were well fed and comfortable, a white overseer had supplied my place; this man through inhumanity and ill-judged avarice, beat and cut the poor slaves most unmercifully; and the consequence was, that everyone got into a large Puriogua canoe, and endeavored to escape; but not knowing where to go, or how to manage the canoe, they were all drowned; in consequence of which the Doctor's plantation was left uncultivated, and he was now returning to Jamaica to purchase more slaves, and stock it again.

On the 14th of October, the *Indian Queen* arrived at Kingston in Jamaica. When we were unloaded I demanded my wages, which amounted to eight pounds five shillings sterling; but Captain Baker refused to give me one farthing, although it was the hardest earned money I ever worked for in my life. I found out Doctor Irving upon this, and acquainted him of the captain's knavery. He did all he could to help me to get my money; and we went to every magistrate in Kingston (and there were nine), but they all refused to do anything for me, and said my oath could not be admitted against a white man. Nor was this all; for Baker threatened that he would beat me severely, if he could catch me, for attempting to demand my money; and this he would have done, but that I got, by means of Doctor Irving, under the protection of Capt. Douglas, of the *Squirrel* man-of-war. I thought this exceeding hard usage, though indeed I found it to be too much the practice there, to pay free Negro men for their labor in this manner.

One day I went with a free Negro tailor, named Joe Diamond, to one Mr. Cochran, who was indebted to him some trifling sum; and the man, not being able to get his money, began to murmur. The other immediately took a horse-whip to pay him with it, but, by the help of a good pair of heels, the tailor got off. Such oppressions as these made me seek for a vessel to get off the island as fast as I could; and by the mercy of God, I found a ship in November bound for England, when I embarked with a convoy, after having taken a last farewell of Doctor Irving. When I left Jamaica he was employed in refining sugars; and some months after my arrival in England, I learned, with much sorrow, that this, my amiable friend, was dead, owing to his having eaten some poisoned fish.

We had many very heavy gales of wind in our passage, in the course of which no material incident occurred, except that an American privateer, falling in with the fleet, was captured and set fire to by his Majesty's ship, the *Squirrel.*

On January the seventh, 1777, we arrived at Plymouth. I was happy once more to tread upon English ground; and, after passing some little time at Plymouth and Exeter, among some pious friends whom I was happy to see, I went to London with a heart replete with thanks to God for past mercies.

CHAPTER 12

Different transactions of the author's life, till the present time—His application to the late Bishop of London to be appointed a missionary to Africa— Some account of his share in the conduct of the late expedition to Sierra Leone—Petition to the Queen—Conclusion.

Such were the various scenes which I was a witness to, and the fortune I experienced until the year 1777. Since that period, my life has been more uniform, and the incidents of it fewer, than in any other equal number of years preceding; I therefore hasten to the conclusion of a narrative which I fear the reader may think already sufficiently tedious.

I had suffered so many impositions in my commercial transactions in different parts of the world, that I became heartily disgusted with the sea-faring life, and was determined not to return to it, at least for some time. I therefore once more engaged in service shortly after my return, and continued for the most part in this situation until 1784.

Soon after my arrival in London, I saw a remarkable circumstance relative to African complexion, which I thought so extraordinary that I beg leave just to mention it. A white Negro woman, that I had formerly seen in London and other parts, had married a white man, by whom she had three boys, and they were every one mulattoes, and yet they had fine light hair.

In 1779, I served Governor Macnamara, who had been a considerable time on the coast of Africa. In the time of my service, I used to ask frequently other servants to join me in family prayer; but this only excited their mockery. However, the Governor, understanding that I was of a religious turn, wished to know what religion I was of; I told him I was a protestant of the church of England, agreeable to the thirty-nine articles of that church; and that whomsoever I found to preach according to that doctrine, those I would hear. A few days after this, we had some more discourse on the same subject; when he said he would, if I chose, as he thought I might be of service in converting my countrymen to the Gospel faith, get me sent out as missionary to Africa. I at first refused going, and told him how I had been served on a like occasion by some white people the last voyage I went to Jamaica, when I attempted (if it were the will of God) to be the means of converting the Indian prince; and said I supposed they would serve me worse than Alexander, the coppersmith, did St. Paul, if I should attempt to go amongst them in Africa.[1] He told me not to fear, for he would apply to the Bishop of London to get me ordained.[2] On these terms I consented to the Governor's proposal, to go to Africa in hope of doing good, if possible, amongst my countrymen; so, in order to have me sent out properly, we immediately wrote the following letters to the late Bishop of London:

To the Right Reverend Father in God, ROBERT, *Lord Bishop of London:*
THE MEMORIAL OF GUSTAVUS VASSA
SHEWETH,
   That your memorialist is a native of Africa, and has a knowledge of the manners and customs of the inhabitants of that country.
   That your memorialist has resided in different parts of Europe for twenty-two years last past, and embraced the Christian faith in the year 1759.
   That your memorialist is desirous of returning to Africa as a missionary, if encouraged by your Lordship, in hopes of being able to prevail upon his countrymen to become Christians; and your memorialist is the more induced to undertake the same, from the success that has attended the like undertakings when encouraged by the Portuguese through their different settlements on the Coast of Africa, and also by the Dutch; both governments encouraging the blacks, who, by their education are qualified to undertake the same, and are found more proper than European clergymen, unacquainted with the language and customs of the country.

---

[1] 1 Timothy 1:18–20, 2 Timothy 4:14. Despite Paul's admonitions, Alexander the coppersmith continued to blaspheme and made "shipwreck concerning the faith."
[2] Robert Lowth (1710–1787), bishop of London.

Your memorialist's only motive for soliciting the office of a missionary is that he may be a means, under God, of reforming his countrymen and persuading them to embrace the Christian religion. Therefore your memorialist humbly prays your Lordship's encouragement and support in the undertaking.

GUSTAVUS VASSA

AT MR. GUTHRIE'S TAYLOR,
NO. 17, HEDGE LANE.

MY LORD,
I have resided near seven years on the coast of Africa, for most part of the time as commanding officer. From the knowledge I have of the country and its inhabitants, I am inclined to think that the within plan will be attended with great success, if countenanced by your Lordship. I beg leave further to represent to your Lordship, that the like attempts, when encouraged by other governments, have met with uncommon success; and at this very time I know a very respectable character, a black priest, at Cape Coast Castle. I know the within named Gustavus Vassa, and believe him a moral good man.

I have the honor to be, my Lord,
Your Lordship's
Humble and obedient servant,
MATT. MACNAMARA

GROVE, 11TH MARCH, 1779.

This letter was also accompanied by the following from Doctor Wallace, who had resided in Africa for many years, and whose sentiments on the subject of an African mission were the same with Governor Macnamara's.

MARCH 13, 1779.

MY LORD,
I have resided near five years on Senegambia on the coast of Africa, and have had the honor of filling very considerable employments in that province. I do approve of the within plan, and think the undertaking very laudable and proper, and that it deserves your Lordship's protection and encouragement, in which case it must be attended with the intended success.

I am, my Lord, your Lordship's
Humble and obedient servant,
THOMAS WALLACE

With these letters, I waited on the Bishop by the Governor's desire, and presented them to his Lordship. He received me with much condescension and politeness; but from some certain scruples of delicacy, and saying the Bishops were not of opinion of sending a new missionary to Africa, he declined to ordain me.

My sole motive for thus dwelling on this transaction, or inserting these papers, is the opinion which gentlemen of sense and education, who are acquainted with Africa, entertain of the probability of converting the inhabitants of it to the faith of Jesus Christ, if the attempt were countenanced by the Legislature.

Shortly after this I left the Governor, and served a nobleman in the Dorsetshire militia, with whom I was encamped at Coxheath for some time; but the operations there were too minute and uninteresting to make a detail of.

In the year 1783, I visited eight counties in Wales, from motives of curiosity. While I was in that part of the country I was led to go down into a coal-pit in Shropshire, but my curiosity nearly cost me my life; for while I was in the pit the coals fell in, and buried one poor man, who was not far from me: upon this, I got out as fast as I could, thinking the surface of the earth the safest part of it.

In the spring of 1784, I thought of visiting old ocean again. In consequence of this I embarked as steward on board a fine new ship called the *London,* commanded by Martin Hopkin, and sailed for New York. I admired this city very much; it is large and well built, and abounds with provisions of all kinds. While we lay here a circumstance happened which I thought extremely singular: one day a malefactor was to be executed on a gallows; but with a condition that if any woman, having nothing on but her shift, married the man under the gallows, his life was to be saved. This extraordinary privilege was claimed; a woman presented herself, and the marriage ceremony was performed.

Our ship having got laden, we returned to London in January 1785. When she was ready again for another voyage, the captain being an agreeable man, I sailed with him from hence in the spring, March 1785, for Philadelphia. On the 5th of April, we took our departure from the lands-end, with a pleasant gale; and about nine o'clock that night the moon shone bright, and the sea was smooth, while our ship was going free by the wind, at the rate of about four or five miles an hour. At this time another ship was going nearly as fast as we on the opposite point, meeting us right in the teeth; yet none on board observed either ship until we struck each other forcibly head and head, to the astonishment and consternation of both crews. She did us much damage, but I believe we did her more; for when we passed by each other, which we did very quickly, they called to us to bring to, and hoist out our boat, but we had enough to do to mind ourselves; and in about eight minutes we saw no more of her. We refitted as well as we could the next day, and proceeded on our voyage, and in May arrived at Philadelphia.

I was very glad to see this favorite old town once more; and my pleasure was much increased in seeing the worthy Quakers freeing and easing the burdens of many of my oppressed African brethren. It rejoiced my heart when one of these friendly people took me to see a free school they had erected for every denomination of black people, whose minds are cultivated here, and forwarded to virtue; and thus they are made useful members of the community.[3] Does not the success of this practice say loudly to the planters, in the language of scripture—"Go ye and do likewise"!

In October 1785, I was accompanied by some of the Africans, and presented this address of thanks to the gentlemen called Friends or Quakers, in Grace Church Court, Lombard street:

GENTLEMEN,

By reading your book, entitled a Caution to Great Britain and her Colonies, concerning the calamitous state of the enslaved Negroes: We, part of the poor, oppressed, needy, and much degraded Negroes, desire to approach you with this address of thanks, with our inmost love and warmest acknowledgment; and with the deepest sense of your benevolence, unwearied labor, and kind interposition, towards breaking the yoke of slavery, and to administer a little comfort and ease to thousands and tens of thousands of very grievously afflicted, and too heavy burthened Negroes.

Gentlemen, could you, by perseverance, at last be enabled under God, to lighten in any degree the heavy burthen of the afflicted, no doubt it would in some measure, be the possible means, under God, of saving the souls of many of the oppressors; and if so, sure we are that the God, whose eyes are ever upon all his creatures, and always rewards every true act of virtue, and regards the prayers of the oppressed, will give to you and yours those blessings which it is not in our power to express or conceive, but which we, as a part of those captivated, oppressed, and afflicted people, most earnestly wish and pray for.

These gentlemen received us very kindly, with a promise to exert themselves on behalf of the oppressed Africans, and we parted.

While in town, I chanced once to be invited to a Quaker's wedding. The simple and yet expressive mode used at their solemnizations is worthy of note. The following is the true form of it:

[3] Benezet had founded this free school for Philadelphia blacks.

After the company have met they have seasonable exhortations by several of the members; the bride and bridegroom stand up, and, taking each other by the hand in a solemn manner, the man audibly declares to this purpose: "Friends, in the fear of the Lord, and in the presence of this assembly, whom I desire to be my witnesses, I take this my friend, M—— N——, to be my wife; promising, through divine assistance, to be unto her a loving and faithful husband till death separate us," and the woman makes the like declaration. Then the two first sign their names to the record, and as many more witnesses as have a mind. I had the honor to subscribe mine to a register in Grace Church Court, Lombard street. My hand is ever free—if any female Debonair wishes to obtain it, this mode I recommend.

We returned to London in August; and our ship not going immediately to sea, I shipped as a steward in an American ship, called the *Harmony*, Captain John Willet, and left London in March 1786, bound to Philadelphia. Eleven days after sailing, we carried our foremast away. We had a nine weeks' passage, which caused our trip not to succeed well, the market for our goods proving bad; and to make it worse, my commander began to play me the like tricks as others too often practise on free Negroes in the West Indies. But, I thank God, I found many friends here, who in some measure prevented him.

On my return to London in August, I was very agreeably surprised to find that the benevolence of government had adopted the plan of some philanthropic individuals, to send the Africans from hence to their native quarter; and that some vessels were then engaged to carry them to Sierra Leone, an act which redounded to the honor of all concerned in its promotion, and filled me with prayers and much rejoicing. There was then in the city a select committee of gentlemen for the black poor, to some of whom I had the honor of being known; and as soon as they heard of my arrival, they sent for me to the committee. When I came there, they informed me of the intention of government; and as they seemed to think me qualified to superintend part of the undertaking, they asked me to go with the black poor to Africa. I pointed out to them many objections to my going; and particularly I expressed some difficulties on the account of the slave dealers, as I would certainly oppose their traffic in human species by every means in my power. However, these objections were over-ruled by the gentlemen of the committee, who prevailed on me to consent to go; and recommended me to the honorable commissioners of his Majesty's Navy, as a proper person to act as commissary for government in the intended expedition; and they accordingly appointed me, in November

1786, to that office, and gave me sufficient power to act for the government, in the capacity of commissary, having received my warrant and the following order:

BY THE PRINCIPAL OFFICERS AND COMMISSIONERS
OF HIS MAJESTY'S NAVY

Whereas you were directed, by our warrant, of the 4th of last month, to receive into your charge from Mr. Joseph Irwin, the surplus provisions remaining of what was provided for the voyage, as well as the provisions for the support of the black poor, after the landing at Sierra Leone, with the clothing, tools, and all other articles provided at government's expense; and as the provisions were laid in at the rate of two months for the voyage, and for four months after the landing, but the number embarked being so much less than we expected, whereby there may be a considerable surplus of provisions, clothing, & c. These are in addition to former orders, to direct and require you to appropriate or dispose of such surplus to the best advantage you can for the benefit of government, keeping and rendering to us a faithful account of what you do herein. And for your guidance in preventing any white persons going, who are not intended to have the indulgence of being carried thither, we send you herewith a list of those recommended by the Committee for the black poor, as proper persons to be permitted to embark, and acquaint you that you are not to suffer any others to go who do not produce a certificate from the Committee for the black poor, of their having their permission for it. For which this shall be your warrant. Dated at the Navy Office, Jan. 16, 1787.

J. HINSLOW
GEO. MARSH
W. PALMER

TO MR. GUSTAVUS VASSA, COMMISSARY
OF PROVISIONS AND STORES FOR THE
BLACK POOR GOING TO SIERRA LEONE.

I proceeded immediately to the executing of my duty on board the vessels destined for the voyage, where I continued till the March following.

During my continuance in the employment of government, I was struck with the flagrant abuses committed by the agent, and endeavored to remedy them, but without effect. One instance, among many which I could produce, may serve as a specimen. Government had ordered to be provided all necessaries (slops, as they are called, included) for 750 persons; however, not being able to muster more than 426, I was ordered to send the superfluous slops, &c., to the king's stores at Portsmouth;

but, when I demanded them for that purpose from the agent, it appeared they had never been bought, though paid for by government. But that was not all; government were not the only objects of peculation; these poor people suffered infinitely more; their accommodations were most wretched, many of them wanted beds, and many more clothing and other necessaries. For the truth of this, and much more, I do not seek credit from my own assertion. I appeal to the testimony of Captain Thompson, of the *Nautilus,* who convoyed us, to whom I applied in February 1787, for a remedy, when I had remonstrated to the agent in vain, and even brought him to be a witness of the injustice and oppression I complained of. I appeal also to a letter written by these wretched people, so early as the beginning of the preceding January, and published in the *Morning Herald,* on the 4th of that month, signed by twenty of their chiefs.

I could not silently suffer government to be thus cheated, and my countrymen plundered and oppressed, and even left destitute of the necessaries for almost their existence. I therefore informed the Commissioners of the Navy of the agent's proceeding, but my dismission was soon after procured, by means of a gentleman in the city, whom the agent, conscious of his peculation, had deceived by letter, and who, moreover, empowered the same agent to receive on board, at the government expense, a number of persons as passengers, contrary to the orders I received. By this I suffered a considerable loss in my property; however the commissioners were satisfied with my conduct, and wrote to Captain Thompson, expressing their approbation of it.

Thus provided, they proceeded on their voyage; and at last, worn out by treatment, perhaps not the most mild, and wasted by sickness, brought on by want of medicine, clothes, bedding, &c., they reached Sierra Leone, just at the commencement of the rains. At that season of the year, it is impossible to cultivate the lands; their provisions therefore were exhausted before they could derive any benefit from agriculture; and it is not surprising that many, especially the Lascars, whose constitutions are very tender, and who had been cooped up in ships from October to June, and accommodated in the manner I have mentioned, should be so wasted by their confinement as not to survive it.

Thus ended my part of the long talked of expedition to Sierra Leone; an expedition which, however unfortunate in the event, was humane and politic in its design, nor was its failure owing to government; everything was done on their part; but there was evidently sufficient mismanagement attending the conduct and execution of it to defeat its success.

I should not have been so ample in my account of this transaction, had not the share I bore in it been made the subject of partial animadversion, and even my dismission from my employment thought worthy of being made by some a matter of public triumph.[4] The motives which might influence any person to descend to a petty contest with an obscure African, and to seek gratification by his depression, perhaps it is not proper here to inquire into or relate, even if its detection were necessary to my vindication, but I thank Heaven it is not. I wish to stand by my own integrity, and not to shelter myself under the impropriety of another; and I trust the behavior of the Commissioners of the Navy to me entitle me to make this assertion; for after I had been dismissed, March 24, I drew up a memorial thus:

> To the Right Honorable the Lord's Commissioners of his Majesty's Treasury.
> The Memorial and Petition of GUSTAVUS VASSA, a black man, late Commissary to the black poor going to Africa.
> HUMBLY SHEWETH,
> That your Lordships' memorialist was, by the Honorable the Commissioners of his Majesty's Navy, on the 4th of December last, appointed to the above employment by warrant from that board;
> That he accordingly proceeded to the execution of his duty on board of the Vernon, being one of the ships appointed to proceed to Africa with the above poor;
> That your memorialist, to his great grief and astonishment, received a letter of dismission from the Honorable Commissioners of the Navy, by your Lordships' orders:
> That, conscious of having acted with the most perfect fidelity and the greatest assiduity in discharging the trust reposed in him, he is altogether at a loss to conceive the reasons of your Lordships having altered the favorable opinion you were pleased to conceive of him, sensible that your Lordships would not proceed to so severe a measure without some apparent good cause; he therefore has every reason to believe that his conduct has been grossly misrepresented to your Lordships, and he is the more confirmed in his opinion, because, by opposing measures of others concerned in the same expedition, which tended to defeat your Lordships' humane intentions, and to put the government to a very considerable additional expense, he created a number of enemies, whose misrepresentations, he has too much reason to believe, laid the foundation of his dismission. Unsupported by friends, and unaided by the advantages of a liberal education, he can only hope for redress from the justice of his cause, in addition to the mortification of having been removed from his employment, and the advantage which he reasonably might have expected to have derived therefrom. He has had the misfortune to have sunk a considerable part of his little property in

[4] See the Public Advertiser, July 14, 1787. [Equiano's note.]

fitting himself out, and in other expenses arising out of his situation, an account of which he here annexes. Your memorialist will not trouble your Lordships with a vindication of any part of his conduct, because he knows not of what crimes he is accused; he, however, earnestly entreats that you will be pleased to direct an enquiry into his behavior during the time he acted in the public service; and, if it be found that his dismission arose from false representations, he is confident that in your Lordships' justice he shall find redress.

Your petitioner therefore humbly prays that your Lordships will take his case into consideration; and that you will be pleased to order payment of the above referred to account, amounting to £32.4s. and also the wages intended which is most humbly submitted.

LONDON, MAY 12, 1787.

The above petition was delivered into the hands of their Lordships, who were kind enough, in the space of some few months afterwards, without hearing, to order me £50 sterling—that is, £18 wages for the time (upwards of four months) I acted a faithful part in their service. Certainly the sum is more than a free Negro would have had in the western colonies!!!

From that period, to the present time, my life has passed in an even tenor, and a great part of my study and attention has been to assist in the cause of my much injured countrymen.

March the 21st, 1788, I had the honor of presenting the Queen with a petition in behalf of my African brethren, which was received most graciously by Her Majesty.[5]

To the Queen's most Excellent Majesty:
MADAM,

Your Majesty's well known benevolence and humanity emboldens me to approach your royal presence, trusting that the obscurity of my situation will not prevent your Majesty from attending to the sufferings for which I plead.

Yet I do not solicit your royal pity for my own distress; my sufferings, although numerous, are in a measure forgotten. I supplicate your Majesty's compassion for millions of my African countrymen, who groan under the lash of tyranny in the West Indies.

The oppression and cruelty exercised to the unhappy Negroes there, have at length reached the British Legislature, and they are now deliberating on its redress; even several persons of property in slaves in the West Indies, have petitioned Parliament against its continuance,

[5] At the request of some of my most particular friends, I take the liberty of inserting it here. [Equiano's note.]

sensible that it is as impolitic as it is unjust—and what is inhuman must ever be unwise.

Your Majesty's reign has been hitherto distinguished by private acts of benevolence and bounty; surely the more extended the misery is, the greater claim it has to your Majesty's compassion, and the greater must be your Majesty's pleasure in administering to its relief.

I presume, therefore, gracious Queen, to implore your interposition with your royal consort, in favor of the wretched Africans; that, by your Majesty's benevolent influence, a period may now be put to their misery—and that they may be raised from the condition of brutes, to which they are at present degraded, to the rights and situation of freemen, and admitted to partake of the blessings of your Majesty's happy government; so shall your Majesty enjoy the heart-felt pleasure of procuring happiness to millions, and be rewarded in the grateful prayers of themselves, and of their posterity.

And may the all-bountiful Creator shower on your Majesty, and the Royal Family, every blessing that this world can afford, and every fulness of joy which divine revelation has promised us in the next.

I am your Majesty's
Most dutiful and devoted servant to command,

GUSTAVUS VASSA
The Oppressed Ethiopian

NO. 53, BALDWIN'S GARDENS

The Negro Consolidated Act, made by the assembly of Jamaica last year, and the new act of amendment now in agitation there, contain a proof of the existence of those charges that have been made against the planters relative to the treatment of their slaves.

I hope to have the satisfaction of seeing the renovation of liberty and justice, resting on the British government, to vindicate the honor of our common nature. These are concerns which do not perhaps belong to any particular office; but, to speak more seriously, to every man of sentiment, actions like these are the just and sure foundation of future fame; a reversion, though remote, is coveted by some noble minds as a substantial good. It is upon these grounds that I hope and expect the attention of gentlemen in power. These are designs consonant to the elevation of their rank and the dignity of their stations; they are ends suitable to the nature of a free and generous government, and, connected with views of empire and dominion, suited to the benevolence and solid merit of the legislature. It is a pursuit of substantial greatness. May the time come—at least the speculation to me is pleasing—when the sable people shall gratefully commemorate the auspicious era of extensive freedom. Then shall those persons[6] particularly be named with praise and honor who generously proposed and stood forth in the cause of humanity, liberty, and good policy, and brought to the ear of the legislature designs worthy of royal patronage and adoption. May Heaven make the British senators the dispersers of light, liberty, and science, to the uttermost parts of the earth: then will be glory to God in the highest, on earth peace, and good will to men. Glory, honor, peace, &c. to every soul of man that worketh good: to the Britons first (because to them the Gospel is preached), and also to the nations. "Those that honor their Maker have mercy on the poor." It is "righteousness exalteth a nation, but sin is a reproach to any people; destruction shall be to the workers of iniquity, and the wicked shall fall by their own wickedness." May the blessings of the Lord be upon the heads of all those who commiserated the cases of the oppressed Negroes, and the fear of God prolong their days; and may their expectations be filled with gladness! "The liberal devise liberal things, and by liberal things shall stand" (Isaiah 32:8). They can say with pious Job, "Did not I weep for him that was in trouble? Was not my soul grieved for the poor?" (Job 30:25).

As the inhuman traffic of slavery is to be taken into the consideration of the British legislature, I doubt not, if a system of commerce was established in Africa, the demand for manufactures will most rapidly augment, as the native inhabitants will sensibly adopt the British fashions, manners, customs, &c. In proportion to the civilization, so will be the consumption of British manufactures.

The wear and tear of a continent, nearly twice as large as Europe and rich in vegetable and mineral production, is much easier conceived than calculated.

A case in point. It cost the Aborigines of Britain little or nothing in clothing, &c. The difference between their forefathers and the present generation, in point of consumption, is literally infinite. The supposition is most obvious. It will be equally immense in Africa—The same cause, *viz:* civilization, will ever have the same effect.

It is trading upon safe grounds. A commercial intercourse with Africa

[6]Granville Sharp, Esq., the Rev. Thomas Clarkson, the Rev. James Ramsay, our approved friends, men of virtue, are an honor to their country, ornamental to human nature, happy in themselves, and benefactors to mankind! [Equiano's note.] The Scottish-born Ramsay (1733–1789) was a doctor and sailor before becoming a parish priest on Nevis and St. Kitts, where his plans to educate slaves raised planters' opposition. He served in the British Navy during the American Revolution and in 1784 wrote *An Essay on the Treatment and Conversion of African Slaves in the British Sugar Colonies.* Ramsay was viciously attacked by slavery's defenders, and he died under the strain of abuse during the opening months of Parliament's 1789 debate on slavery.

opens an inexhaustible source of wealth to the manufacturing interest of Great Britain;[7] and to all which the slave trade is an objection.

If I am not misinformed, the manufacturing interest is equal, if not superior, to the landed interest, as to the value, for reasons which will soon appear. The abolition of slavery, so diabolical, will give a most rapid extension of manufactures, which is totally and diametrically opposite to what some interested people assert.

The manufactures of this country must and will, in the nature and reason of things, have a full and constant employ, by supplying the African markets.

Population, the bowels and surface of Africa, abound in valuable and useful returns; the hidden treasures of centuries will be brought to light and into circulation. Industry, enterprise, and mining will have their full scope, proportionably as they civilize. In a word, it lays open an endless field of commerce to the British manufacturers and merchant adventurer. The manufacturing interest and the general interests are synonymous. The abolition of slavery would be in reality an universal good.

Tortures, murder, and every other imaginable barbarity and iniquity, are practised upon the poor slaves with impunity. I hope the slave trade will be abolished. I pray it may be an event at hand. The great body of manufacturers, uniting in the cause, will considerably facilitate and expedite it; and as I have already stated, it is most substantially their interest and advantage, and as such the nation's at large (except those persons concerned in the manufacturing neck yokes, collars, chains, handcuffs, leg bolts, drags, thumb screws, iron muzzles, and coffins; cats, scourges, and other instruments of torture used in the slave trade). In a short time one sentiment will alone prevail, from motives of interest as well as justice and humanity. Europe contains one hundred and twenty million of inhabitants. Query: How many millions doth Africa contain? Supposing the Africans, collectively and individually, to expend £5 a head in raiment and furniture yearly when civilized, &c., an immensity beyond the reach of imagination! This I conceive to be a theory founded upon facts, and therefore an

---

[7] "In the ship *Trusty*, lately for the new Settlement of Sierra Leone, in Africa, were 1,300 pair of shoes (an article hitherto scarcely known to be exported to that country) with several others equally new, as articles of export. Thus will it not become the interest, as well as the duty, of every artificer, mechanic, and tradesman, publicly to enter their protest against this traffic of the human species? What a striking—what a beautiful contrast is here presented to view, when compared with the cargo of a slave ship! Every feeling heart indeed sensibly participates of the joy, and with a degree of rapture reads of barrels of *flour* instead of *gunpowder*—*biscuits and bread* instead of *horse beans*—*implements of husbandry* instead of *guns* for destruction, rapine, and murder—and various articles of *usefulness* are the pleasing substitutes for the *torturing thumbscrew*, and the *galling chain*, &c." [Equiano's note.]

infallible one. If the blacks were permitted to remain in their own country, they would double themselves every fifteen years. In proportion to such increase will be the demand for manufactures. Cotton and indigo grow spontaneously in most parts of Africa; a consideration this of no small consequence to the manufacturing towns of Great Britain. It opens a most immense, glorious, and happy prospect—the clothing, &c., of a continent ten thousand miles in circumference, and immensely rich in productions of every denomination in return for manufactures.

Since the first publication of my *Narrative*, I have been in a great variety of scenes in many parts of Great Britain, Ireland, and Scotland, an account of which might not improperly be added here;[8] but this would swell the volume too much, I shall only observe in general, that in May 1791, I sailed from Liverpool to Dublin, where I was very kindly received, and from thence to Cork, and then travelled over many counties in Ireland. I was everywhere exceedingly well treated, by persons of all ranks. I found the people extremely hospitable, particularly in Belfast, where I took my passage on board of a vessel for Clyde, on the 29th of January, and arrived at Greenock on the 30th. Soon after I returned to London, where I found persons of note from Holland and Germany, who requested me to go there; and I was glad to hear that an edition of my *Narrative* had been printed in both places, also in New York. I remained in London till I heard the debate in the House of Commons on the slave trade, April the 2d and 3d. I then went to Soham in Cambridgeshire, and was married on the 7th of April to Miss Cullen, daughter of James and Ann Cullen, late of Ely.[9]

I have only therefore to request the reader's indulgence and conclude. I am far from the vanity of thinking there is any merit in this narrative: I hope censure will be suspended, when it is considered that it was written by one who was as unwilling as unable to adorn the plainness of truth by the coloring of imagination. My life and fortune have been extremely checkered, and my adventures various. Nay even those I have related are considerably abridged. If any incident in this little work should appear uninteresting and trifling to most readers, I can only say, as my excuse for mentioning it, that almost every event of my life made an impression on my mind, and influenced my conduct. I early accustomed myself to look at the hand of God in the minutest occurrence, and to learn from it a lesson of

---

[8] *Viz.* Some curious adventures beneath the earth, in a river in Manchester, and a most astonishing one under the Peak of Derbyshire—and in September 1792, I went 90 fathoms down St. Anthony's Colliery, at Newcastle, under the river Tyne, some hundreds of yards on Durham side. [Equiano's note.]

[9] See *Gentleman's Magazine* for April 1792, *Literary and Biographical Magazine,* and *British Review* for May 1792, and the *Edinburgh Historical Register* or *Monthly Intelligencer* for April 1792. [Equiano's note.]

morality and religion; and in this light every circumstance I have related was to me of importance. After all, what makes any event important, unless by its observation we become better and wiser, and learn "to do justly, to love mercy, and to walk humbly before God"? To those who are possessed of this spirit, there is scarcely any book or incident so trifling that does not afford some profit, while to others the experience of ages seems of no use; and even to pour out to them the treasures of wisdom is throwing the jewels of instruction away.

THE END

An Equiano Chronology

THE EARLY ATLANTIC SLAVE TRADE

The slave trade began long before Europeans reached the New World. Portuguese ships began trading with Africans for gold and captives in the early 1400s and by 1441 had brought African captives to Lisbon as slaves. In 1452 Pope Nicholas V had given Portugal a monopoly on trade with Africa and by 1456 approved the Portuguese practice of enslaving "pagans and unbelievers inimical to Christ." In 1505 the Spanish crown sent seventeen black slaves, probably all born in either Spain or Portugal, to the island of Hispaniola. By 1515 Hispaniola was producing sugar, and three years later the Portuguese began bringing slaves directly from West Africa to this Spanish colony. The Africans resisted (the first recorded slave revolt happened in 1522), and other Europeans challenged the Portuguese monopoly: England sent a vessel to West Africa in the 1550s, and the Dutch quickly followed.

In 1607 England established a colony in Jamestown, Virginia; in 1619 a Dutch ship brought the colony its first Africans. In 1625 England colonized Barbados; within a generation 20,000 African slaves worked that island's sugar plantations. By the early eighteenth century the English and the Dutch had replaced the Portuguese as the New World's slave traders, though not without resistance from slaves (who revolted in Barbados in 1675, in Jamaica in the 1730s, and in South Carolina in 1739) as well as from within their own societies. Bostonian Samuel Sewall wrote an antislavery pamphlet, *The Selling of Joseph*, in 1701, and the Quakers condemned the slave trade in 1727. In the 1730s, 52,200 Africans were brought to the New World.

OLAUDAH EQUIANO AND THE ANTISLAVERY MOVEMENT (1740–1797)

1741–1750: 53,600 Africans transported to the New World each year.

1745: Olaudah Equiano born in Isseke, Nigeria.

1751–1760: 52,900 Africans transported to the New World each year.

1754: Quaker John Woolman writes *Some Considerations on the Keeping of Negroes.*

1756: Olaudah Equiano kidnapped, taken to a slave ship. After crossing the Atlantic to Barbados, he is sent to Virginia.

1756–1763: Seven Years' War.

1757: Equiano bought by Michael Henry Pascal, a British naval officer, who names him Gustavus Vassa and takes him to England.

1758–1762: Equiano serves in British navy.

1759: Olaudah Equiano baptized at St. Margaret's Church, London.

1761–1770: 63,500 Africans transported to the New World each year.

1763–1766: Working for Robert King in Montserrat, Equiano trades between West Indies and mainland American colonies.

1765: In Savannah, Equiano hears evangelist George Whitefield preach.

1766, July 11: Equiano buys his freedom.

1766: Quaker abolitionist Anthony Benezet writes *Historical Account of Guinea.*

1767: Equiano shipwrecked in Bahamas. Last visit to Savannah, buries black child. Sails for London.

1768: Equiano sails to the Mediterranean. St. Patrick's Day slave uprising on Montserrat.

1771–1780: 58,000 Africans transported to the New World each year.

1772: *Somerset* decision declares that slavery cannot exist in England and that a slave setting foot in England is free and cannot be returned to slavery.

1773: Equiano on expedition to Arctic. Massachusetts slaves petition legislature for emancipation.

1774: John Annis kidnapped by his former master and taken to the West Indies, where he is tortured to death. Equiano sails for Spain, has vision of Christ October 6. Methodist John Wesley writes *Thoughts upon Slavery.*

1774–1776: Pennsylvania Quakers bar slaveholders from membership.

1775–1783: American Revolution.

1775: Equiano admitted to communion in Westminster Church. Equiano voyages to Mosquito Coast (Nicaragua) with Dr. Irving to establish a plantation.

1776, June: Equiano leaves Nicaragua for London.

1776: American Declaration of Independence declares that "all men are created equal."

1780: Pennsylvania passes gradual emancipation law.

1781–1790: 88,800 Africans transported to the New World each year.

1781: *Zong* massacre: captain orders 132 slaves drowned so ship owners can collect on insurance.

1783: Equiano tells abolitionist Granville Sharp of *Zong* massacre. American Quakers call on Congress to end slavery and honor its commitment to "universal liberty." Massachusetts says that slavery violates the state constitution, which holds all men to be "free and equal."

1784: Equiano sails for New York. Rev. James Ramsay publishes *Essay on the Treatment and Conversion of African Slaves in the Sugar Colonies*. Methodists declare slavery contrary to God's law, give members twelve months to free slaves. Pennsylvania Society for Promoting Abolition of Slavery formed. Connecticut and Rhode Island pass gradual emancipation laws.

1785: Equiano in Philadelphia. New York Society for Promoting Manumussion of Slaves formed. Methodists petition Virginia legislature for emancipation. James Tobin's *Cursory Remarks* attacks abolitionists, defends slavery.

1786: Committee for Relief of the Black Poor appoints Equiano commissary to Sierra Leone expedition. Thomas Clarkson publishes *Essay on the Slavery and Commerce of the Human Species*.

1787: Equiano dismissed from Sierra Leone expedition after he publicizes mismanagement. With other Africans in London, Equiano organizes Sons of Africa. Ottabah Cugoano writes antislavery *Thoughts and Sentiments on the Evil of Slavery*. Society for the Abolition of the Slave Trade formed in England. U.S. Congress bans slavery north of the Ohio River after 1800. New U.S. Constitution does not mention slavery, allows slaveholders more representation in Congress, requires the return of fugitive slaves, and forbids Congress to end the slave trade before 1807.

1788: Equiano presents antislavery petition to England's Queen Charlotte. Abolitionists petition the British Parliament to end the slave trade. Massachusetts, Connecticut, New York, and Pennsylvania bar citizens from participating in the slave trade. French abolitionists form *Société des Amis des Noirs*.

1789: Equiano publishes *Interesting Narrative*. Parliament decides to regulate the English slave trade, not to end it. Baptists say that slavery is inconsistent with republican government. The French Revolution begins.

1790: Equiano's *Narrative* is printed in Dutch and is published in third English edition. Quakers and the Pennsylvania Society for Promoting Abolition, led by Benjamin Franklin, petition Congress to end the slave trade.

1791–1800: 76,400 Africans transported to the New World each year.

1791: Equiano speaks in Ireland; *Narrative* printed in New York.

1791–1803: Slave revolt in the French colony of St. Domingue.

1792, April 7: Equiano marries Susan Cullen of Ely, Cambridgeshire.

1793: Anna Maria Vassa born.

1795: Johanna Vassa born. Susan Cullen Vassa dies.

1796: House of Commons defeats bill abolishing the slave trade. St. George

Tucker, Virginia law professor, proposes a plan to end slavery in the United States by 1896.

1797: Equiano dies in London on April 31. Anna Maria Vassa dies on July 21.

SLAVERY, ABOLITION, AND EQUIANO'S *NARRATIVE* (1797–1837)

1799: New York (21,000 slaves, total population 589,000) adopts gradual emancipation law. (Law revised 1817; slavery ends July 4, 1827.)

1800: Slave revolt in Richmond, Virginia.

1801–1810: 61,700 Africans transported to the New World each year.

1802: France restores slavery to West Indian colonies.

1804: French driven from St. Domingue, which is proclaimed the independent republic of Haiti. New Jersey (11,000 slaves, total population 211,000) adopts gradual emancipation law.

1807: Britain and United States abolish the slave trade.

1810: Portugal agrees to gradual abolition of the slave trade. Mexican revolutionaries issue emancipation order before Spain crushes rebellion.

1811–1820: 53,600 Africans transported to the New World each year.

1814: Equiano's *Narrative* republished in England as part of a new protest and petition drive against slavery.

1816: Johanna Vassa turns twenty-one, inherits £950 from parents' estate. Barbados slave revolt. Simon Bolívar in Venezuela and José San Martín in Chile promise freedom to slaves who join revolution.

1817: American Colonization Society formed to emancipate American slaves and colonize them outside the United States.

1820: U.S. Congress admits Missouri as a slave state and forbids slavery in territory north of 36°30'. First American Colonization Society expedition to West Africa, forms colony of Liberia.

1821–1830: 64,600 Africans transported to the New World each year.

1821: American abolitionist Benjamin Lundy starts a newspaper, *Genius of Universal Emancipation.*

1822: Free blacks and slaves conspire to burn Charleston, S.C. Illinois debates whether to establish institution of slavery.

1823: Chile adopts emancipation. Slave revolt in British Guiana.

1824: Slavery abolished in Central America.

1829: Abridged edition of Equiano's *Narrative* published as prize for children in New York's Free African Schools. Free black David Walker publishes *Appeal to the Colored Citizens of the U.S.* Mexico abolishes slavery.

1831–1840: 54,600 Africans transported to the New World each year.

1831: Slaves revolt in Jamaica and Virginia. Virginia legislature rejects gradual emancipation bill. American abolitionist William Lloyd Garrison begins publishing a newspaper, *The Liberator.*

1833: Britain emancipates West Indian slaves (780,000 in colonies).

1837: Isaac Knapp, Garrison's partner, reprints Equiano's *Narrative.*

THE END OF SLAVERY (1837–1886)

Though Pope Gregory XVI condemned the slave trade in 1839, slaves continued to come into the New World legally (43,300 each year in the 1840s) until Brazil stopped buying slaves in 1851. By then only Surinam, Brazil, Cuba, and the United States were slaveholding countries. Slavery seemed to be dying everywhere but in the United States, which annexed Texas from Mexico in 1845 and made it a slave state, and some Americans pushed for annexing Central America and Cuba as well. In 1857 the U.S. Supreme Court ruled that Congress could not prohibit slavery in any territories. Only the Civil War (1861–1865) would stop the spread of slavery in the United States. Brazil abolished slavery in 1881, and Cuba in 1886, nearly a century after Equiano wrote his *Narrative.*

Questions for Consideration

1. What are Equiano's arguments against slavery? Which of his arguments do you find most convincing?
2. How does Equiano define himself? Is he African? Is he European? How would you define him?
3. What audience is Equiano trying to reach? Which of his arguments do you think would have been most convincing to his various readers, and why?
4. Equiano's first name, Olaudah, imples "good fortune," and he considered himself "a particular favorite of heaven." In what ways was he lucky? Would you consider him a lucky man?
5. How is literacy crucial to Equiano's life?
6. Pro-slavery writers often challenged the authenticity of testimony by former slaves. How does Equiano prevent challenges to his account of life in the West Indies? What proof does he give that his is a true story?
7. Why does Equiano devote so much of his book to his life after slavery, to his experiences in Turkey, Nicaragua, and on the polar expedition? What do these experiences add to his story of his life as a slave?
8. In a letter to the *Public Advertiser* a few months before he wrote his *Narrative,* Equiano proposed interracial marriage as a solution to the race problem. What solutions does he offer in his book?
9. If Parliament had abolished the slave trade in 1788 or 1789, as Equiano wanted, would that have solved the problems he discusses in the *Narrative?*
10. Discuss Equiano's continuing involvement in slavery after he becomes free in 1766. How does he justify his work for Robert King and Charles Irving?
11. What is the significance of the full title of the *Narrative?*
12. What does the *Narrative* tell us about religion and commerce in the eighteenth century?
13. What is Equiano's relationship with nature? How does he view the natural world? Does his relationship with nature change as he moves through the world?
14. How important are dreams to Equiano's life? What role do dreams play in his *Narrative?*

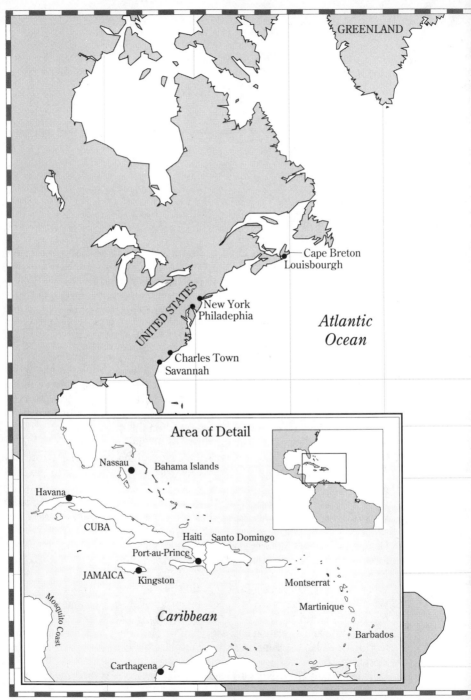

Map of Equiano's Travels.

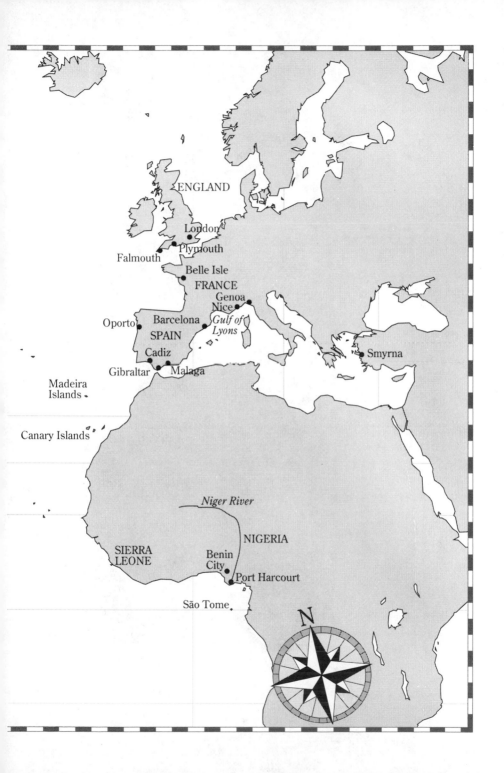

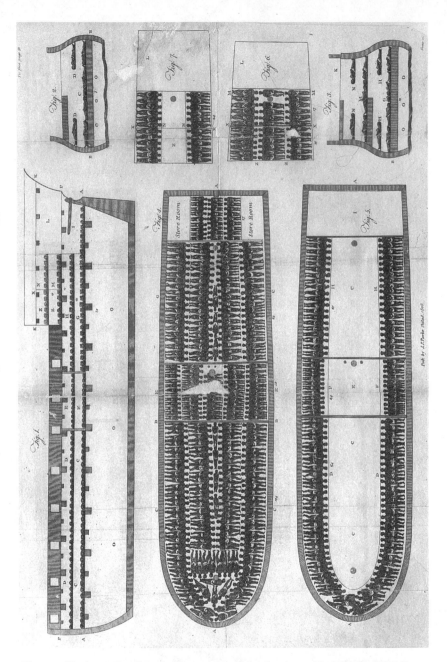

Thomas Clarkson distributed this cross section of a slave ship with his 1786 *Essay on the Slavery and Commerce of the Human Species*. It was also reprinted as a broadside and in many abolitionist pamphlets.

Josiah Wedgwood (1730–1795), manufacturer of English ceramics, designed this medallion as the antislavery movement's symbol. The symbol appeared on the title page of the 1814 edition of Equiano's *Narrative* and remained the symbol for the abolition movement through the American Civil War.

This picture shows one particularly brutal form of slave torture. Equiano's friend, John Annis, perished on a similar rack in St. Kitts.

William Blake, (1757–1827), English poet, painter, and engraver, made this illustration for John Stedman's account of his service to the British planters in Surinam. The skulls are displayed as warnings, and a ship sits off the coast.

Blake Sculp!

Europe supported by Africa & America.

Blake knew, like Equiano, that Africa and America supported Europe. This engraving by Blake suggests both the bondage of Americans and Africans to Europeans, but also the possibility of mutual support and harmony.

This popular 1790s mezzotint, sold both in London and Paris, shows shipwrecked English people saved by humane Africans. It points to the ironic inhumanity of the slave trade: these same English might enslave these same Africans who had saved their lives.

Selected Bibliography

AFRICAN HISTORY

Acholonu, Catherine Obianuju. *The Igbo Roots of Olaudah Equiano: an Anthropological Research.* Owerri, Nigeria: Afa Publications, 1989.
Curtin, Philip D., ed. *Africa Remembered.* Madison: University of Wisconsin Press, 1962.
Inikori, Joseph E., ed. *Forced Migration: The Impact of the Export Slave Trade on African Societies.* London: Hutchinson, 1982.
Manning, Patrick. *Slavery and African Life: Occidental, Oriental, and African Slave Trades.* Cambridge: Cambridge University Press, 1990.
Thornton, John. *Africa and Africans in the Making of the Atlantic World.* Cambridge: Cambridge University Press, 1992.

AFRO-AMERICAN LITERATURE

Andrews, William L. *To tell a free story: The first century of Afro-American Autobiography, 1760–1865.* Urbana: University of Illinois Press, 1986.
Baker, Houston A., Jr. *Blues, Ideology, and Afro-American Literature: A Vernacular Theory.* Chicago: University of Chicago Press, 1984.
Costanzo, Angelo. *Surprizing Narrative: Olaudah Equiano and the Beginnings of Black Autobiography.* Westport, Conn.: Greenwood Press, 1987.
Fichtelberg, Joseph. "Word between Worlds: The Economy of Equiano's Narrative." *American Literary History* 5 (1993).
Fisher, Dexter, and Robert B. Stepto, eds. *Afro-American Literature: The Reconstruction of Instruction.* New York: Modern Language Association, 1978.

SLAVERY AND THE SLAVE TRADE

Berlin, Ira, and Ronald Hoffman, eds. *Slavery and Freedom in the Era of the American Revolution.* Urbana: University of Illinois Press for the United States Capitol Historical Society, 1986.
Craton, Michael. *Sinews of Empire: A Short History of British Slavery.* Garden City, N.Y.: Anchor Press, 1974.
Curtin, Philip D. *The Atlantic Slave Trade: A Census.* Madison: University of Wisconsin Press, 1969.

Davidson, Basil. *The African Slave Trade.* Boston: Little, Brown, 1980.
Davis, David Brion. *The Problem of Slavery in the Age of Revolution, 1770–1823.* Ithaca: Cornell University Press, 1975.
———. *Slavery and Human Progress.* New York: Oxford University Press, 1984.
Donnan, Elizabeth. *Documents Illustrative of the History of the Slave Trade to America.* 4 vols. Washington, D.C.: Carnegie Institute, 1930–1935.
Drescher, Seymour. *Capitalism and Antislavery: British Mobilization in Comparative Perspective.* New York: Oxford University Press, 1987.
———. *Econocide: British Slavery in the Era of Abolition.* Pittsburgh: University of Pittsburgh Press, 1977.
Dunn, Richard S. *Sugar and Slaves: The Rise of the Planter Class in the English West Indies, 1624–1713.* New York: W. W. Norton, 1973.
Inikori, Joseph E., and Stanley L. Engerman, eds. *The Atlantic Slave Trade: Effects on Economies, Societies, and Peoples in Africa, the Americas, and Europe.* Durham: Duke University Press, 1992.
Klein, Herbert S. *The Middle Passage: Comparative Studies in the Atlantic Slave Trade.* Princeton: Princeton University Press, 1978.
Littlefield, Daniel F. *Rice and Slaves: Ethnicity and the Slave Trade in Colonial South Carolina.* Baton Rouge: Louisiana State University Press, 1981.
Patterson, Orlando. *Slavery and Social Death: A Comparative Study.* Cambridge: Harvard University Press, 1982.
Williams, Eric. *Capitalism and Slavery.* Chapel Hill: University of North Carolina Press, 1944.

RACE RELATIONS

Berlin Ira. "Time, Space, and the Evolution of Afro-American Society on British Mainland North America." *American Historical Review* 85 (1980).
Fredrickson, George. *The Black Image in the White Mind: The Debate on Afro-American Character and Destiny, 1814–1917.* New York: Harper and Row, 1971.
Fryer, Peter. *Staying Power: The History of Black People in Britain.* London: Pluto Press, 1984.
Jordan, Winthrop D. *White over Black: American Attitudes toward the Negro, 1550–1812.* Chapel Hill: University of North Carolina Press, 1969.
Macleod, Duncan. *Slavery, Race, and the American Revolution.* London: Cambridge University Press, 1974.
Morgan, Edmund S. *American Slavery, American Freedom: The Ordeal of Colonial Virginia.* New York: W. W. Norton, 1975.
Nash, Gary B. *Forging Freedom: The Formation of Philadelphia's Black Community, 1720–1840.* Cambridge: Harvard University Press, 1988.
———. *Race and Revolution.* Madison, Wisc.: Madison House, 1990.
Quarles, Benjamin. *The Negro in the American Revolution.* Chapel Hill: University of North Carolina Press, 1961.
Robinson, Donald L. *Slavery in the Structure of American Politics, 1765–1820.* New York: W. W. Norton, 1971.

Shyllon, Folarin. *Black People in Britain, 1555–1833*. London: Oxford University Press for the Institute for Race Relations, 1977.

Tise, Larry E. *Proslavery: A History of the Defense of Slavery in America, 1701–1840*. Athens: University of Georgia Press, 1987.

Walvin, James, ed. *Slavery and British Society, 1776–1846*. Baton Rouge: Louisiana State University Press, 1982.

Wood, Peter H. *Black Majority: Negroes in Colonial South Carolina from 1670 through the Stono Rebellion*. New York: W. W. Norton, 1975.

ANTISLAVERY MOVEMENT

Anstey, Roger. *The Atlantic Slave Trade and British Abolition, 1760–1810*. Atlantic Highlands, N.J.: Humanities Press, 1975.

Blackburn, Robin. *The Overthrow of Colonial Slavery, 1776–1848*. London: Verso, 1988.

Bolt, Christine, and Seymour Drescher, eds. *Anti-Slavery, Religion, and Reform: Essays in Memory of Roger Anstey*. Hamden, Conn.: Archon Books, 1980.

Bruns, Roger, ed. *Am I Not a Man and a Brother: The Antislavery Crusade of Revolutionary America, 1688–1788*. New York: Chelsea House Publishers, 1977.

James, C. L. R. *Black Jacobins: Toussaint l'Ouverture and the San Domingo Revolution*. New York: Vintage Books, 1963.

Midgely, Clare. *Women against Slavery: The British Campaigns, 1780–1870*. London: Routledge, 1992.

Turley, David. *The Culture of English Antislavery, 1780–1860*. London: Routledge, 1991.

Zilversmit, Arthur. *The First Emancipation: The Abolition of Slavery in the North*. Chicago: University of Chicago Press, 1967.

Index